Called of God

An LDS Perspective on America's Founding

Paperback ISBN-10: 0-9972126-0-8
Paperback ISBN-13: 978-0-9972126-0-0

Cover Design by BespokeBookCovers.com

Acknowledgements

Special thanks to my wife, Natalie, who was determined to be the first to read (and to like) my book. Additional thanks to friends and family who read early drafts and provided valuable feedback. Finally, thanks to Dayton and Tim who, quite unknowingly, contributed greatly to this work.

Disclaimer

I am a member of The Church of Jesus Christ of Latter-day Saints. Many refer to me as Mormon, but I will hereafter refer to myself and those of my faith as Latter-day Saints or LDS.

The Church's full and official name is The Church of Jesus Christ of Latter-day Saints. Many refer to it as the Mormon Church. I will hereafter refer to it as the Church. All references to the Church should be considered as being made to The Church of Jesus Christ of Latter-day Saints unless otherwise noted or specified.

The content contained in this work consists of my own interpretations of, and my own conclusions drawn from, the doctrines and teachings related to and promulgated by The Church of Jesus Christ of Latter-day Saints. I do not, however, speak for the Church. I am not an official spokesman for the Church on any matters contained herein and the Church is unaware that I am producing this work and is in no way affiliated with this work. This work is not to be viewed as being sanctioned or endorsed by The Church of Jesus Christ of Latter-day Saints or by any of its leaders.

All that being said, I do believe this to be a correct interpretation of LDS doctrine. Otherwise, obviously, I wouldn't have written it.

Primer For Non-LDS Readers

This brief primer is provided for the non-LDS reader as a basis for the LDS beliefs from which all of the subsequent arguments are presented. This background information is intended to inform the reader and not to convince. I will not provide evidence but will merely state some of the basic beliefs held by Latter-day Saints so that the non-LDS reader might be aware of the foundation upon which I am building my arguments.

Basic Beliefs

First and foremost, we (Latter-day Saints) believe in God the Eternal Father. We believe that He is our Father in a very real sense and that our spirits are His literal offspring. We believe in a very personal God who loves His children and is concerned for their wellbeing. He is involved in our lives, though many fail to recognize His hand and influence. We often refer to God the Father as our Heavenly Father or our Father in Heaven.

We believe in Jesus Christ. We consider ourselves, therefore, to be Christian. We believe that Jesus Christ is the Son of God and the Savior of mankind. We believe that God and Jesus Christ are distinct individuals united in purpose and righteousness. We believe that Jesus Christ is the only way by which we might return to live in the presence of our Heavenly Father. We believe that He atoned for our sins and took upon Himself all of our infirmities, ailments, and afflictions. He has suffered all things which we can suffer and therefore has a perfect knowledge of our suffering. This allows Him to understand us perfectly, to guide, console, and teach us each individually in exactly the manner best suited to each individual.

We believe in the Holy Ghost or Holy Spirit. We believe that He is the third, distinct member of the Godhead. It is through the Holy Ghost that God and Jesus Christ testify of eternal truths, teach us, comfort us, and lead us to ever greater happiness when we are willing to follow.

We believe that these three beings comprise the Godhead. They are individual and distinct beings but are united as one in purpose and in righteousness.

We believe that God calls prophets and apostles upon the earth to accomplish His eternal designs. He did this anciently in Israel. They taught the Israelites, testified of Him, exhorted them to live His commandments, and called on them to repent when they did not. Many of the teachings and doings of these prophets and apostles were recorded and compiled over many centuries and the resulting volume of scripture is the Bible.

The Book of Mormon: Another Testament of Jesus Christ

We believe the Bible to be the word of God, however, we also believe that through many centuries of translations, alterations, and other designs of men (of both good and ill intent), the truths originally contained in the Bible have been rendered somewhat difficult to understand and often ambiguous.

We believe that God called prophets and apostles among peoples other than the ancient Israelites.[1] They too taught and prophesied of Jesus Christ and recorded their doings and teachings into volumes of scripture. One such volume is *The Book of Mormon: Another Testament of Jesus Christ*, the volume from which Latter-day Saints receive the "Mormon" moniker.[2]

The Book of Mormon relates histories of several different peoples but primarily treats one particular group referred to as Nephites or the People of Nephi. This people trace their lineage to an Israelite prophet named Lehi and his son, Nephi, who is called by God to be a prophet to his descendants. Lehi and Nephi lead a small group of people out of Israel around 600 B.C., shortly before Babylon conquers and enslaves the southern kingdom of Judah. They are led by God across the ocean to a "land of promise,"[3] which is held by the Church to be somewhere on the American continents.

The Book of Mormon tells of this journey and a small portion of the doings and teachings of this group and their descendants over a roughly 1000-year period until the Nephite authors and their people are exterminated by their enemies due to unrighteousness in the 4th century A.D., an occurrence similar to the fates of their Israeli and Jewish counterparts in the Old World.

Among the prophets that contributed to The Book of Mormon was one named Mormon. Mormon was a historian who compiled and abridged portions of Nephite record into the volume that carries his name today.

The Restoration

We believe that Christ, during His mortal ministry, established His Church among the Jewish people. We believe that in order for a Church to be Christ's Church, it must be established by Him and not by man. We believe that Christ also established His Church among the Nephite people somewhere in the American

---

1 John 10:16 (14-16); 3 Nephi 15:21 (15:13-16:3)

2 2 Nephi 29

3 1 Nephi 2:20; 4:14; 5:5, 22

hemisphere and that He then went and established it among other peoples of whom we yet do not know.[4]

We believe that the Church organization that Christ established was ultimately lost due to wickedness by its adherents and that the world then went through a period of time where Christ's Church was not to be found. We refer to this loss of the Gospel's true principles and Christ's true Church as the Apostasy.

Since the true Gospel and true Church organization were not found in the world it was necessary that they be restored. The only one with the authority to do so was Christ Himself. We believe that, following the same pattern that He had previously, Christ called prophets and apostles to again establish His Church organization and to clarify and expand principles of His Gospel. We refer to this reestablishment of His Church as the Restoration and believe The Church of Jesus Christ of Latter-day Saints to be the same Church organization established by Christ Himself among the Jews and other ancient peoples, only reestablished, or restored, in the latter days in preparation for His Second Coming and Millennial reign.

It is common among Latter-day Saints to use the term "restoration" as a distinguishing qualifier to differentiate between people, such as prophets and apostles, who have been called and scripture that has been revealed either as part of or since the restoration of Christ's Church. Therefore, in LDS vernacular are often found the terms "restoration prophets" or "restoration scripture" to distinguish between prophets called and scripture revealed in the latter days and those called and revealed anciently in Israel.

We believe since God has set His hand again in the latter days to establish His kingdom, he has called modern day prophets and apostles and revealed new volumes of scripture. Within the organization of The Church of Jesus Christ of Latter-day Saints, the prophet on the earth is also the president of the Church. There is only ever one prophet on the earth at a time and he is always assisted by two counselors, the three together making up what Latter-day Saints refer to as the First Presidency. Additionally, we believe there to be twelve apostles on the earth just as in ancient Israel. Within the organization of the Church, they make up the body known as the Quorum of the Twelve Apostles or, more commonly known in the past, as the Council of the Twelve Apostles. I will use the more modern "Quorum" even when referring to apostles who served long enough ago to have been referred to as being in the "Council". The two terms are interchangeable and refer to the same body. Apostles are referred to with the preceding title of "Elder." The title "Elder," however, can refer to a broad range

[4] 3 Nephi 16:1-3

of leaders in the Church organization. Therefore, I will generally specify when a quoted speaker or writer is, at the time of the quotation, a member of The Quorum of the Twelve Apostles or serving in some other capacity. Any unqualified references to an elder should be assumed to mean an apostle. Similarly, each member of the First Presidency is commonly referred to with the title of President. For the sake of simplicity, I will refer only to the prophet and president of the Church as "President" and to all other apostles, including counselors in the First Presidency, as "Elder." It is generally sufficient to know that the quoted speaker is an apostle of the Lord Jesus Christ. Further distinction between members of the First Presidency and the Quorum of the Twelve Apostles typically will not bear much significance on the quotation being cited. Any unqualified references to a president should be assumed to mean the prophet.

Every six months (usually in April and October), members of the Church hear from the prophet, apostles, and other general authorities of the Church through a forum called General Conference. Speeches from General Conference are subsequently printed in Conference Reports. Teachings from General Conference are considered by Latter-day Saints as being akin to scripture in that they are words spoken by God's servants in their official capacities.[5]

The first of the restoration prophets was Joseph Smith who was tasked, among other things, with translating the ancient Nephite record compiled and abridged by Mormon and thus bringing to light a new volume of scripture called The Book of Mormon.

As a prophet of God, we believe that Joseph Smith received revelation from God. Many of the revelations he received were recorded and assembled into a single work now known as The Doctrine and Covenants (often shortened to D&C), another volume of restoration scripture.

Another volume of scripture used by Latter-day Saints is called The Pearl of Great Price and consists of writings of both Moses and Abraham.

Please refer to Appendix I for the complete body of scripture used in the LDS canon and for descriptions of the notations used to refer to each volume.

Temples and Temple Work

One of the unique characteristics of The Church of Jesus Christ of Latter-day Saints is the penchant we have for building temples. Temples are the object of some curiosity and fascination on the part of those looking from outside the

---

[5] Deuteronomy 8:3; Matthew 4:4; D&C 98:11, 68:4; TG *Revelation*

Church into it. We believe temples to be special and sacred buildings where the most holy of God's work and our worship is conducted.

We believe that in order to return to the presence of our Heavenly Father and Jesus Christ we must participate in certain ordinances, such as baptism as taught by the Savior during His mortal ministry. Many of these ordinances can only be performed in the LDS temples. Unique to temples, however, is the ability to effect these ordinances for both living and dead recipients. In temples, we perform vicarious ordinances for people (usually family members and ancestors) that have already passed on from this life.

When Latter-day Saints refer to doing temple work, they are referring to these ordinances that are performed either by the living for themselves or vicariously on behalf of the deceased. We believe that every individual then has the opportunity to accept or reject the ordinances performed on his or her behalf.

Final Thoughts

I hope this primer will provide the non-LDS reader with sufficient background on LDS beliefs to understand where the arguments contained herein are originating. Unfortunately, there will still be many esoteric terms and concepts used throughout much of this book. I will do my best to provide brief explanations where I think them necessary. For the reader more interested in the history over LDS doctrine, I recommend chapters 4, 5, and 7, which focus more on the Founders, their work and legacy, and addressing present criticisms against them.

Preface

I don't have any profound, single experience to share or fantastic vision received that impelled me to undertake this project. I am not claiming any new revelation on the subject at hand and I do not offer this work as prophetic commentary on things that are to come. I do have a number of reasons for writing this book, however, many of which will no doubt seem rather mundane to the reader. I will not declare all of my reasons for writing this book, but I will discuss a few.

The principal reason I wrote this book is because I believe it. I believe the arguments that I make in this book to be true and therefore endeavor to make a reasoned and intelligent case for them based on revelation and teachings from God and His servants.

I believe that through modern revelation, Latter-day Saints have been given much knowledge and information on civil government that no other people has. Particularly, the Latter-day Saints of America have a unique perspective on matters of civil government as a result of their culture, their heritage, and their history. I believe that "of him unto whom much is given much is required,"[1] and that therefore a certain responsibility falls on Latter-day Saints to first, understand the principles that have been revealed and second, to advocate the implementation of those principles around the world.

Once again, I do not claim to have had any visions or grand revelations that called me to produce this work. I do feel, however, that through personal experiences and guidance from God I have found a "good cause" to be "anxiously engaged in" without the need of a command to do so.[2]

The Lord stated in a revelation given to Joseph Smith:

> Teach ye diligently and my grace shall attend you, that you may be instructed more perfectly in theory, in principle, in doctrine, in the law of the gospel, in all things that pertain unto the kingdom of God, that are expedient for you to understand;
>
> Of things both in heaven and in the earth, and under the earth; things which have been, things which are, things which must shortly come to pass; things which are at home, things which are abroad; the wars and the perplexities of the nations, and the judgements which are on the land; and a knowledge also of countries and of kingdoms-

---

[1] D&C 82:3; Luke 12:48

[2] D&C 58:26-27

That ye may be prepared in all things when I shall send you again to magnify the calling whereunto I have called you, and the mission with which I have commissioned you.[3]

President Gordon B. Hinckley said of those verses, "It is apparent that we are obligated not only to learn of ecclesiastical matters but also of secular matters."[4] It is my belief that righteous civil government, founded on eternal principles, will one day be required to establish Zion and to carry the Church from its current role as a strictly ecclesiastical institution into the governing Kingdom of Heaven that it is prophesied to become.[5] In order for that to occur, God will need honest and devoted civil servants who understand the principles of just and sound civil government, many of whom will likely be drawn from the members of His Church.

Furthermore, I believe that the Gospel of Jesus Christ has much to offer on matters of sound civil government. As quoted by Elder Dallin H. Oaks in the April, 2015 General Conference of The Church,

> Catholic leader Charles J. Chaput said, "I want to stress again the importance of really living what we claim to believe. That needs to be a priority—not just in our personal and family lives but in our churches, *our political choices*, our business dealings, our treatment of the poor; in other words, in everything we do."[6]

Finally, I do not consider this book to be an exhaustive work on matters of civil government. Instead, what I hope this book to accomplish is to foster a more complete understanding of righteous, revealed principles as pertaining to civil government, renew and strengthen testimonies among Latter-day Saints of God's hand in the Founding of America and the instruction of the Founders, and to spark a fervor of desire among members of the Church for continued study of, understanding of, and action on the Founding principles of America as delivered to us by God.

---

[3] D&C 88:78-80

[4] Gordon B. Hinckley, *Why We Do Some of the Things We Do*, General Conference, October-1999

[5] See *Kingdom of Heaven* or *Kingdom of God* in Bible Dictionary

[6] Dallin H. Oaks, *The Parable of the Sower*, General Conference, April-2015 (emphasis added)

Introduction

My primary audience are members of The Church of Jesus Christ of Latter-day Saints to whom I will refer as Latter-day Saints. Therefore, LDS beliefs are treated herein as axiomatic and will not be discussed with any intent of convincing the reader of their veracity. I will not offer evidence or proofs for LDS beliefs and doctrine, but will rather use those doctrines and beliefs as accepted premise from which to present my case with the hope of convincing many other Latter-day Saints of the things I believe to be true.

Nevertheless, it is my hope that this work will garner at least some attention from Christians of other faiths and anyone who believes in the divine heritage of the United States of America. Therefore, LDS beliefs and doctrines will be presented with some, very minimal, background information, not to convince, but to inform and to help the non-LDS reader better understand the principles from which my arguments are drawn. This background information will also serve to remind the LDS reader of the principles being used in the arguments made and make for a more complete and sound argument.

These objectives make for a somewhat unique format for this work. As mentioned above, LDS beliefs and doctrines will be treated as true principles, however, those principles and beliefs will often be laid out in very basic terms to lay the foundation on which to construct further arguments and draw conclusions.

The format I will use is to describe principles, doctrines, and beliefs at a basic enough level that they can be comprehended by LDS and non-LDS readers alike, tie multiple beliefs and doctrines together, and then draw conclusions from the resulting combinations. All the while I will be providing supporting evidence from scripture and apostolic teachings.

As these arguments are presented, I will give preference to restoration scripture[1] and teachings over the Bible. This may present a problem for some non-LDS readers and for that I apologize but, as already stated, my primary audience are Latter-day Saints. I believe this to make a more convincing argument for Latter-day Saints. I also feel that restoration scripture is clearer and easier to understand than the Bible. Indeed, I consider The Book of Mormon

---

[1] Please refer to the previous Primer for non-LDS Readers for a description of what is meant by "restoration scripture."

and other restoration scripture to be more "plain and precious"[2] than that which is found in the Bible.

As for apostolic teachings, I will endeavor to use quotes and teachings where it is clear that the speaker is teaching by the Spirit and not merely expressing an opinion. This is mostly determined by the setting in which the teaching is delivered. The general rule I apply is to ask whether the teaching could be considered to be an official statement made by the Church organization. As expected, this will tend to include many addresses of General Conference and will be limited to only individuals who are considered to be sustained authorities and sanctioned spokesmen for the Church as a whole.

References to General Conference addresses will include the speaker's name, the title of the address if there is one (many older Conference addresses carry no title), and the month and year of the Conference when the speech was delivered, not the publication date of the corresponding Conference Report. At the time of this writing, all Conference addresses as far back as 1971 can be found on the official website of The Church of Jesus Christ of Latter-day Saints.[3] The actual Conference Reports can be viewed and downloaded as far back as 1880 from the Internet Archive.[4]

References to addresses delivered at Brigham Young University will be cited similarly to Conference addresses. The original speeches can be found on the BYU Speeches website.[5]

For historical citations and quotes from the Founding Fathers and their contemporaries, the more discerning reader might notice a generous use of secondary source references. This is intentional. The intent of this book is to make a very specific, and somewhat narrow, argument to a target audience. The main thrust of that argument is that God was significantly involved in preparing and teaching the American Founders and that He justifies and approves the work that they accomplished, namely the U.S. Constitution. In order to make this argument, I found it necessary to give a historical treatment of the Founders and some of their work. This treatment is very brief, however, and I consider it to be extremely introductory, barely scratching the surface of the history available to us for research and study. I hope this treatment together with the surrounding context of this entire book, will lead readers to further pursue their own research into many or all of the tangential topics introduced. For this reason, I

---

[2] 1 Nephi 13:28 (13:1-42)

[3] https://www.lds.org/general-conference

[4] https://archive.org/details/conferencereport

[5] https://speeches.byu.edu

deliberately reference sources that I have found to be educational and informative.

I am confident in the historicity of the quotes and references that I have used throughout this work. I have validated them myself and have removed or not included any that I was unable to satisfactorily verify. In addition, the reader should note that spelling and grammar has changed since the time of the Founding. The conventional method to alert readers to archaic spelling and grammar in quotations is the use of a Latin abbreviation, *sic*, after anything appearing to be an error to inform the reader that the transcription of the quote is true and that the error or unusual spelling is in the original text. Because the spelling of so many words has changed over the years, I have opted to not make extensive use of this convention in order to avoid it being everywhere and too distracting to the faithful reading of quotations. I make a sparing use of it to point out some of the more error apparent spellings.

Finally, for reference and comparison I have included a number of Appendices at the end of this book. I consider these Appendices a very good place to start for the reader who is new to this subject matter. I especially recommend continued reading and study of the resources listed in Appendix IX.

Chapter 1 – Agency

This chapter will treat the principle of agency. Agency, or the freedom to choose and to act according to one's choices, is foundational to the argument presented throughout this book. The pre-mortal existence and the conflict that began there with the presentation of opposing plans for mankind are both examined in an effort to learn more of the importance of agency. A definition of agency is also detailed as can be extracted from scripture and teachings of general leaders of The Church of Jesus Christ of Latter-day Saints.

The Plan of Salvation

Before coming to this mortal life, we existed as a family in the eternal realm with the Father of our spirits, whom we call God. We grew in knowledge and progressed to a point where we could progress no further without a physical body and the tests of mortality. Our loving Heavenly Father, our God, then laid out a plan by which we could continue our progress and increase in joy and happiness by receiving a physical body and entering into a probationary state wherein we are proven to see whether we will "do all things whatsoever the Lord [our] God shall command [us]."[1]

This plan is most commonly known among Latter-day Saints as the Plan of Salvation, the Plan of Happiness, or the Plan of Redemption. Central to the Plan of Salvation is the necessity of a Savior. We would fall short. It was known in the initial planning stages that we would fail our probationary tests on our own and would therefore require the intervention of a Savior.

Abraham 3:27 reads:

> And the Lord said: Whom shall I send? And one answered like unto the Son of Man: Here am I, send me. And another answered and said: Here am I, send me. And the Lord said: I will send the first.[2]

Moses 4:1-2 fills in some of the details:

> Satan ... came before me, saying—Behold, here am I, send me, I will be thy son, and I will redeem all mankind, that one soul shall not be lost, and surely I will do it; wherefore give me thine honor.

---

[1] Abraham 3:25

[2] Abraham 3:27

> But, behold, my Beloved Son, which was my Beloved and Chosen from the beginning, said unto me—Father, thy will be done, and the glory be thine forever.[3]

Two individuals volunteered to fulfill the role of Savior. The first agreed with the plan as it had been presented to us and honored our Father for creating it.[4] The second proposed alterations to the plan and demanded the glory be his. The former was Jesus Christ, our Lord, our Savior, our brother. The latter was Lucifer, Son of the Morning, also our brother, and thereafter known as Satan.

What ensued has since come to be known as the War in Heaven.[5] We have little revealed detail on the nature of this war. But, we do know the principal issues over which the war was fought and some of the immediate consequences that it engendered.

Moses 4:3-4 reads:

> Wherefore, because that Satan rebelled against me, and sought to destroy the agency of man, which I, the Lord God, had given him, and also, that I should give unto him mine own power; by the power of mine Only Begotten, I caused that he should be cast down;
>
> And he became Satan, yea, even the devil, the father of all lies, to deceive and to blind men, and to lead them captive at his will, even as many as would not hearken unto my voice.[6]

So began the ongoing confrontation between good and evil, the one side championed by Jesus Christ and the other side led by Satan. No individual, no matter what they may pretend, can remain neutral in this struggle. We, by our actions, choose every day to follow one side or the other.

This story is not new to Latter-day Saints. Members of the Church are taught this story, or portions of it, from a very early age. The LDS reader will not find anything new or controversial in this brief retelling. There are, however, several finer points in this story that are often overlooked by a casual reading or consideration.

There were two plans presented to our eternal family with one fundamental difference, and that difference was agency. The Plan of Salvation presented by God and Jesus Christ exalted agency as supreme and would not allow any violation of it. The plan of the opposition, presented by Lucifer, rejected the importance of agency and sacrificed it for the "greater good" of saving all

---

[3] Moses 4:1-2

[4] Moses 4:2

[5] Revelation 12:7

[6] Moses 4:3-4

mankind. This opposition plan will be treated in more detail shortly. To better understand the fundamental difference between these opposing plans it is useful to define and understand agency itself. Agency is defined in the Book of Helaman as follows:

> And now remember, remember, my brethren, that whosoever perisheth, perisheth unto himself; and whosoever doeth iniquity, doeth it unto himself; for behold, ye are free; ye are permitted to act for yourselves; for behold, God hath given unto you a knowledge and he hath made you free.
>
> He hath given unto you that ye might know good from evil, and he hath given unto you that ye might choose life or death; and ye can do good and be restored unto that which is good, or have that which is good restored unto you; or ye can do evil, and have that which is evil restored unto you.[7]

Agency is here defined as the freedom an individual has to act for himself and to choose for himself based on the knowledge that God has given him regarding good and evil. Many references are made throughout the scriptures to this freedom that man has to choose for himself.[8]

Another concept to note is that agency comes with an associated responsibility or accountability. In this passage from the book of Helaman above, agency is described as only a portion of a larger argument that while we are free to choose and act for ourselves, we will at some point have "restored" unto each of us that which we have chosen. In other words, we will one day "reap what we sow" as the saying goes.[9] Agency is very frequently spoken of in the scriptures this way, closely associated with the eventual inevitability of being held accountable for the choices we have made. In the April, 2013 General Conference of the Church, Elder Boyd K. Packer of the Quorum of the Twelve Apostles summarized this point when he said, "We are free to choose what we will and to pick and choose our acts, but we are not free to choose the consequences. They come as they will come."[10]

Another definition of agency is given by the Prophet Joseph Smith as "that free independence of mind which heaven has so graciously bestowed upon the human family as one of its choicest gifts."[11]

---

[7] Helaman 14:30-31

[8] See Genesis 2:16; 2 Nephi 10:23; Alma 12:31; TG *Agency*

[9] Galatians 6:7

[10] Boyd K. Packer, *These Things I know*, General Conference, April-2013

[11] Joseph Smith, *Scriptural Teachings of the Prophet Joseph Smith*, 1993, p. 62

One more great definition of agency, and its relationship to accountability, is found in the Book of Alma when Alma is counseling his son, Corianton. Alma teaches his son:

> Therefore, O my son, whosoever will come may come and partake of the waters of life freely; and whosoever will not come the same is not compelled to come; but in the last day it shall be restored unto him according to his deeds.[12]

Alma, in this verse, again teaches that we are free to choose between good and evil, but that eventually we will have "restored unto [us]" according to that which we choose. He also points out that we will not be compelled to do even something so good and worthy as partaking of the waters of life.

One additional item of importance is to recognize the source of man's agency. Agency, or the ability to choose between good and evil, was given to man by God. God stated in the verses above that "I, the Lord God, had given him"[13] his agency. This principle can also be found later in the book of Moses where we read, "in the Garden of Eden, gave I unto man his agency."[14] We are also taught this by Nephi who said, "Wherefore, the Lord God gave unto man that he should act for himself."[15] It is clear from these verses, and a number of others throughout the scriptures, that God is the source of man's agency. He gave agency to man and granted to each individual to be owner and steward of his or her own agency.

Agency is central to the Plan of Salvation that was presented to us by our Heavenly Father and advocated by Jesus Christ. Lehi taught the necessity of agency in God's plan to his son, Jacob, in the second chapter of the Second Book of Nephi. Lehi teaches that "men are instructed sufficiently that they know good from evil,"[16] that a law is given for man to live by, and that redemption is provided to make up for what man lacks in living up to that law. He also teaches that there must be "opposition in all things."[17] There must be good and evil, there must be right and wrong, so that man may exercise agency in choosing between the two. Only in this manner can man progress toward his ultimate goal of exaltation and becoming like God, by proving that he will choose good over evil while possessing the freedom to do either.

---

[12] Alma 42:27
[13] Moses 4:3
[14] Moses 7:32
[15] 2 Nephi 2:16
[16] 2 Nephi 2:5
[17] 2 Nephi 2:11

There is, of course, much more to Lehi's teaching than this, but it satisfies this work's purposes to reinforce the necessity of agency in God's Plan of Salvation. In fact, slightly further along in Lehi's teachings to Jacob, it is found that one of the purposes of the Atonement itself was to preserve man's agency.

He teaches:

> And the Messiah cometh in the fullness of time, that he may redeem the children of men from the fall. And because that they are redeemed from the fall they have become free forever, knowing good from evil; to act for themselves and not to be acted upon, save it be by the punishment of the law at the great and last day, according to the commandments which God hath given.[18]

Alma also teaches this principle to his son, Corianton:

> These are they that are redeemed of the Lord; yea, these are they that are taken out, that are delivered from that endless night of darkness; and thus they stand or fall; for behold, they are their own judges, whether to do good or do evil.[19]

It is clear from these passages that at least part of being redeemed is maintaining our freedom to act for ourselves and choose whether to do good or evil. The redemption made possible for us by Jesus Christ is that we remain agents unto ourselves with our agency intact. Lehi teaches that this is one of the things accomplished when we are redeemed from the fall, that we remain free to choose and to act for ourselves. Alma teaches that being redeemed of the Lord is to become our own judges or, in other words, to judge and choose for ourselves. The Plan of Salvation grants agency to man and then because of the inevitability of man misusing and abusing that agency, a Redeemer is provided to redeem mankind and allow them to maintain their freedom to choose, their agency.

The Plan of the Opposition

True to Lehi's teaching of "opposition in all things," we were presented with an opposing plan to the Plan of Salvation. The opposing plan was presented by Lucifer and the key characteristic for consideration of this plan is the concept of force. Where Christ's plan was based on agency, Satan's plan was based on force. Force and compulsion are the opposition to agency.

---

[18] 2 Nephi 2:26

[19] Alma 41:7

Satan proposed that force be used to ensure that all mankind would do what they were supposed to do and thereby be eligible for exaltation, having fulfilled and kept all of God's commandments. It is important to note here that the force that Satan proposed to inflict on all of mankind was to force them to do good and to keep the commandments, saving "all mankind, that one soul shall not be lost."[20]

This is extremely important because it shows that force, in and of itself, is the evil and not what man would be forced to do. Few would disagree that it would have been best for all of God's children to be saved. Surely this is what God Himself would most desire, for all of His children to return to Him and be exalted. But, it was more important to Him, and so should be more important to us, that His children choose to return to Him and not be forced or compelled to do so.

The War in Heaven

As mentioned above, the presentation of two opposing plans caused a rift in our eternal family to develop and sides to be chosen. A conflict ensued and it is very instructive to observe the behavior on both sides of the dispute.

First, God Himself cites only two issues that were central to the conflict known as the War in Heaven. One is that Lucifer desired God's glory for his own. The other is agency. The initial division between good and evil, the Savior and the Devil, was caused by a dispute over man's agency. This is significant. Not all evil acts can be broken down to a question of agency versus force, however, God and the devil initially parted ways over the question of whether to let man choose to do good or to force him to do good. It should be noted once again that the behavior proposed to be forced onto mankind was not to do evil, but to force him to do *good*.

God is omniscient and "know[s] the end from the beginning,"[21] in part because He knows His children and how they will react to all circumstances and the decisions they will make in all situations. Therefore, it follows that God knew beforehand that the result of His decision to reject Lucifer's plan would be the immediate loss of one third[22] of His children with no hope for their salvation. Furthermore, He knew that after passing through mortality and the trials associated therewith, many more of His children would be lost and never return to Him. Fully aware of these dismal prospects for the exaltation of His children—because of choices *they* would make—God upheld the principle of agency in direct opposition to a plan claiming to provide for the redemption of every last

---

[20] Moses 4:1

[21] Abraham 2:8 (reference is made to Jehovah but LDS doctrine asserts that Jehovah possesses no characteristic or quality that the Father lacks and vice versa)

[22] D&C 29:36

one of His children. In choosing this way, God the Father established agency, the freedom to choose for oneself, as one of the supreme and essential principles of Eternity.

Satan, on the other hand, put forth the plan to "redeem all mankind, that one soul shall not be lost."[23] What's noteworthy about this claim is the seeming worthiness of the stated end to "redeem all mankind." But this end is only achieved through the unstated means of enslaving that very same mankind through the removal of their agency. Here Satan reveals his cunning nature and sinister tactic of promising a tantalizing prize, but at an undisclosed cost that is too great to bear, in this case man's agency. The attack on mankind's agency was so serious an offense that it resulted not merely in the rejection of Satan's plan but the rejection of the plan coupled with the expulsion of its author from God's presence forever. Coinciding with these events, all of God's children were able to exercise their agency to choose whether to follow Jesus Christ or Satan. One third of God's children chose to follow Satan and thereby forfeited any opportunity to live in mortality and gain a physical body. The other two thirds chose the Savior's plan and includes anyone who has ever come or ever will come to this Earth to live through mortality and gain a physical body.

Agency is Essential

Here some readers may be tempted to ask whether the redemption of all mankind was even possible without agency. The answer to this question is irrelevant to the objectives of this writing. If it's not possible, then agency is a necessary prerequisite to redemption. If it is possible, then God considered agency too high a price to pay for that universal redemption. Either scenario reinforces agency as an essential and fundamental principle to God's plan and a principle that God was unwilling to sacrifice or be moved on.

In the April, 2015 General Conference of the Church, Elder Robert D. Hales of the Quorum of the Twelve Apostles expresses gratitude for agency in the opening remarks of his talk, "We worship Him, grateful for our freedom of religion, freedom of assembly, freedom of speech, and our God-given right of agency."[24] He continues a little later with, "we must not forget that moral agency is an essential part of God's plan for all His children. That eternal plan, presented to us in the premortal Council in Heaven, included the gift of agency."[25] In this Conference address, Elder Hales affirms that agency is

---

[23] Moses 4:1

[24] Robert D. Hales, *Preserving Agency, Protecting Religious Freedom*, General Conference, April-2015

[25] Ibid.

essential to God's plan for His children and exhorts Latter-day Saints to not forget that it is.

In the October, 1947 General Conference of the Church, Elder Henry D. Moyle, then of the Quorum of the Twelve Apostles, stated, "free agency is as necessary for our eternal salvation as is our virtue. And just as we guard our virtue with our lives, so should we guard our free agency."[26] Elder Moyle uses the term "free agency" as was more common during this period in the Church's history. The present work will give preference to the terms "agency" and "moral agency" but still considers "free agency" as meaning the same thing and will consider this term equal and interchangeable as it is used more often in older quotes and statements. Elder Moyle also affirms the necessity of agency to the salvation of man and counsels Church members that we should guard our agency similarly to how we guard our virtue, that is with our very lives.

In a speech delivered at Brigham Young University in 1957, Elder Marion G. Romney of the Quorum of the Twelve Apostles, said, "One of the fundamental doctrines of the revealed truth is that, in the Garden of Eden, God endowed men with free agency. The preservation of this free agency is more important than the preservation of life itself."[27] Very similar to the previous quote by Henry D. Moyle, Elder Romney states his belief that agency is more important than life itself and should be prioritized as such if ever one should need to be risked in order to preserve the other.

In a fireside address given at Brigham Young University, Elder Dallin H. Oaks of the Quorum of the Twelve Apostles said the following:

> [A]gency, the power to choose, is a gift of God, conferred on his children and exercised by them in the premortal existence. It is an essential precondition of the further progression we seek in mortality. But free agency cannot be exercised unless there is opposition in all things. That opposition is provided by Satan, who once sought to destroy our free agency. His effort continues. He tries to persuade us to do evil, and to make those choices that will finally give him the mastery he was denied in the premortal existence—to have all power over us, to lead us captive at his will.[28]

In this address, Elder Oaks adds his voice to those of others and reiterates that agency is essential for our continued progression. He points out that agency is essential but so also is the opposition provided by Satan. Satan, according to

[26] Henry D. Moyle, General Conference, October-1947

[27] Marion G. Romney, *Your Quest for Truth*, BYU, May-1957

[28] Dallin H. Oaks, *Free Agency and Freedom*, BYU, October-1987

Elder Oaks, continues to persist in his effort to destroy man's agency and achieve the mastery over us that he began fighting for in the premortal existence.

In the *Improvement Era* magazine, a publication of the Church, President David O. McKay wrote, "Next to the bestowal of life itself, the right to direct that life is God's greatest gift to man ... Freedom of choice is more to be treasured than any possession earth can give. It is inherent in the spirit of man. It is a divine gift to every normal being ... Everyone has this most precious of all life's endowments—the gift of free agency—man's inherited and inalienable right."[29] President McKay echoes the sentiments of the others that have been quoted above. Agency is among the greatest gifts given to man by God and so should be highly treasured.

Accountability

It should be noted that agency carries with it a corollary principle of accountability. When asked about Latter-day Saint beliefs, Joseph Smith penned thirteen Articles of Faith that have since been canonized and serve as the core principles of the LDS religion. Article of Faith number 2 reads:

> We believe that men will be punished for their own sins, and not for Adam's transgression.[30]

This belief was put forth as a counter argument to the widely believed Christian doctrine of original sin and therefore refers to Adam specifically. It can be expanded, however, to say that we believe men will be punished for their own sins, and not for anyone else's. When combined with the principle of agency and its associated principle of accountability, it can be further expanded to say that we believe that God has made man free to act according to his own desires, but that each individual is responsible for the resulting consequences of their own chosen actions. Each individual will likewise be accountable for their own sins and not for anybody else's. This is the system of moral agency and accountability that was established in pre-mortality as a central and essential part of God's plan.

President Boyd K. Packer taught this very principle in the April, 2013 General Conference as was quoted previously. Consequences to our freely chosen acts will "come as they will come."[31] We are not free to choose what those consequences are, when they will come, or whether we will be responsible for

[29] David O. McKay, *Free Agency ... the Gift Divine*, *Improvement Era*, February-1962
[30] Articles of Faith 1:2
[31] Boyd K. Packer, *These Things I know*, General Conference, April-2013

them. The consequences and our responsibility for them are already established by eternal law.

Additionally, in a devotional address delivered at Brigham Young University in 2006, Elder D. Todd Christofferson stated, "When we use the term moral agency, then, we are appropriately emphasizing the accountability that is an essential part of the divine gift of agency. We are moral beings and agents unto ourselves, free to choose but also responsible for our choices."[32]

Summary and Conclusions

Agency is an essential and a fundamental principle of eternity. It is necessary for the continued progression of man. It was given to man by God and to rebel against the principle of man's agency meant the forfeiture of any opportunity for further progression. God has demonstrated by His behavior that he takes man's agency very seriously. He has instructed His servants to teach regarding its essential nature and its supernal status.

The opposite of agency is force or compulsion. It is force and compulsion that was sought after by Lucifer to control mankind and lead them according to his own will. What he proposed was to force mankind to do good, so the evil was in the compulsion itself and not necessarily in the act to be forced. This is an important distinction that will be revisited later.

God has given agency to man, the freedom and ability to choose and to act. God considers agency as vital to His plans for us and has taken very serious measures against those who have made threats against it or supported plans to destroy it. It does not suit the purposes of this writing to get into why agency is important to God's plans, but sufficient evidence has been given to show that it is important and that God considers it to be so, His prophets and apostles have taught it to be so, and it is therefore this author's opinion that Latter-day Saints should also consider it to be so.

---

[32] D. Todd Christofferson, *Moral Agency*, BYU, January-2006

Chapter 2 – Liberty

After having arrived in the Promised Land and shortly before his death, Lehi taught and prophesied a few final things to his posterity. Among his prophecies and teachings are found ones on the Promised Land itself. Specifically, Lehi describes how "this land" is reserved for people who are brought here by the Lord, that it is a land of prosperity to the righteous, and that "it shall be a land of liberty."[1]

The purpose of this chapter is to define and treat the principle of liberty. Liberty is a principle that is often overlooked in the scriptures. It is not a principle that is often well defined and expounded on by itself, but rather it is usually merely made mention of. When examined as a principle in its own right, however, and in the surrounding context in which it is made mention, many things can be learned about liberty, its importance to the Gospel plan, and the high regard in which it was held by the authors of The Book of Mormon.

This chapter will attempt to extract a definition and view of liberty as held by The Book of Mormon prophets. There is no real hard and fast definition of liberty in the scriptures, nowhere that an author merely states what liberty is or what it means. For this reason it becomes necessary to conduct a close examination of how the term liberty is used and how the principle of liberty is applied. Additionally, antithetical concepts such as oppression, bondage, and captivity will be examined in an effort to inform the corollary definition of liberty.

Religion & Worship

There are a few concepts that are used various times in association with liberty and freedom. One of those concepts, which is to be expected in a religious text like The Book of Mormon is the freedom to worship God according to the desires of the people themselves. This association is found in the Book of Alma where King Lamoni, a Lamanite king that had been converted to the Gospel, granted religious freedom to all those people under his rule. The reader should note that after having converted to Christ's Gospel, King Lamoni did not dictate that all of his subjects should do the same but rather granted unto them "that they might have the liberty of worshipping the Lord their God according to their desires."[2]

---

[1] 2 Nephi 1:7 (6-9)

[2] Alma 21:22

A concise but complete description of the religious freedom enjoyed by the Nephite people can be found in the thirtieth chapter of the book of Alma, where it reads:

> Now there was no law against a man's belief; for it was strictly contrary to the commands of God that there should be a law which should bring men on to unequal grounds.
>
> For thus saith the scripture: Choose ye this day, whom ye will serve. Now if a man desired to serve God, it was his privilege; or rather, if he believed in God it was his privilege to serve him; but if he did not believe in him there was no law to punish him.
>
> But if he murdered he was punished unto death; and if he robbed he was also punished; and if he stole he was also punished; and if he committed adultery he was also punished; yea, for all this wickedness they were punished.
>
> For there was a law that men should be judged according to their crimes. Nevertheless, there was no law against a man's belief; therefore, a man was punished only for the crimes which he had done; therefore all men were on equal grounds.[3]

The Nephite people and their system of government clearly valued freedom of conscience. Their laws were constructed in such a way as to allow citizens to be free in their thoughts and their beliefs and to be punished only for actions committed in violation of the law. Note the assertion that to punish based solely on belief would introduce inequality into the society.

Another mention of worshipping God in connection with liberty is found in a description of what the Nephites were defending as they prepared for war against the invading Lamanites. Among the things they were said to be preserving was 'their liberty, that they might worship God according to their desires."[4]

Doctrine and Covenants contains an expression of the Church's position on religious freedom, it reads:

> We believe that religion is instituted of God; and that men are amenable to him, and to him only, for the exercise of it, unless their religious opinions prompt them to infringe upon the rights and liberties of others; but we do not believe that human law has a right to interfere in prescribing rules of worship to bind the consciences of men, nor dictate forms of public or private devotion; that the civil

---

[3] Alma 30:7-11

[4] Alma 43:9 (see also Alma 43:30, 45)

> magistrate should restrain crime, but never control conscience; should punish guilt, but never suppress the freedom of the soul.[5]

It is important to recognize that while freedom of religion and worship is important, it also has its limitations in a just and peaceful society. Freedom of religion cannot be used as a justification to do anything that is in the name of a religion, but must be restrained when used to compel or permit actions against the rights and liberties of others.

Property

Another association made in conjunction with liberty is that of property or, as the Nephites referred to it, lands and possessions. This association is found in the Book of Alma, where Mormon states that "it was the only desire of the Nephites to preserve their *lands*, and their liberty, and their church..."[6] Further in the same chapter, in verse 48, Captain Moroni inspires the Nephites from their fear with "thoughts of their *lands*, their liberty, yea, their freedom from bondage."[7] Again in chapter 58 we read "and to maintain our *lands*, and our *possessions*, ... and the cause of our liberty."[8]

Control of lands and possessions, or in other words private property, is viewed here as one aspect of liberty. It is closely associated with "the cause of our liberty" and with "freedom from bondage." It is also noteworthy that the preservation of private property was a justification for a military defense.

This principle is also found in the book of Doctrine and Covenants where we read that "no government can exist in peace, except such laws are framed and held inviolate as will secure to each individual ... the right and control of property."[9]

Taxes

Taxes are mentioned several times in The Book of Mormon and each time there is a negative sentiment toward the party imposing the tax or, in one case, a positive sentiment toward the one trying to alleviate or prevent taxation.

The first time they are mentioned is by King Benjamin when he states, "I ... have labored with mine own hands that I might serve you, and that ye should not be laden with taxes, and that there should nothing come upon you which was grievous to be borne."[10]

---

[5] D&C 134:4
[6] Alma 43:30 (emphasis added)
[7] Alma 43:48 (emphasis added, see also Alma 43:45, 49; 48:10)
[8] Alma 58:12 (emphasis added, see also Alma 44:5)
[9] D&C 134:2
[10] Mosiah 2:14

The next mention of taxes is among a small group of Nephites who accompanied a man named Zeniff to possess the land of their inheritance, or the Land of Nephi, which at the time was occupied by the Lamanites. These Nephites are later rediscovered by Ammon. King Limhi, the grandson of Zeniff and king at the time when Ammon makes contact, says to Ammon, "we are in bondage to the Lamanites, and are taxed with a tax which is grievous to be borne."[11] He continues a few verses later, "we at this time do pay tribute to the king of the Lamanites."[12]

In Zeniff's record, we find his description of the initial event that brought his people into bondage, he states, "therefore, they [the Lamanites] were desirous to bring us into bondage, that they might glut themselves with the labors of our hands."[13] In this passage, the word "tax" is not used but it is reasonably presumed that it would be through taxation that the Lamanites would "glut themselves" with the Nephites' labor.

In the above recounting of the experiences of Zeniff and those Nephites who followed him to regain the lands of their forefathers, references to taxation are made in association with bondage to the Lamanites. Contrast this with the prior mention of King Benjamin who worked himself as a service to his people for the express purpose of preventing a tax being laid on them.

There are also examples of taxation being associated with wickedness in The Book of Mormon. Between Zeniff and Limhi was King Noah, who ruled over this group of Nephites in Lamanite territory for a time. Mormon describes Noah as a wicked man who "did not keep the commandments of God."[14] Among Noah's sins, "he laid a tax of one fifth part of all they possessed."[15]

Sometime long before the Nephites, Riplakish was a king over the Jaredites, The Jaredite record found as the Book of Ether states that he "did not do that which was right in the sight of the Lord, ... he did tax them with heavy taxes."[16]

Throughout The Book of Mormon record, when taxes are mentioned, they are always mentioned in association with some form of oppression (captivity, bondage, etc.) or wickedness. The argument is not being made that all taxes are inherently evil or that they are always used for wicked purposes. Indeed, the references above all carry with them qualifiers such as "grievous" and "heavy." It is not a part of the current writing to make any attempt to delineate between good and evil uses of taxes or to attempt to identify the threshold at which taxes

---

[11] Mosiah 7:15
[12] Mosiah 7:22
[13] Mosiah 9:12; Alma 30:27
[14] Mosiah 11:2
[15] Mosiah 11:3
[16] Ether 10:5

become grievous, heavy, or burdensome. It is sufficient to point out that the authors of The Book of Mormon saw taxes as a vehicle that could and is used for great evil, and the only way taxes are mentioned in the record is in conjunction with such evil.

Kings

One of the most discussed concepts related to liberty in The Book of Mormon is the idea of kings as rulers. For example, Jacob reiterates Lehi's earlier prophecy by stating that "this land shall be a land of liberty unto the Gentiles,"[17] but Jacob further clarifies the meaning by adding, "and there shall be no kings upon the land."[18] Similarly, Alma later desires that the people with whom he had fled King Noah "stand fast in this liberty wherewith ye have been made free, and that ye trust no man to be a king over you."[19]

In later chapters of the book of Alma, we find a group of people known as king-men who "were desirous that the law should be altered in a manner to overthrow the free government and to establish a king over the land."[20] The king-men are subsequently described as being "of high birth, and they sought to be kings; and they were supported by those who sought power and authority over the people."[21] The king-men are treated in more detail later in this chapter, but here note the incompatibility between those seeking power and authority and free government.

Later, while the Nephites are struggling with the Gadianton Robbers and corruption within their own government, a group of chief judges, high priests, and lawyers conspire together to condemn prophets to death while simultaneously working to free their own associates from the legal system after having committed murders and other crimes. Their actions are summarized in the verse below.

> And they did set at defiance the law and the rights of their country; and they did covenant one with another to destroy the governor, and to establish a king over the land, that the land should no more be at liberty but should be subject unto kings.[22]

Once again note the contrast and incompatibility of kings and liberty. As illustrated by these several examples given above, one element of the principle

---

[17] 2 Nephi 10:11
[18] 2 Nephi 10:11
[19] Mosiah 23:13
[20] Alma 51:5
[21] Alma 51:8
[22] 3 Nephi 6:30 (20-30)

of liberty as defined by The Book of Mormon is the absence of kings. Conversely, where people are subject to kings, liberty does not exist.[23]

The most detailed and explicit treatment of kings as rulers in The Book of Mormon is found in the final chapter of the Book of Mosiah, which consists largely of a circulation written by King Mosiah—the final king of the Nephites—on the subject of kingship and his proposal that the Nephites do away with it in favor of a system of judges that would make them more free. The Nephites follow King Mosiah's counsel in this and establish a system of judges, doing away with kings. This event is of such significance that from this time forward, the Nephites reckon their time based on which year it is since the establishment of the judges. This continues until the coming of Christ, when they begin to reckon their time based on His appearance instead.

This may seem like an insignificant point to a twenty-first century student of The Book of Mormon, so far removed from Nephite culture, history, and day-to-day living. But, the reader here is encouraged to ponder on just how significant an event must be to cause a society to begin measuring their time from it. Clearly the impact of this change to Nephite government was perceived by them to be far reaching and substantial. The change amounted to a substantive shift in the balance of power between the government and the citizenry and was thereby marked as an extremely significant point in their history.

In his writing, Mosiah goes into specific detail as to why kingship is inferior and how kings tend to interfere with liberty. First, he points out that "the judgements of man are not always just" and "because all men are not just it is not expedient that ye should have a king or kings to rule over you."[24]

Mosiah's wording in this passage is very interesting. He states that we should not have "a king or *kings* to rule over [us]," explicitly adding the plural reference. In so doing, Mosiah appears to be saying that it doesn't really matter whether it is an individual or a group, the unrighteous rule by either will produce the same outcome. It is all too easy when reading this scripture to lend too much attention to the title "king" and suppose that as long as that title isn't found in a particular form of government, then there is nothing to fear. But the more salient point that Mosiah is making here is not to have anyone—king or kings, individual or a group—"rule over you." Why? Because "men are not just." The emphasis here should be not on the positional title of king, but more on the principle of one individual or group being setup as ruler or rulers over others. The principle that Mosiah is teaching to the Nephites is this: you cannot trust

---

[23] See also Alma 51:5
[24] Mosiah 29:12,16

men to be righteous and just, and so it is not right to have some men rule over others, therefore don't trust any man or group to be ruler over you.

The criticism that Mosiah is making is not of kings specifically, but of the more general concept of imperfect, unjust men being made into rulers over other men. In other words, governing bodies and individuals should not be made into rulers. As is demonstrated below, one party being a ruler or rulers over another party includes, among other things, the ruling party forcing behavior onto the subject party.

King Mosiah goes into detail as to why he makes this criticism in verse 23:

> And he enacteth laws, and sendeth them forth among his people, yea, laws after the manner of his own wickedness; and whosoever doth not obey his laws he causeth to be destroyed; and whosoever doth rebel against him he will send his armies against them to war, and if he can he will destroy them; and thus an unrighteous king doth pervert the ways of all righteousness.[25]

In this verse Mosiah is again speaking in reference to a singular king, however, all of the wrongs that he cites as the evil in which a wicked king may engage can just as easily by perpetrated by a body of rulers or "kings" as opposed to a single individual. For example, a governing body or group also enacts laws and sends them among the people. If that body or group of governors, or "kings" is wicked to any degree then the laws will be reflective of that wickedness. Disobedient or rebellious subjects are destroyed. This is a pattern easily recognizable throughout mankind's history that has been repeated by both individuals and groups alike.

The principal reason cited by Mosiah for his criticism of kingship is that of a top-down use of force and coercion to control the behavior of people, more particularly to make that behavior more wicked. The reader is here encouraged to recall the discussion on the principle of agency in chapter 1 and the two plans presented for the redemption of mankind. Satan's plan was designed around this very concept of forced behavior. It is important to remember that Satan was expelled from Heaven and became the source of wickedness in our world and that his plan was to force the children of men to keep the commandments, not to do evil. Therefore, it was the force of man's will that was the wickedness for which he was expelled and not for explicit wickedness that he was going to force them to perform. The forcing of behavior onto an individual is inherently evil regardless of the type of behavior being forced.

---

[25] Mosiah 29:23

The Book of Mormon contains several examples of the issue of kingship being treated by prophets or other prominent figures. Nephi's followers wanted to make him their king, but Nephi refused and "was desirous that they should have no king."[26]

Alma led many converts away from King Noah and his wicked priests. The converts that he led away desired that he would be their king. Alma refused and said to them, "it is not expedient that we should have a king; for thus saith the Lord: Ye shall not esteem one flesh above another, or one man shall not think himself above another; therefore I say unto you it is not expedient that ye should have a king."[27] Several verses later, Alma exhorts the people, "ye should stand fast in this liberty wherewith ye have been made free, and that ye trust no man to be a king over you."[28]

Amlici, who was "a very cunning man, yea, a wise man as to the wisdom of the world,"[29] and "being a wicked man,"[30] wanted to make himself a king over the Nephite people. He tried to do so by vote and when that attempt failed he tried to establish his rule by force of arms. The "Nephites, or the people of God"[31] armed themselves and fought off Amlici and his followers, killing many of them.

The early Jaredites desired that Jared and his brother anoint one of their sons to be a "king over them."[32] This they eventually did, but very reluctantly. The brother of Jared said, "Surely this thing leadeth into captivity."[33] All of the sons of Jared and his brother refused to be kings except for one son of Jared whose name was Orihah.

It is important to note that none of the sons of Jared and his brother were at this time considered to be wicked that we know of. In fact, Orihah, who was the one anointed in the end, is described as one who "did walk humbly before the Lord"[34] and "did execute judgement upon the land in righteousness."[35]

Why then was the brother of Jared so concerned? The brother of Jared saw the danger in vesting a single individual with too much power and in making that individual into a ruler over the rest of the people. He knew that the people could not always count on righteous kings having righteous successors. He knew that kingship was passed down from one king to the next often by familial heritage

---

[26] 2 Nephi 5:18
[27] Mosiah 23:6-7
[28] Mosiah 23:13
[29] Alma 2:1
[30] Alma 2:4
[31] Alma 2:11
[32] Ether 6:22
[33] Ether 6:23 (22-27)
[34] Ether 6:30
[35] Ether 7:1

and the people being ruled would have no control over the character of their rulers and successors.

The fears of Jared's brother proved justified as subsequent rulers, who either inherited the kingship or forced it through violence because of a belief of their right to it, were indeed evil. They forced their wickedness onto the entire Jaredite nation and the result was misery and captivity among the citizens, and their ultimate destruction as a nation and a people.

Judges

Mosiah doesn't stop at merely criticizing kingship and rulers, but goes on to propose an alternative to the top down approach of rulers possessing all the power over their subjects. In place of kingship, Mosiah proposes to "appoint judges, to judge this people according to our law."[36] More significantly, he counsels, "choose you by the voice of this people, judges..."[37]

Mosiah proposes, and the Nephites subsequently establish, a fundamental shift in the basis of Nephite government. The new system is a system of judges in place of a king and is referred to by the Nephite record keepers as the reign of the judges. This new system, however, is not a mere change in title and plurality from a single individual being called king to a group of people carrying the title of judges. Instead, it is a complete shift in the government's role, and its source of power and authority.

Most significant is the fact that the new judges were elected by the people as opposed to receiving the office by inheritance or some other arbitrary method unrelated to character or capacity to govern. Mosiah goes so far as to recommend making it the law that they do all "business by the voice of the people."[38] With respect to the new system of judges and the new manner of doing business, Mosiah teaches:

> And now if ye have judges, and they do not judge you according to the law which has been given, ye can cause that they may be judged of a higher judge.
>
> If your higher judges do not judge righteous judgements, ye shall cause that a small number of your lower judges should be gathered together, and they shall judge your higher judges, according to the voice of the people.[39]

---

[36] Mosiah 29:11
[37] Mosiah 29:25
[38] Mosiah 29:26
[39] Mosiah 29:28-29

Here Mosiah describes a form of government where the governing power originates with the people. The people are to elect the judges, the people are to make sure they are judging according to the law, and the people are to cause them to judge each other when they do not judge according to the law. It is clear that Mosiah is instituting a system of government where the government is accountable to the people.

Very interestingly, Mosiah also describes a system of internal checks within the government itself. The government is not instituted with the sole purpose of ruling or judging the people, but is expected to also judge and maintain checks on itself, "according to the voice of the people."

It is important to note here that "business by the voice of the people" is not to be understood as advocacy for pure and direct democracy, where the people vote on all matters of policy. There is no evidence in The Book of Mormon that the people were voting on every matter of policy. Instead they voted to elect representatives as is described in verse 39.

> Therefore, it came to pass that they assembled themselves together in bodies throughout the land, to cast in their voices concerning who should be their judges, to judge them according to the law which had been given them; and they were exceedingly rejoiced because of the liberty which had been granted unto them.[40]

The system proposed by Mosiah and ultimately implemented by the Nephites was a representative system of government where sovereignty rested with the people who delegated some of their authority to elected representatives to act in their name and on their behalf in a governing capacity. As previously pointed out, this was a very significant occurrence among the Nephites. "They were exceedingly rejoiced because of the liberty which had been granted unto them." They rejoiced so much in this liberty, that they began reckoning their time based on this change.

Self-Government

Toward the end of his writings, Mosiah makes an interesting statement that is then followed up by Mormon as he interjects into the abridgement. Mosiah repeats how the people's sins are often caused by their kings and then states that "their iniquities are answered upon the heads of their kings."[41] Mosiah then continues, "And now I desire that this inequality should be no more in this land,

---

[40] Mosiah 29:39
[41] Mosiah 29:31

especially among this my people; but I desire that this land be a land of liberty, and every man may enjoy his rights and privileges alike..."[42]

Then Mormon summarizes a little by saying "many more things did king Mosiah write unto them, unfolding unto them all the trials and troubles of a *righteous* king ... but that the burden should come upon all the people, that every man might bear his part."[43]

What Mosiah and Mormon are both advocating for is self-government. First, Mosiah denounces the inequality of having rulers force people to commit sins so that those sins are answered on the rulers' heads. Instead, Mosiah desires that "every man may enjoy his rights and privileges alike." Every individual should share in the same rights and privileges. Every individual should have to follow the same laws and be subject to the same consequences of breaking those laws. Everyone should be equally protected and equally treated under the law. In short, institutionalized government should provide the same benefits to every individual being governed, and every individual subject to a government and its laws should be treated equally by that government and those laws.

But Mosiah is not satisfied with listing only the benefits of good government. We don't have his writings on this because he wrote "many more things" that aren't included here. Mormon, however, states how King Mosiah—very interestingly—described all the "troubles of a *righteous* king!" When a king rules righteously, he carries an undue portion of the burden of government. Mormon paraphrases Mosiah in saying that this "burden should come upon all the people, that every man might bear his part." Here we see that in Mormon's view of a free society, each member of the society bears responsibility in contributing to and upholding that society. In a free and self-governing society, if the people are to maintain their sovereignty, they must be willing to participate in the governing process and each "bear his part."

In summary, Mormon and Mosiah are saying that under good government everyone has the same rights and privileges and should enjoy them alike. Everyone also has certain responsibilities to participate in that government and should bear their part of the burden. This is self-government. Instead of having rulers rule over people, the people participate in and enjoy the benefits of their own government. The people establish the government and then delegate some of their power and authority, through election, to certain individuals to act in governing capacities. The people, however, should remain the source of authority and retain the power to control the government and correct it when it goes astray.

---

[42] Mosiah 29:32

[43] Mosiah 29:33-34 (emphasis added)

The result of Mosiah's writings and teachings was that the people "relinquished their desires for a king, and became exceedingly anxious that every man should have an equal chance throughout all the land; yea, and every man expressed a willingness to answer for his own sins."[44] As has been demonstrated already, this is an integral characteristic of agency, that each individual be accountable for their own sins and not for the sins of others.

Every man had an equal chance to be elected into office, instead of a kingship which is decided by birth, political intrigue, or violence. Every man also was willing to accept more responsibility and be accountable for his actions.

Interestingly, the government system advocated by Mosiah can be seen to be "of the people, by the people, [and] for the people."[45] It was of the people because the judges were to be elected from among the people and each individual had an equal chance to participate, by the people because everything was to be done by the voice of the people, and for the people in that it was meant to preserve the rights, privileges, and freedoms of all the people in equal measure.

Bondage & Captivity

The words bondage and captivity are used quite often throughout The Book of Mormon. This section will list and discuss the various manners in which they are used. This section is not intended to be an exhaustive list of every use of these terms and will be limited to those uses where clarifying or informative descriptions are found in association.

Bondage is first used in reference to the Israelite condition during their sojourn in Egypt.[46] This reference needs little to no explanation as the Israelites were in complete and total bondage to the Egyptians who owned, controlled, and ruled over them in every way. The Israelites during this period were slaves, used for hard labor, and forced into poor living conditions.

The next people who are described as being in bondage are the group of Nephites who accompanied Zeniff to possess the land of their inheritance and were discussed previously in conjunction with taxation.

Later in the record, Captain Moroni is said to know the intentions of the Lamanites who were at the time making war against the Nephite people. He said "that it was their intention to destroy their brethren, or to subject them and

---

[44] Mosiah 29:38

[45] Compare to *Gettysburg Address* by Abraham Lincoln

[46] 1 Nephi 17:24-25; 19:10

bring them into bondage that they might establish a kingdom unto themselves over all the land."[47]

Zarahemna was the military leader leading the Lamanite armies at this time. Zarahemna's designs were described so that "he might gain power over the Nephites by bringing them into bondage."[48]

In all these scenarios above, bondage is associated with power and control that one group exerts over another.[49]

Finally, Nephi prophecies of the pilgrims who would one day settle the American Colonies, he refers to them as Gentiles who "went forth out of captivity."[50] They were fleeing the monarchies of Europe and a world where religious doctrine was dictated by the state. Nephi does not get into details as to why he said they were in captivity, but quite a bit about the early pilgrims is known from more modern history. What they were fleeing from when they came to America were many of the same things observed here among Book of Mormon peoples. They were laden with heavy taxes, subject to arbitrary rulers, and forced into state mandated religious beliefs or persecuted for "heresy," which was any belief or system of thought or expression that was not approved of or not considered sanctioned by the state.

Captain Moroni

One very notable personality in The Book of Mormon is Captain Moroni. Moroni was made military commander over all the armies of the Nephites, at the age of 25[51], during the first century BC. Moroni was also well admired by Mormon, the Nephite historian who abridged the Nephite records into what is now The Book of Mormon. Mormon wrote of Captain Moroni:

> And Moroni was a strong and a mighty man; he was a man of a perfect understanding; yea, a man that did not delight in bloodshed; a man whose soul did joy in the liberty and the freedom of his country, and his brethren from bondage and slavery;
>
> Yea, a man whose heart did swell with thanksgiving to his God, for the many privileges and blessings which he bestowed upon his people; a man who did labor exceedingly for the welfare and safety of his people.

---

[47] Alma 43:29
[48] Alma 43:8
[49] See also Alma 51:8
[50] 1 Nephi 13:13,16,19,29,30
[51] Alma 43:17

> Yea, and he was a man who was firm in the faith of Christ, and he had sworn with an oath to defend his people, his rights, and his country, and his religion, even to the loss of his blood...
>
> Yea, verily, verily I say unto you, if all men had been, and were, and ever would be, like unto Moroni, behold, the very powers of hell would have been shaken forever, yea, the devil would never have power over the hearts of the children of men.[52]

Clearly Mormon thought very highly of Moroni, the probable namesake of his own son who completed The Book of Mormon record and prepared it for future generations. A full twenty chapters (Alma 43-62) are filled with the character and doings of Captain Moroni, roughly ten percent of the record as a whole. Few Book of Mormon persons are featured so prominently.

The verses cited above deserve some further analysis as they reveal valuable insight into Mormon's esteem of freedom and liberty. These verses are always correctly interpreted as glowing praise for Captain Moroni, but often the reason and source of that praise is too easily overlooked.

First, Mormon refers to Moroni as "a man of a perfect understanding." What's noteworthy about this is that Mormon does not follow this up with details of an ecclesiastical ministry, doctrinal dissertations, or Gospel preaching. Rather, Mormon points out how Moroni was "a man whose soul did joy in the liberty and the freedom of his country ... and he had sworn with an oath to defend his people, his rights, and his country ... even to the loss of his blood." Then Mormon spends 20 chapters demonstrating just how devoted Moroni was to the "cause of liberty"[53] among his people and his country.

It's clear that a significant theme in Mormon's praising description of Captain Moroni is the latter's love, understanding of, and devotion to liberty and freedom, rights, and his country. After praising Moroni such, and providing his reasoning behind his praise, Mormon then makes the bold and familiar (among Latter-day Saints) declaration that "if all men had been, and were, and ever would be, like unto Moroni, behold, the very powers of hell would have been shaken forever, yea, the devil would never have power over the hearts of the children of men."

After such a powerful and resounding declaration, attention again needs to be drawn to the fact that Captain Moroni was not a prophet or ecclesiastical leader (that we know of), and that the focus of Mormon's praise is directed at Moroni

---

52 Alma 48:11-13,17

53 Alma 51:17; 58:12

as a military commander and a staunch defender of rights, privileges, liberty, and freedom.

The content of the chapters that contain Captain Moroni focus largely on an ongoing war that the Nephites are required to wage in defense of their nation from enemy aggressors both from without and from within. These chapters comprise the majority of the portion of The Book of Mormon that is sometimes referred to as the "war chapters" by Latter-day Saints.

One well known episode in The Book of Mormon is when Captain Moroni establishes what he calls the title of liberty, causes the people to covenant to uphold it, and then raises it in many cities throughout all the land of the Nephites while recruiting for his army to defend against the Lamanites. The initial raising of the title of liberty is found in the forty-sixth chapter of the Book of Alma. Moroni heard report of a man named Amalickiah, who had amassed a number of followers and together with them he was seeking "to destroy the foundation of liberty which God had granted unto them."[54]

> And now it came to pass that when Moroni, who was the chief commander of the armies of the Nephites, had heard of these dissensions, he was angry with Amalickiah.
>
> And it came to pass that he rent his coat; and he took a piece thereof, and wrote upon it—In memory of our God, our religion, and freedom, and our peace, our wives, and our children—and he fastened it upon the end of a pole.
>
> And he fastened on his head-plate, and his breastplate, and his shields, and girded on his armor about his loins; and he took the pole, which had on the end thereof his rent coat, (and he called it the title of liberty) and he bowed himself to the earth, and he prayed mightily unto his God for the blessings of liberty to rest upon his brethren, so long as there should a band of Christians remain to possess the land...
>
> And therefore, at this time, Moroni prayed that the cause of the Christians, and the freedom of the land might be favored."[55]

Note the frequency of references to liberty and freedom in these verses. Also note the close association that is here established between freedom and religion, particularly Christianity, and how it is treated as a principle on par with and of similar importance to God and the Christian religion.

To summarize, Captain Moroni was a man highly esteemed by the Nephite people, by Mormon, and presumably by God if Mormon's description and praise

---

[54] Alma 46:10

[55] Alma 46:11-13,16

of him when introduced can be considered an indicator. Captain Moroni is used as an instructional figure in The Book of Mormon, which book contains the fullness of the Gospel. In detailing Captain Moroni's achievements and characteristics, The Book of Mormon intently focuses on his love for, understanding of, and defense of freedom and liberty as opposed to his spiritual beliefs, teachings, and works. His treatment and stature in The Book of Mormon record is a testament to the importance of liberty to the Gospel plan and the merit of understanding and defending liberty as considered by God and His prophets.

Amalickiah

One of Captain Moroni's early antagonists is a man named Amalickiah. Briefly mentioned above as the catalyst for Moroni's title of liberty, Amalickiah is an antithetical figure that Mormon seemingly places in the record with the intent of contrasting him with Moroni. Amalickiah likewise deserves some attention here to demonstrate that contrast.

Where Mormon's introduction of Captain Moroni is filled with praise and admiration, his subsequent introduction of Amalickiah is less than affectionate. Below are the verses in which Amalickiah and his followers make their entry into The Book of Mormon record.

> And Amalickiah was desirous to be a king; and those people who were wroth were also desirous that he should be their king; and they were the greater part of them the lower judges of the land, and they were seeking for power.
>
> And they had been led by the flatteries of Amalickiah, that if they would support him and establish him to be their king that he would make them rulers over the people.
>
> Thus they were led away by Amalickiah to dissensions...[56]

Amalickiah wanted to be king over the Nephite people and was able to enlist many followers who also wanted him to be king. Many of his followers were made up of existing judges in the lower courts of the land and were enticed by Amalickiah's promises of reciprocation of political favors and power.

In these verses and subsequent verses, references are made to the "flatteries of Amalickiah." Many people were led to believe in the "flattering words of

[56] Alma 46:4-6

Amalickiah."[57] After introducing and describing Amalickiah and his followers, Mormon summarizes with the following:

> Yea, we see that Amalickiah, because he was a man of cunning device and a man of many flattering words, that he led away the hearts of many people to do wickedly; yea, and to seek to destroy the church of God, and to destroy the foundation of liberty which God had granted unto them, or which blessing God had sent upon the face of the land for the righteous' sake.[58]

Amalickiah led many to do wickedly. Among the wickedness that is ascribed to him is that he sought "to destroy the foundation of liberty which God had granted unto them, or which blessing God had sent upon the face of the land for the righteous' sake." Note again how closely liberty is associated with God and His Church. Also note how liberty is considered a blessing from God and that it is given for the benefit of the righteous. The foundation of liberty being referred to here is in the context of the Nephite system of government at the time of having elected and representative judges and not kings. Finally, note the contrast that Mormon portrays between Moroni, a man of perfect understanding who fights to defend liberty, and Amalickiah, a man of cunning deceit and wickedness, who works to undermine and destroy liberty.

In the following chapters Moroni and Amalickiah have a brief confrontation. Afterwards, Amalickiah and his followers defect to the Lamanites where Amalickiah employs more deceit, intrigue, and ultimately murder to usurp the position of king over the Lamanites. He then manipulates the Lamanites into invading the Nephites and the end result is the long and drawn out war fought over the next 15 years or so and comprising a large portion of Captain Moroni's military career.

King-men and Freemen

Another episode in The Book of Mormon is extremely instructive regarding how its authors valued freedom and liberty. During the first century BC, there arose a group of people, known as king-men, who "were desirous that the law should be altered in a manner to overthrow the free government and to establish a king over the land."[59]

---

[57] Alma 46:7

[58] Alma 46:10

[59] Alma 51:5

The king-men are described in a following verse as "those of high birth, and they sought to be kings; and they were supported by those who sought power and authority over the people."[60]

Opposing the king-men were another group of people who came to call themselves freemen. "[T]he freemen had sworn or covenanted to maintain their rights and the privileges of their religion by a free government."[61]

Note the contrast between the two groups. The king-men considered themselves more worthy of governing roles because of their lineage. They thought they were better equipped to determine how society should be and sought to impose their views on others through the force of government, specifically monarchical government. The freemen were concerned with preserving and maintaining everyone's rights and freedom and had committed to do so through oath or covenant. The similarity between these two groups and the two sides that formed to fight the war in Heaven is not easily ignored.

At the same time that the conflict between king-men and freemen was raging, the aforementioned Amalickiah was preparing to invade Nephite territory with the Lamanites of whom he had taken control and manipulated into a state of war with the Nephites.

What follows is extremely significant and is detailed in the verses below.

> And it came to pass that when the men who were called king-men had heard that the Lamanites were coming down to battle against them, they were glad in their hearts; and they refused to take up arms, for they were so wroth with the chief judge, and also with the people of liberty, that they would not take up arms to defend their country.
>
> And it came to pass that when Moroni saw this, and also saw that the Lamanites were coming into the borders of the land, he was exceedingly wroth because of the stubbornness of those people whom he had labored with so much diligence to preserve; yea, he was exceedingly wroth; his soul was filled with anger against them.
>
> And it came to pass that he sent a petition, with the voice of the people, unto the governor of the land, desiring that he should read it, and give him (Moroni) power to compel those dissenters to defend their country or to put them to death...
>
> And it came to pass that the armies did march forth against them; and they did pull down their pride and their nobility, insomuch that as they did lift their weapons of war to fight against the men of Moroni they were hewn down and leveled to the earth.

---

[60] Alma 51:8

[61] Alma 51:6

> And it came to pass that there were four thousand of those dissenters who were hewn down by the sword; and those of their leaders who were not slain in battle were taken and cast into prison...[62]

The king-men took advantage of the invading Lamanites to make an attempt to undermine and sabotage the government, and thereby their country with which they were displeased, by refusing to fight. For a solution, Moroni, with permission from the chief judge and the people, marched with his armies on his own people and put to death those that refused to defend their country and fight for liberty.

Before any of this is misunderstood or misconstrued, this is not intended to be a case for using any sort of violence against people of differing political opinions. The discussion of why or when such actions as this might be appropriate is a separate discussion and not considered important to the purposes of this writing. The more important point here is that there exist circumstances at all where it is justifiable to use deadly force and put to death those that would undermine the liberty of their country and fellow citizens.

Also important is to note the behavior on both sides of the liberty argument in these passages of scripture. The king-men saw an opportunity with the invading Lamanites and devised to essentially hold the Nephite people ransom by withholding their support of the defense effort as a means to get their way, which was to eliminate the form of government with which they were unhappy. Captain Moroni, along with Pahoran and the people of liberty, saw this behavior as grievous enough that they were willing to root it out by the sword.

The king-men and the freemen constitute another stark contrast between those who desire to force behavior on others and those that will fight for and defend freedom and liberty. The two groups are very similar to the two sides formed in the war in Heaven that was fought over agency. The episode between these two groups and its inclusion in The Book of Mormon is another example of the importance of liberty in the Gospel and which side God's people and followers are expected to be on.

Ammonihah

There is one final story in The Book of Mormon that serves well to illustrate the importance of liberty and where God Himself stands on liberty. Alma is one of the prophets in The Book of Mormon and was called at one point to preach to the people in a city named Ammonihah.

---

[62] Alma 51:13-15,18-19

The spiritual conditions of the city of Ammonihah are described in the following verse of scripture. "Now Satan had gotten great hold upon the hearts of the people of the city of Ammonihah; therefore they would not hearken unto the words of Alma."[63] The people of Ammonihah reject Alma and Alma leaves the city in search of more agreeable audiences elsewhere. During his travel away from the city of Ammonihah, Alma is visited by an angel who commands him to return to Ammonihah and continue his preaching there. The angel gives a specific message to deliver to the inhabitants of Ammonihah. He says:

> And behold, I am sent to command thee that thou return to the city of Ammonihah, and preach again unto the people of the city; yea, preach unto them. Yea, say unto them, except they repent the Lord God will destroy them.
>
> For behold, they do study at this time that they may destroy the liberty of thy people, (for thus saith the Lord) which is contrary to the statutes, and judgments, and commandments which he has given unto his people.[64]

The message that Alma is to carry back to the residents of Ammonihah is that they will be destroyed by God if they do not repent. The interesting part is why they will be destroyed, "[f]or behold, they do study at this time that they may destroy the liberty of thy people."

Alma returns to the city and meets a righteous man named Amulek who becomes his companion in preaching the Gospel. Amulek testifies against the people of Ammonihah with a direct warning, saying, "And now behold, I say unto you, that the foundation of the destruction of this people is beginning to be laid by the unrighteousness of your lawyers and your judges."[65] It is worthy of note that the root of the wickedness that was leading to the aforementioned destruction is found in the government. It should also be noted that their wickedness was in their working against "the statutes, and judgements, and commandments" that the Lord had given to the people.

Not much detail is given into what the unrighteousness of the lawyers and judges actually is. One example is given whereby the judges were manipulating the people into using their services more because they were paid by the amount of time they spent deliberating and judging cases.[66] By today's standards, this is a seemingly small infraction on the part of the judges, however, it was serious enough to earn its place as the sole example of the wickedness for which the

---

[63] Alma 8:9
[64] Alma 8:16-17
[65] Alma 10:27
[66] See Alma 11:20

people of Ammonihah were threatened with destruction by the Lord. Surely there was more to it, but it is reasonable to presume that a lot of it had to do with the lawyers and judges manipulating the levers and mechanisms of government for their own benefit and gain at the expense of the people, as was the case in this example above. Whatever they were doing, it was a threat to the liberty of the Nephite people and for this reason the Lord promised to destroy them Himself if they failed to repent. The people of Ammonihah did not repent and, not long after the preaching of Alma and Amulek, were destroyed by an invading force of Lamanites.[67]

The story of Ammonihah is not completely unique in The Book of Mormon record. The central culminating event of The Book of Mormon is the visit of the Resurrected Lord Himself to the Nephite people. After His mortal ministry, death, and subsequent resurrection in Jerusalem, He visited the Nephite people and established His Church among them. At the time of the Crucifixion, there was great destruction around the lands of the peoples of The Book of Mormon. Many cities were destroyed. Prior to His actual visit and ministry among the Nephites, Jesus Christ spoke to them and listed many of the cities that had been destroyed by His hand and why. For the discussion in this book, one of them in particular, Jacobugath, is very interesting. In the book of 3 Nephi can be found the Lord's description of His destruction of the city of Jacobugath as follows.

> And behold, that great city Jacobugath, which was inhabited by the people of king Jacob, have I caused to be burned with fire because of their sins and their wickedness, which was above all the wickedness of the whole earth, because of their secret murders and combinations; for it was they that did destroy the peace of my people and the government of the land; therefore I did cause them to be burned, to destroy them from before my face, that the blood of the prophets and the saints should not come up unto me any more against them.[68]

Of all the cities listed in this chapter by the Lord, only Jacobugath earns the status of being "above all the wickedness of the whole earth." Also unique to Jacobugath is that they employed secret combinations to destroy the free government of the Nephites.

Agency and Liberty

It is necessary now to distinguish between agency and liberty. Liberty is a principle very akin to agency, though the two are not identical. As demonstrated

---

[67] See Alma 16:2-3

[68] 3 Nephi 9:9

in chapter 1, agency is given to man by God and therefore cannot be forcibly taken from him. Liberty, on the other hand, can be severely restricted or all together taken from one man by another. As an example, a man can be placed in a jail cell or in shackles and so be extremely limited in his liberty while retaining possession of his agency to love and forgive his captors or to hate, despise, and seek revenge on them.

Agency is the power, granted by God, for us to choose who to be, how to feel, what to think, and how to act. Liberty, or freedom, is the ability to carry out those choices through physical acts. Liberty is largely dependent on external circumstances whereas agency is an internal power intrinsic to every human being and inseparable from that being.

The two principles are very similar and there is a fair amount of overlap in their definitions. The line dividing agency and liberty is a fine line that is often difficult to define. Elder Dallin H. Oaks has distinguished between the two concepts by defining agency as "an exercise of the will, the power to choose" and freedom as the "power and privilege to carry out our choices."[69] He then further clarifies with the following:

> Because free agency is a God-given precondition to the purpose of mortal life, no person or organization can take away our free agency in mortality...
>
> What can be taken away or reduced by the conditions of mortality is our freedom, the power to act upon our choices. Free agency is absolute, but in the circumstances of mortality freedom is always qualified.
>
> Freedom may be qualified or taken away ... by the action of others, including governments...
>
> A loss of freedom reduces the extent to which we can act upon our choices, but it does not deprive us of our God-given free agency.[70]

A little further down in the same address, Elder Oaks cites a couple of examples:

> Interferences with our freedom do not deprive us of our free agency. When Pharaoh put Joseph in prison, he restricted Joseph's freedom, but he did not take away his free agency. When Jesus drove the money changers out of the temple, he interfered with their freedom to engage in a particular activity at a particular time in a particular place, but he did not take away their free agency.[71]

---

[69] Dallin H. Oaks, *Free Agency and Freedom*, BYU, October-1987

[70] Ibid.

[71] Ibid.

Though the two principles are very similar, it is important to properly distinguish between them in order to correctly frame arguments regarding liberty. After giving a detailed background in agency and freedom, including the quotes and examples above, Elder Oaks states:

> Freedom is obviously of great importance, but as these examples illustrate, freedom is always qualified in mortality. Consequently, when we oppose a government-imposed loss of freedom, it would be better if we did not conduct our debate in terms of a loss of our free agency, which is impossible under our doctrine. We ought to focus on the legality or the wisdom of the proposed restriction of our freedom.[72]

Agency is granted to man by God and cannot be taken by other men or manmade institutions, including governments. Liberty, or freedom, may be lost while in mortality or taken by others, including governments. Losing liberty will restrict or diminish the ability to exercise one's agency but cannot deprive an individual of that agency.

Summary and Conclusions

Mormon was compiling a record with very limited space and was using as his sources all the records of the Nephites that had been produced over roughly a thousand years. Mormon admits that he can only include very little information In his abridgement.[73] Additionally, the record that Mormon compiled was intended to be spiritual and was to be taken from the spiritual portion of the Nephite histories.[74] Given these constraints, it is telling that Mormon chose to include all that he did on the subject of liberty, including the entire 29th chapter of the Book of Mosiah and 20 chapters worth of Captain Moroni and his struggles with and for the Nephite people for the express purpose of preserving their liberty.

Liberty is a principle that is not treated lightly by the authors of The Book of Mormon nor, evidently, by the Nephite people. From the evidence presented in this chapter, it is clearly a principle that is closely related to the Gospel of Jesus Christ and also tied to the more supernal principle of agency. Liberty is worth defending unto bloodshed and even is expected to be defended by righteous Christians.

---

[72] Ibid.

[73] See Words of Mormon 1:5 (3-10); 3 Nephi 5:8; Jacob 3:13, 4:1

[74] See Words of Mormon 1:3-6; 1 Nephi 6:3, 9:2-4

Below is a list of characteristics in a society that have been examined in this chapter as aspects of liberty as taught by The Book of Mormon:

- The absence of kings or rulers
- Power and authority resting with the people—popular sovereignty
- The free election of representative officials (in the Nephites' case, judges)
- Each individual having an equal chance to be elected
- The equal treatment of each individual under the law
- Everyone participating in the governing process
- Freedom of religion and worship
- Ownership and control of property (lands and possessions)
- The absence of burdensome taxes

These are the characteristics that the Nephite people and Book of Mormon authors considered indicative of a free society. Note, however, that while the structure of a society can be free or conducive to freedom it still remains vulnerable to deceit and corruption and those that desire power for the sake of having power, or for the purpose of ruling over others. Mormon and other Book of Mormon personalities recognized this and at times experienced and fought against such corruption. As an example, please refer to the previously cited episode of corrupt judges found in the book of 3 Nephi.[75]

This vulnerability is absolutely critical to recognize so that false complacency is not suffered when the structure of a society has all the markers and characteristics of being free. Free government can be usurped by despots and others with less than righteous intentions. Indeed there is a political equivalent to the spiritual warning given by Jesus to beware of wolves in sheep's clothing.[76]

Freedom's preservation requires an aware and active citizenry. In a truly free society, power rests with the people that comprise the society. For them to remain free and self-governing, the people need to be judicious in whom they are electing as representatives so that the representatives don't slowly usurp the people's authority and make themselves into rulers.

In a 1938 edition of the *Improvement Era* magazine, Elder Albert E. Bowen of the Quorum of the Twelve Apostles taught:

> So important is the principle of liberty, so essential is it to man's higher self-realization and so inexorably necessary to dignity of his

[75] 3 Nephi 6:20-30
[76] Matthew 7:15; 3 Nephi 14:15; See also Alma 5:60

> status as the issue of Deity that the omnipotent God Himself does not countenance compulsion. Ample ancient and modern evidences of this have been scripturally recorded.[77]

In a 1962 edition of the *Improvement Era* magazine, President David O. McKay wrote:

> Next to the bestowal of life itself, the right to direct that life is God's greatest gift to man. One of the most urgent needs today is the preservation of individual liberty. Freedom of choice is more to be treasured than any possession earth can give. It is inherent in the spirit of man. It is a divine gift to every normal being. Whether born in abject poverty or shackled at birth by inherited riches, everyone has this most precious of all life's endowments—the gift of free agency—man's inherited and inalienable right...
>
> Force, on the other hand, emanates from Lucifer himself. Even in man's pre-existent state, Satan sought power to compel the human family to do his will by suggesting that the free agency of man be inoperative. If his plan had been accepted, human beings would have become mere puppets in the hand of a dictator, and the purpose of man's coming to earth would have been frustrated. Satan's proposed system of government, therefore, was rejected, and the principle of free agency established in its place.[78]

Liberty and agency are principles established by God. Force and compulsion are tools used by the Adversary. Liberty is a principle prominently featured and taught in The Book of Mormon but sometimes overlooked or discounted by its readers and adherents. The authors and prophets of The Book of Mormon, however, esteemed liberty as a high ideal, granted by God and worthy of defense by military force and arms. There are several instances in The Book of Mormon where the enemies of liberty, and those who attempt to undermine it, are treated with severity and ultimately pay with their lives. This treatment is advocated and carried out by prophets and other servants of God and even by God Himself. The Book of Mormon, which contains the fullness of the Gospel of Jesus Christ, provides ample evidence that liberty is a principle inextricably linked to that Gospel and the principles of Heaven and Eternity.

---

[77] Jerreld L. Newquist, *Prophets, Principles and National Survival*, 1964, p. 127

[78] Ibid., pp. 135, 136-137

Chapter 3 – America

This chapter will focus on the nation of the United States of America, the prophecies regarding its establishment and the means employed to establish it.

Prophecy Regarding the Nation

Some 2,600 years ago, a prominent Book of Mormon prophet named Nephi testified that "the Lord God will raise up a mighty nation among the Gentiles, yea, even upon the face of this land."[1] That mighty nation has since been understood to be the United States of America. Nephi prophesied of the establishment of this nation in the then distant future and, while doing so, attested to the fact that this nation would be raised up by God Himself.

Roughly 600 years later, during the Savior's ministry among the Nephite people, He taught "For it is wisdom in the Father that they [the Gentiles] should be established in this land, and be set up as a free people by the power of the Father."[2] Here the Savior testifies that the American people, to whom He referred as the Gentiles, would be established "by the power of the Father" and that it is by God the Father's own design, and again by His power, that they be made a "free people."

In 1833 the Lord Jesus Christ, in a revelation to His prophet, Joseph Smith, declared that *He* "established the Constitution of this land" and that *He* "raised up" the Founders "unto this very purpose."[3]

It is clear, by these scripture references, that God Himself claims credit for establishing the United States of America. It was always a part of his plan to do so. He founded this country in His wisdom and did so to accomplish His purposes. It was likewise in His wisdom and by His power that America was made a free nation.

Even a cursory examination of America's Founding reveals one, single, overarching principle upon which the Founders intended to construct the fledgling nation of America. That principle is liberty. A more in depth investigation into the Founders and their work reveals just how critical and divine that principle of liberty was believed by them to be. That investigation will come later.

---

[1] 1 Nephi 22:7

[2] 3 Nephi 21:4

[3] D&C 101:80

America's Constitution

At this point, a question begs to be asked. Is it mere coincidence that God the Father exalted agency as one of the supreme principles of Eternity, reveals through prophets and scripture the importance of liberty to the Gospel plan, and then that same God establishes a nation that is founded overwhelmingly on the principle of liberty over all other designs and intentions of men?

To begin to answer this question, let's look into the Lord's purposes behind establishing America. The 101st section of Doctrine and Covenants contains a revelation wherein the Lord reveals His purposes for "rais[ing] up [the] mighty nation" now known as the United States of America. It should be noted that the scripture passage cited below actually refers to America's Constitution rather than the nation itself, however, these will be treated as one and the same for purposes here. It has been established that God has claimed responsibility and credit for establishing the United States as a nation. The Constitution is considered, as will be further demonstrated later, among the principle means utilized for that end. D&C 101:77-80 reads:

> According to the laws and constitution of the people, which I have suffered to be established, and should be maintained for the rights and protection of all flesh, according to just and holy principles;
>
> That every man may act in doctrine and principle pertaining to futurity, according to the moral agency which I have given unto him, that every man may be accountable for his own sins in the day of judgment.
>
> Therefore, it is not right that any man should be in bondage one to another.
>
> And for this purpose have I established the Constitution of this land, by the hands of wise men whom I raised up unto this very purpose, and redeemed the land by the shedding of blood.[4]

The First important principle contained in this passage is that one revealed objective of the Constitution, by God's own mouth, is the "rights and protection of all flesh." Elder Dallin H. Oaks of the Quorum of the Twelve Apostles has elaborated on this matter on more than one occasion. Following are two examples.

In a February, 1992 *Ensign* article, he wrote:

> The United States Constitution was the first written constitution in the world. It has served Americans well, enhancing freedom and prosperity during the changed conditions of more than two hundred

[4] D&C 101 77-80

> years. Frequently copied, it has become the United States' most important export. After two centuries, every nation in the world except six have adopted written constitutions, and the U.S. Constitution was a model for all of them. No wonder modern revelation says that God established the U.S. Constitution and that it "should be maintained for the rights and protection of all flesh, according to just and holy principles."[5]

Then again in a speech on religious freedom delivered on the campus of BYU-Idaho in 2009:

> In 1833, when almost all people in the world were still ruled by kings or tyrants, few could see how the infant United States Constitution could be divinely designed "for the rights and protection of all flesh." Today, 176 years after that revelation, almost every nation in the world has adopted a written constitution, and the United States Constitution profoundly influenced all of them. Truly, this nation's most important export is its constitution, whose great principles stand as a model "for the rights and protection of all flesh."[6]

God directed through revelation that the U.S. Constitution "should be maintained for the rights and protection of all flesh." God also directed Joseph Smith to pray that "the Constitution of our land ... be established forever."[7] This very direct counsel speaks to a purpose for the Constitution that is both greater in scope and more eternal in nature than is generally credited to it, even by many Latter-day Saints.

Elder Oaks interprets "all flesh" to signify all the people of the world, or all of mankind. He does not use this particular phraseology but his meaning is quite clear from his message that was delivered on at least those two distinct occasions.

The other half of that statement is direct counsel from the Lord that the U.S. Constitution "should be maintained." If the Lord Himself says that it should be maintained, then it follows that His faithful disciples will be prominent among the ones maintaining it.

But, to what rights is the Lord referring, and from what exactly does mankind require protection? These questions will be addressed below.

The Second principle revealed to be imbued in and upheld by the U.S. Constitution is "that every man may act ... according to the moral agency which

---

[5] Dallin H. Oaks, *The Divinely Inspired Constitution*, *Ensign*, February-1992

[6] Dallin H. Oaks, *Religious Freedom*, BYU-Idaho , October-2009

[7] D&C 109:54

[God has] given unto him." Here agency resurfaces as one of very few reasons, as cited by God, for His hand in establishing the U.S. Constitution. In fact, a more careful reading of these verses reveals that the protection of agency is the primary reason for God's establishment of the Constitution. The first part of this passage, already discussed above, merely defines the scope of the intended effect—all mankind—and then attests that what follow are the "just and holy principles" upon which the Constitution is founded. What directly follows this is the statement on agency and that God is He who gave agency to man.[8]

What follows next is, "that every man may be accountable for his own sins in the day of judgement." But this is not really a new principle. Instead, it serves as further clarification as to why agency is so important in the eternal Plan of Salvation and why it should be protected for "all flesh." The reader is encouraged to refer back to chapter 2 and Mosiah's writings on how kings, or rulers, can disrupt the system of moral agency and accountability by forcing behavior onto their subjects. That agency is essential and associated with accountability is not new to Latter-day Saints, it is a central tenet of the LDS faith and was treated in detail in chapter 1. A government system where rulers are prescribing behavior for the ruled frustrates the concept of moral agency and thus is at odds with the designs of God.

The next part of this passage declares, "therefore, it is not right that any man should be in bondage one to another." Once again, this is not revealing a new principle so much as continuing the elaboration on agency and applying that principle into a practical context. No one should be in bondage to another because the captor or ruler will disrupt the agency and accountability system by forcing the captive or ruled party to behave in a certain way. Note that it is irrelevant whether the forced behavior is to behave in a manner that is perceived as either good or bad. The real problem is the compulsion itself. God does not approve of forced behavior and does not ever state that it's acceptable to force another to behave in any way, be it good or evil. Recall that Satan's plan was to force mankind to keep the commandments and it was still rejected and caused his expulsion from Heaven.

Finally, the Lord concludes by stating: "for this purpose have I established the Constitution." For what purpose? For the purpose of protecting man's God-given moral agency.

Let's return to the questions asked above as they have now been sufficiently answered. First, is it a coincidence that God exalted agency as one of the supreme principles of Eternity, teaches liberty as a similar eternal principle

[8] See also Moses 7:32

through prophets and scripture, and then takes credit for establishing a nation founded overwhelmingly on the principle of liberty above all else? No, it is not. As has been shown, God explicitly revealed that the protection of man's agency is His primary reason for establishing the Constitution of the United States and thereby the country that resulted from it. He taught that He gave agency to man and that man needs to act according to that agency and therefore should not be in bondage to anyone else. He should be free to make his own decisions and to suffer or enjoy the resulting consequences of those decisions. One individual should never be forced by another to behave a certain way, whether good or bad.

Agency was previously established, in chapter 1, as being of essential import to God's designs and to our salvation. The reader will recall that it was of such grave import that to rebel against the principle of agency meant eternal expulsion from God's presence and the complete revocation of any hope for redemption. Those who sided against agency, against man's freedom to choose for himself, during the war in Heaven will forevermore be known as sons of perdition.[9]

While it isn't possible to revoke a man's agency it is possible to restrict him in his liberty so that he is unable to exercise that agency to its fullest extent. Bondage may come in many forms ranging from physical restraint to monetary compulsion. Chapter 2 listed and reviewed several forms of bondage and captivity as defined and described by the authors of and characters in The Book of Mormon. Regardless of the form of bondage, the forcing of behavior, beliefs, or practices by one party onto another party is a violation of the supreme law of moral agency and an encroachment on the offended party's freedom.

Second, to what rights does the Lord refer when He directs us to maintain the Constitution "for the rights and protection of all flesh?" The only one declared in these verses is the right to exercise one's agency to its fullest extent, or in more temporal terms, liberty. This conclusion is drawn from these scripture verses and the abundance of evidence presented in chapter 2 that the earthly principle of liberty is an extension of the eternal principle of agency.

The rights referred to here and similarly referred to several times in The Book of Mormon are never specifically enumerated, however, referring back to chapter 2, many aspects of liberty are defined as well as what is considered to be bondage or captivity. It is reasonable then to deduce that some of the rights that are being referred to here are those that are considered in The Book of Mormon as requisite for people to be free. These rights include the right to self-

[9] D&C 76:25-26, 76:32-33

government (as it is considered bondage to be subject to rulers), the right of religious worship and observance, the right to own and control property and not have excessive taxation to limit that ownership and control of one's property. A more comprehensive list will be made in following chapters.

Third, from what does mankind need protection? Anyone who would violate these rights and thereby place man into bondage to rulers. The Constitution is to serve as a protection against kings or rulers. In the Book of 2 Nephi the Lord states that "he that raiseth up a king against me shall perish"[10] when describing how this land would be a free land for the Gentiles in the Latter Days. The Lord has made His stand against kingship in America by establishing the Constitution.

Another passage on the Constitution can be found in the 98th section of the Doctrine and Covenants, which reads:

> And now, verily I say unto you concerning the laws of the land, it is my will that my people should observe to do all things whatsoever I command them.
>
> And that law of the land which is constitutional, supporting that principle of freedom in maintaining rights and privileges, belongs to all mankind, and is justifiable before me.
>
> Therefore, I, the Lord, justify you, and your brethren of my church, in befriending that law which is the constitutional law of the land;
>
> And as pertaining to the law of man, whatsoever is more or less than this, cometh of evil.[11]

This is an interesting declaration from the Lord. Here He states that the constitutional law supporting freedom and maintaining the rights and privileges of man is justifiable before Him and that He justifies His Church in befriending it. This is an extremely important point because at the present time in the world's history, the U.S. government as far as it is rooted in the U.S. Constitution is the only form of government on the earth that God has deemed justifiable to Him. It's important to note, however, that this is not a blanket justification of the U.S. government and any act that it commits. Rather this justification is a justification of the laws embedded in the U.S. Constitution and the *form* of government that is appropriately and correctly derived from that law and Constitution at the time that it was produced by the Founders.

The degree to which the present U.S. government adheres to the Constitution is a matter of considerable discussion and controversy and will not be treated in this book. It is hoped, however, that the reader will be left with a better sense of

---

[10] 2 Nephi 10:14

[11] D&C 98:4-7

how important it is for Latter-day Saints to understand the Constitution and what is meant by constitutional law so that increased understanding of what is and is not constitutional might be achieved through further research and study. One of the goals of this present work is to leave the reader better equipped to address and answer just such questions.

It is significant that there is only one form of civil law that has been explicitly justified by God. In fact, the Lord went even further and stated that "as pertaining to the law of man, whatsoever is more or less than this, cometh of evil." The Lord, Jesus Christ, has defined the line between good and evil as pertaining to civil law or, as He states it, "the law of man," and that line is the Constitution of the United States of America.

One final note on this passage of scripture cannot go unstated. The justification of U.S. constitutional law by the Lord Jesus Christ and the unequivocal declaration that the U.S. Constitution is the line between good and evil with regards to civil law and government were both communicated by direct revelation from God to His prophet and then canonized into scripture. Neither of these declarations have since been rescinded nor has any further revelation been received that would negate, nullify, or render obsolete this revelation where these two statements were made. Furthermore, the Lord's justification of the U.S. Constitution was at a time very shortly after it had been authored and does not necessarily justify each and every amendment to or interpretation of the same that has occurred since.

Surely it is with this scriptural background and divine origin of the Constitution in mind that President Heber J. Grant strongly warned:

> I counsel you, I urge you, I plead with you, never, so far as you have voice or influence, permit any departure from the principles of government on which this nation was founded, or any disregard of the freedoms which, by the inspiration of God our Father, were written into the Constitution of the united States[12]

Similarly, in 1956, President David O. McKay stated, "Next to being one in worshipping God, there is nothing in this world upon which this Church should be more united than in upholding and defending the Constitution of the United States!"[13]

And finally, in the April, 1950 General Conference of the Church, then Elder David O. McKay, while serving as Second Counselor in the First Presidency, said,

---

[12] Heber J. Grant, General Conference, October-1944

[13] Jerreld L. Newquist, *Prophets, Principles and National Survival*, 1964, p. 101

"No greater immediate responsibility rests upon members of the Church ... than to protect the freedom vouchsafed by the Constitution of the United States."[14]

America's Founders

In addition to revealing that He was the one that established the U.S. Constitution, the Lord has also revealed the means by which he did so, which were "by the hands of wise men whom [He] raised up unto this very purpose."[15]

D&C 101:80 comprises all of the revelation that the scriptures have to offer on the Founders and at first glance seems to not give much information. But there is more revealed in this one brief declaration by God than is immediately obvious.

First, God refers to the Founders as "wise men." The author can find only one other instance in all the scriptures where God, by His own mouth, refers directly to a specific individual as wise. That reference is made to King Solomon and refers to him.[16] There are several more general references wherein it is taken to mean that wise men can indeed be found in the world, especially among God's people, however, in no other case is this compliment paid by God to specific, identifiable individuals, save for these two.[17]

There are a number of other references that label individuals or groups as wise but in a way that is clearly pejorative and not in a manner of praise. These references identify people as "wise ... as to the wisdom of the world"[18] or "wise in their own eyes"[19] or similar. These references are clearly not to praise and compliment and are therefore not included in the above count of people to whom the Lord has referred as wise.

Therefore, to be described as wise by God's own voice is not a trivial matter and places the recipient of such praise in a very small and select group of individuals. The Founders of the United States are included in this exclusive group.

Now the question must be asked: in what things were they made wise? Their calling in this life was to establish the Constitution, and thereby a form of government and a nation that, as previously seen, was founded on "just and holy principles" and intended for the "rights and protection of all flesh." It was therefore necessary that they be instructed and schooled in these same just and holy principles upon which they would construct a nation and the rights of man

---

[14] David O. McKay, General Conference, April-1950
[15] D&C 101:80
[16] 1 Kings 3:12
[17] See Exodus 28:3, 31:6; Matthew 23:34; D&C 45:57, 98:10, 101:73, 103:23, 105:28
[18] Alma 2:1
[19] 2 Nephi 15:21

that needed protecting. Furthermore, it stands to reason that they would be made wise as to things pertaining to these principles, man's rights, and how government is best implemented to protect them. It would be strange indeed if these men were to be foreordained to the work they were to perform and then God had left them ill equipped for that work. So, presumably, they understood man's rights and they understood the just and holy principles upon which government should be founded. Particularly, they understood the just and holy principle of agency, which they referred to as liberty, at least as far as it pertained to civil governments. This is evidenced by the scripture passage discussed in detail above wherein God expounds on agency as the chief principle and purpose behind the Constitution and then immediately thereafter declares how He established it through the wise men who are the Founders. And finally, they understood these things because they were instructed in them by God's Holy Spirit.

Next, God states that He "raised [them] up unto this very purpose" of establishing the Constitution and thereby the nation of the United States. What is not revealed is exactly what God did to raise them up for this purpose. It can reasonably be assumed, however, that He prepared the Founders in ways similar to how He's prepared others for their works and callings.

In the book of Abraham, chapter 3, it reads:

> Now the Lord had shown unto me, Abraham, the intelligences that were organized before the world was; and among all these there were many of the noble and great ones;
>
> And God saw these souls that they were good, and he stood in the midst of them, and he said: These I will make my rulers; for he stood among those that were spirits, and he saw that they were good; and he said unto me: Abraham, thou art one of them; thou wast chosen before thou wast born.[20]

This passage of scripture is often referenced for instruction on the principle of foreordination, the doctrine that we were all foreordained to, and prepared for, specific callings and work according to God's foreknowledge of our personalities, strengths, weaknesses, and the work that He knew from the beginning needed to be done. This passage describes direct testimony from God to Abraham on his own foreordination.

Jeremiah was also a recipient of a witness to his own foreordination to be a prophet to the nations:

---

[20] Abraham 3:22-23

> Before I formed thee in the belly I knew thee; and before thou camest forth out of the womb I sanctified thee, and I ordained thee a prophet unto the nations.[21]

Additionally, Alma offers some elaboration on the principle of foreordination in one of the more detailed explanations found in the scriptures on this principle:

> And this is the manner after which they were ordained—being called and prepared from the foundation of the world according to the foreknowledge of God, on account of their exceeding faith and good works; in the first place being left to choose good or evil; therefore they having chosen good, and exercising exceedingly great faith, are called with a holy calling...
>
> And thus they have been called to this holy calling on account of their faith, while others would reject the Spirit of God on account of the hardness of their hearts and blindness of their minds...[22]

Here Alma teaches that not only are individuals called and set apart for certain work prior to coming into mortality, but that they are "called *and prepared* from the foundation of the world" for that work. A glimpse into this preparation process is found in the Doctrine and Covenants:

> Even before they were born, they, with many others, received their first lessons in the world of spirits and were prepared to come forth in the due time of the Lord to labor in his vineyard for the salvation of the souls of men.[23]

The preparation for foreordained work is, at least in part, to receive lessons in the spirit world before coming into mortality. The lessons received would most likely be tailored in such a way as to deliver to each recipient the doctrine and spiritual truths that most pertain to the work to which each individual is foreordained. The Founders of America, therefore, must have been instructed in agency and liberty, and all things that pertain to sound and just civil government.

In addition to adding the preparation part of foreordination, Alma instructs that foreordination is implemented "according to the foreknowledge of God." As mentioned previously, this foreknowledge includes a knowledge of who His children are and who they would become. It also includes a detailed and intimate knowledge of the Plan of Salvation, including when and where each of

---

[21] Jeremiah 1:5
[22] Alma 13:3-4
[23] D&C 138:56

His children would be born into mortality, what they would do with their lives, and how they would react to influences from the Spirit.

After describing the manner in which individuals are foreordained to "holy calling[s]", Alma teaches that individuals qualified for those callings by "exercising exceedingly great faith" and by "having chosen good" over evil and also because God knew beforehand that while "others would reject the Spirit of God" these individuals would not. This last part is also instructive in how preparation and guidance for these callings continue in mortality: by God's Holy Spirit.

Based on the revelation currently possessed, it is reasonable to deduce that the Founding Fathers of America were foreordained to the work that they performed, that their foreordination included receiving their callings and their first lessons and preparations for fulfilling those callings in pre-mortality before coming to this world, that this process of calling, educating, and influencing these men was a process directed by God and was the process by which He raised them up and made them wise. In fact, not only is this deduction well within reason, but it would be wholly outside the bounds of reason to suppose that they were called or prepared in any way other than this revealed manner.

In 1952 in the Church News publication, Elder J. Reuben Clark, then a counselor in the First Presidency, stated:

> Moses was no more prepared by the training and experience gained in the Court of Pharaoh for his great service of leading Israel from the bondage of Egypt, than were the framers of the Constitution prepared by training and experience for their work of providing a form of government that would "secure the Blessings of Liberty to ourselves and our Posterity," as they proclaimed to the world in the classic Preamble to the Constitution ... This was a choice lot of men ...[24]

An experience had by Wilford Woodruff in the St. George temple in 1877 serves as a good illustration of the stature of the spirits that the Founders were. He recounts the story as follows:

> Two weeks before I left St. George, the spirits of the dead gathered around me, wanting to know why we did not redeem them. Said they, "You have had the use of the Endowment House [temple] for a number of years, and yet nothing has ever been done for us. We laid the foundation of the government you now enjoy, and we never

---

[24] Jerreld L. Newquist, *Prophets, Principles and National Survival*, 1964, pp. 69-70

> apostatized from it, but we remained true to it and were faithful to God.
>
> Every one of those men that signed the Declaration of Independence, with General Washington, called upon me as an Apostle of the Lord Jesus Christ, in the Temple at St. George, two consecutive nights, and demanded at my hands that I should go forth and attend to the ordinances of the House of God for them.
>
> I straightway went into the baptismal font and called upon Brother McCallister to baptize me for the signers of the Declaration of Independence, and fifty other eminent men, making one hundred in all, including John Wesley, Columbus, and others.
>
> When Brother McAllister had baptized me for the 100 names I baptized him for 21, including General Washington and his forefathers and all the Presidents of the United States–except three. Sister Lucy Bigelow Young went forth into the font and was baptized for Martha Washington and her family and 70 of the 'eminent women' of the world.[25]

Some years later, in the April 1898 General Conference, then President Wilford Woodruff testified of the character of those men while referring back to this experience:

> I am going to bear my testimony to this assembly, if I never do it again in my life, that those men who laid the foundation of this American government and signed the Declaration of Independence were the best spirits the God of heaven could find on the face of the earth. They were choice spirits, not wicked men. General Washington and all the men that labored for the purpose were inspired of the Lord ... Would those spirits have called up on me, as an Elder in Israel to perform that work if they had not been noble spirits before God? They would not.[26]

Even more recently, Ezra Taft Benson referred back to the experience had by Wilford Woodruff:

> I was deeply moved on that occasion to realize that these great men returned to this promised land by permission of the Lord and had their ordinance work done for them. If they had not been faithful men, if they had not been God-fearing men, would they have come to the elders of Israel to seek their temple blessings? I think not. The Lord raised them up, sanctioned their work, and proclaimed them "wise men" ... When one casts doubt about the character of these noble

---

[25] Joseph Smith Academy, *Eminent Spirits Appear to Wilford Woodruff*, www.josephsmithacademy.org

[26] Wilford Woodruff, General Conference, April-1898

> sons of God, I believe he or she will have to answer to the God of heaven for it. Yes, with Lincoln I say: 'To add brightness to the sun or glory to the name of Washington is . . . impossible. Let none attempt it. In solemn awe pronounce the name and in its deathless splendor, leave it shining on.' ... [27]

Elder Benson concludes from the experience, "I think the Lord expects us to take an active part in preserving the Constitution and our freedom."[28]

Vicki Jo Anderson has performed a large amount of research into the experience Wilford Woodruff had. Using his journals and temple records, she was able to compile a list of the men and women who appeared to the Apostle that night and had their temple work done. Among those present were the familiar names listed below:

1. George Washington
2. John Hancock
3. John Adams
4. Samuel Adams
5. Benjamin Franklin
6. Thomas Jefferson
7. James Madison
8. James Monroe

It should also be noted that George Washington and Benjamin Franklin were both ordained to the office of high priest at this time (interestingly, so was Christopher Columbus).[29]

Summary and Conclusions

It is beneficial at this point to summarize the argument that has been presented so far in the first three chapters.

From chapter 1 it is seen that agency is an eternal principle, established as such by God the Father and central to His plan for our redemption and happiness. When the plan was presented to our eternal family, an opposing plan was also presented and a dispute erupted that grew into the War in Heaven with God's and Jesus Christ's side supporting agency and Satan's side opposing it, and instead supporting the use of force and compulsion to control behavior in order to achieve a desired end, in this case the salvation of all mankind. Though the

---

[27] Joseph Smith Academy, *Eminent Spirits Appear to Wilford Woodruff*, www.josephsmithacademy.org
[28] Ibid.
[29] Ibid.

goal was worthy, agency was too high a cost to achieve it. Satan and those who supported his plan were expelled from God's presence forever.

Chapter 2 demonstrated that liberty is an earthly principle that is related to but not exactly the same as agency. Agency is given to man by God and cannot be taken away by other men. Liberty is the ability to act on choices we make using our agency. If a man be deprived of his liberty, he is restricted in the exercise of his agency but not deprived of his agency all together, which cannot be separated from any one individual. Chapter 2 also extracted a definition of liberty from The Book of Mormon, the volume of scripture containing the fullness of the Gospel of Jesus Christ. Liberty is also shown in The Book of Mormon to be of extreme import, closely associated with the Gospel of Jesus Christ, and defended by Christ and His most righteous followers.

In chapter 3 it is shown that there is ample evidence in restoration scripture and teachings from Church authorities to support the claim that the United States of America is a nation founded by God. Several prophets in The Book of Mormon prophesied of the event and Jesus added His own prophecies to the list. He additionally stated that the Founding of America was part of the Father's plan and that it was in the Father's wisdom and by the Father's power that America was made a free nation.

The Constitution of the United States is one of the means used by God the Father and Jesus Christ to found America as a free nation. The purpose stated by the Lord of establishing the U.S. Constitution is the protection of man's ability to act according to the agency that was given to him by God. He also revealed that the U.S. Constitution is intended for the use of all mankind and directed His people to maintain and support it.

The American Founders, who authored the Constitution were raised by God for that specific work. They were foreordained in the premortal existence and prepared by God to do so. God referred to them as wise men and it is presumed that He meant they were wise as pertaining to the just and holy principles that comprise good civil government and the principles that they were called on by God to imbue into the Constitution, chief among those principles being liberty or freedom.

The U.S. Constitution is the only form of government on the earth today that has been personally approved and justified by God and the only one that He claims to have had a hand in founding through those men whom He called.

For spiritual matters of the Gospel, God has always taught through prophets and apostles and servants that He calls. As for matters of civil government, He foreordained and prepared the Founding Fathers of America. They are the servants He called for that work, they are His apostles of civil government in that

He did that work through them. It is for this reason that this author believes that when questions of moral, sound, and good civil government arise, there is but one resource that God has provided for instruction on the matter and that resource is comprised of the Founding Fathers and their work.

Chapter 4 – The Founders

In the previous chapter, it was well established that the Founding Fathers of America were foreordained and prepared for the work that they were called to do on the Earth during mortality. Naturally, since they were called by God to do a portion of His work in the world, Satan can be found actively laboring to destroy that work as "it must needs be, that there is an opposition in all things."[1]

One way that he works to destroy their work is by attacking their character. Therefore, the Founding Fathers of the United States are among the most viciously maligned men of present day America. It has become largely fashionable, especially in intellectual and academic circles, to question the integrity, motives, character, and intelligence of those men. Most notable, in the context of the content of this writing, is that they are often said to be non-religious men who intended a secular society free from the influences of religion. The religious worldviews that are assigned to the Founders include atheism, deism, Unitarianism, anti-Christian, or simply anti-religion all together. Additionally, They are accused of many moral indiscretions, dishonesty, racial oppression, and an ardent self-interest to preserve their own wealth and status.

Much of what is heard today about the Founders is difficult to reconcile with the narrative presented previously that they were wise men called and taught by God. This should not come as a surprise to Latter-day Saints, however. As pointed out briefly above, if they were indeed called by God to do His work, then Satan will be working against them and it is not surprising to find him working against them in ways similar to how he has worked against God's prophets, apostles, missionaries, and other servants. Similar attacks are made on the character and dispositions of restoration prophets and apostles, most notably, Joseph Smith and many of his contemporaries from the early days of the Restoration.

The author has found that many of these negative claims made about the Founding Fathers struggle greatly to hold up to factual scrutiny. Nevertheless, it is beyond the scope of this work to treat each and every defamation directed at America's Founders. The body of work on the Founding Fathers is very large and includes many opinions ranging from supportive to critical to indifferent. This

[1] 2 Nephi 2:11

writing is not intended to be biographical in nature and will not attempt a detailed biographical examination of the Founders themselves.

The aim of this writing is to demonstrate that the Founders were wise men called by God who were in tune with and directed by His Spirit, and to arouse enough interest in the reader that further research is pursued into the Founders and their work. The object of this chapter is to present supporting evidence to the argument already given, to give samples of the Founders' character and personalities, and especially their religion. The evidence presented in this chapter is anecdotal and it is acknowledged that the information in this chapter alone is not proof of who the Founders were. As noted above, the extant body of work on the Founders is enormous and a complete, exhaustive examination of arguments both supportive and critical of them is well outside the scope of this writing.

What the author has found through years of study and research is that when taken in their proper historical context, and when examined through original sources and without parsing out small phrases here and there and separating them from the surrounding context in which those phrases were spoken or written, the Founding Fathers are exactly what God and the LDS religion proclaim them to be: a group of wise, intelligent, and moral men who were in tune with God's Spirit and who completed a great and a holy work.

It is hoped that the evidence and quotes in this chapter, together with the surrounding argument that comprises this book, will pique the interest of the reader who is encouraged to judiciously research who the Founders were and what they believed and taught regarding civil government and related issues. The reader is also encouraged to conduct this research and study together with prayer and guidance from the Lord since, as this book endeavors to demonstrate, it is a subject that is related to the Gospel and one on which the Lord has given and will give revelation.

The author does not have any illusions that the Founders were perfect men. Certainly, if one searches, instances can be found where they made mistakes or were found to be subject to the same weaknesses and errors that we all are as part of human mortality. That being said, it is the opinion of the author that no other group of men, in the history of the world, were better suited or prepared to do the work that was done by the Founders. No other group of men or philosophers anywhere had the knowledge or understanding of those men with regards to man's rights, sound government, and the "just and holy principles" on which the Constitution was established because they were instructed by Almighty God in those very matters. The Founders were "wise men" who were "raised up" by God to perform a specific work and they did just that.

Religion

Much has been said of the religion of the Founding Fathers. As noted above, they have had many varying systems of belief attributed to them ranging from atheist and agnostic to Unitarian and deist. The historical evidence, however, shows that the Founding Fathers were overwhelmingly Christian.

David Barton,[2] on his WallBuilders website,[3] teaches that there were 56 signers of the Declaration of Independence. Of those 56 signers, 29 held what today would be considered seminary or Bible school degrees. Judge Thomas McKean delivered Gospel messages in the courtroom; John Witherspoon was responsible for two American translations of the Bible, including America's first family Bible; Benjamin Rush founded America's first Bible Society and began the Sunday School movement; Francis Hopkinson produced the first purely American hymn book, setting the entire Book of Psalms to music.[4]

Of the signers of the Constitution, John Langdon and Charles Cotesworth Pinckney were founders of the American Bible Society; Rufus King was a founder of the New York Bible Common Prayer Book Society; James McHenry founded the Maryland Bible Society; Alexander Hamilton urged the formation of the Christian Constitutional Society to elect people to office who would support the Christian religion and the Constitution; Abraham Baldwin served as a military chaplain during the American Revolution; Roger Sherman wrote the doctrinal creed for his evangelical denomination in Connecticut.[5]

In addition to the above statistical data, abundant evidence can be found in a number of quotes and writings. Below are quotes from a number of the Founding Fathers that serve to illustrate that they were indeed Christian men. Furthermore, note that in many cases, these quotes are taken from public settings when these men were acting in government capacities. This contradicts the increasingly popular argument that the U.S. Founders intended a purely secular society. This topic will be treated in more detail later, for now it is enough to take note, as mentioned, of the public setting and capacities in which some of the following quotes are given.

The sampling of Founders in this book amount to somewhere between maybe 5 and 10% of the entire body of men and women that can be considered

---

[2] From his WallBuilders website: David Barton is the Founder and President of WallBuilders, a national pro-family organization that presents America's forgotten history and heroes, with an emphasis on our moral, religious and constitutional heritage ... His exhaustive research has rendered him an expert in historical and constitutional issues and he serves as a consultant to state and federal legislators, has participated in several cases at the Supreme Court, was involved in the development of the History/Social Studies standards for states such as Texas and California, and has helped produce history textbooks now used in schools across the nation.

[3] www.wallbuilders.com

[4] Ibid.

[5] Ibid.

America's Founders. This figure varies between groups because of differing definitions of what exactly constitutes being a Founding individual. In this work, the attempt is made to examine individuals where there can be little question, such as those who contributed to the creation of or signed significant Founding documents like the Declaration of Independence or the Constitution. While the sample size may seem small when considered as a percentage of all Founding individuals, an examination of all individuals who participated in America's Founding could by itself constitute an entire separate book, and a substantial one at that. The examples given below were not chosen because they were the most religious of this group, but more for the accessibility of easily citable information. Much more evidence could be given for these and for many other Founders, but the number of examples is limited to be an appropriate portion of the present writing. It should be noted, that at the beginning of the American Revolution, 99.8% of Americans were professing Christians.[6] It does not come as a surprise to find that the overwhelming majority of American Founders were also Christian as such was the case for all of the American Colonies at that time.

Josiah Barlett was a governor of the state of New Hampshire and signed the Declaration of Independence. While serving as the chief executive of that state, he delivered a proclamation in which he called on New Hampshire citizens "to confess before God their aggravated transgressions and to implore His pardon and forgiveness through the merits and mediation of Jesus Christ" and "that the knowledge of the Gospel of Jesus Christ may be made known to all nations."[7]

Elias Boudinot served as President of the Continental Congress and, while later serving in the U.S. House of Representatives, contributed greatly to the framing of the Bill of Rights. Boudinot helped found the American Bible Society and served as one of its Presidents. Boudinot also authored *The Age of Revelation* as a response to Thomas Paine's *The Age of Reason*. In a speech that Boudinot gave in the First Provincial Congress of New Jersey, he said:

> Let us enter on this important business under the idea that we are Christians on whom the eyes of the world are now turned ... [L]et us earnestly call and beseech Him, for Christ's sake, to preside in our councils ... We can only depend on the all powerful influence of the Spirit of God, Whose Divine aid and assistance it becomes us as a Christian people most devoutly to implore. Therefore I move that

---

[6] Peter A. Lillback, Jerry Newcombe, *George Washington's Sacred Fire*, 2006, p. 29

[7] David Barton, *A Few Declarations of Founding Fathers and Early Statements on Jesus, Christianity, and the Bible*, 2008, www.wallbuilders.com

> some minister of the Gospel be requested to attend this Congress every morning ... in order to open the meeting with prayer.[8]

Boudinot also proposed a day of thanksgiving for the nation after Congress voted to recommend the First Amendment of the Constitution to the states. He said that he "could not think of letting the session pass over without offering an opportunity to all the citizens of the United States of joining, with one voice, in returning to Almighty God their Sincere thanks for the many blessings he had poured down upon them."[9]

Charles Carroll signed the Declaration of Independence and helped in framing the Bill of Rights. He said, "Grateful to Almighty God for the blessings which, through Jesus Christ Our Lord, He had conferred on my beloved country in her emancipation."[10]

John Dickinson served as a general in the Revolutionary War, as Governor of both Delaware and Pennsylvania, and signed the Constitution. In his will, he wrote:

> Rendering thanks to my Creator for my existence and station among His works, for my birth in a country enlightened by the Gospel and enjoying freedom, and for all His other kindnesses, to Him I resign myself, humbly confiding in His goodness and in His mercy through Jesus Christ for the events of eternity.[11]

Dickinson also stated on another occasion that government "could not give the rights essential to happiness ... We claim them from a higher source: from the King of Kings, and Lord of all the earth."[12]

Elbridge Gerry served as a member of the Constitutional Convention, he signed the Declaration of Independence, and contributed to the framing of the Bill of Rights. He served as the Governor of Massachusetts and as Vice President of the United States. In a proclamation for a day of thanksgiving and praise delivered to the state of Massachusetts while serving as Governor of that state, Gerry wrote:

> [W]ith one heart and voice may we prostrate ourselves at the throne of heavenly grace and present to our Great Benefactor sincere and unfeigned thanks for His infinite goodness and mercy towards us from

---

[8] Ibid.
[9] Ibid.
[10] Ibid.
[11] Ibid.
[12] Ibid.

> our birth to the present moment for having above all things illuminated us by the Gospel of Jesus Christ.[13]

Alexander Hamilton served as a general in the Revolutionary War, signed the Constitution, and was one of the authors of *The Federalist Papers*, which work greatly aided in the ratification of the Constitution. On his deathbed, Hamilton is quoted as saying, "I have a tender reliance on the mercy of the Almighty, through the merits of the Lord Jesus Christ."[14]

Hamilton also proposed the formation of the Christian Constitutional Society with the stated goals of supporting the Christian religion and supporting the U.S. Constitution. The intent of the society was to organize chapters throughout each state in the Union and work to elect to office individuals who would do the same.

John Hancock served as a general in America's Revolution, as the President of the Congress that produced and signed the Declaration of Independence, and as the Governor of Massachusetts. He also signed the Declaration of Independence himself and is perhaps best known for his comparatively large, flourishing signature. Hancock wrote in the Independent Chronicle of Boston, "Sensible of the importance of Christian piety and virtue to the order and happiness of a state, I cannot but earnestly commend to you every measure for their support and encouragement."[15]

Hancock also issued numerous proclamations for days of prayer, fasting, and thanksgiving while serving as Governor of Massachusetts. In those proclamations can be found language admonishing the citizens of that state to pray for outcomes such as "that all nations may bow to the scepter of our Lord and Savior Jesus Christ and that the whole earth may be filled with his glory"; "that the spiritual kingdom of our Lord and Savior Jesus Christ may be continually increasing until the whole earth shall be filled with His glory"; "to confess their sins and to implore forgiveness of God through the merits of the Savior of the World"; "to cause the benign religion of our Lord and Savior Jesus Christ to be known, understood, and practiced among all the inhabitants of the earth"; "to confess their sins before God and implore His forgiveness through the merits and mediation of Jesus Christ, our Lord and Savior"; and "that the kingdom of our Lord and Savior Jesus Christ may be established in peace and righteousness among all the nations of the earth."[16]

John Hart signed the Declaration of Independence. In his last will and testament, he wrote, "Thanks be given unto Almighty God therefore, and

---

[13] Ibid.
[14] Ibid.
[15] Ibid.
[16] Ibid.

knowing that it is appointed for all men once to die and after that the judgement ... principally, I give and recommend my soul into the hands of Almighty God who gave it and my body to the earth to be buried in a decent and Christian like manner ... to receive the same again at the general resurrection by the mighty power of God."[17]

Patrick Henry was a Revolutionary War general and served as Governor of Virginia. He was a prominent leader of the opposition against the 1765 Stamp Act and is credited with substantial influence in moving the Revolution forward, particularly with his famous speech in which he boldly declared, "give me liberty, or give me death!"

Patrick Henry said that being a Christian "is a character which I prize far above all this world has or can boast" and that "the great pillars of all government ... [are] virtue, morality, and religion."[18]

Samuel Huntington signed the Declaration of Independence and served as President of Congress and as Governor of Connecticut. In a proclamation for a day of fasting and prayer signed while Governor of Connecticut, Huntington wrote, "it becomes a people publicly to acknowledge the over-ruling hand of Divine Providence and their dependence upon the Supreme Being as their Creator and Merciful Preserver ... and with becoming humility and sincere repentance to supplicate the pardon that we may obtain forgiveness through the merits and mediation of our Lord and Savior Jesus Christ."[19]

John Jay served as President of Congress and the very first Chief Justice of the U.S. Supreme Court. He was also the Governor of New York and another one of the authors of *The Federalist Papers*. In his will he wrote, "unto Him who is the author and giver of all good, I render sincere and humble thanks for His manifold and unmerited blessings, and especially for our redemption and salvation by His beloved Son ... Blessed be His holy name."[20]

On another occasion, to the Committee of the Corporation of the City of New York, Jay stated, "I recommend a general and public return of praise and thanksgiving to Him from whose goodness these blessings descend. The most effectual means of securing the continuance of our civil and religious liberties is always to remember with reverence and gratitude the source from which they flow."[21]

John Jay also expressed his opinion on electing government officials as follows: "Providence has given to our people the choice of their rulers, and it is the duty

---

[17] Ibid.
[18] Ibid.
[19] Ibid.
[20] Ibid.
[21] Ibid.

as well as the privilege and interest of our Christian nation, to select and prefer Christians for their rulers."[22]

William Samuel Johnson signed the U.S. Constitution and helped to frame the Bill of Rights. He said, "I .. am endeavoring ... to attend to my own duty only as a Christian ... let us take care that our Christianity ... be not shaken."[23]

George Mason was a delegate at the Constitutional Convention and is considered to be the father of the Bill of Rights. In his will, he wrote "I give and bequeath my soul to Almighty God that gave it me, hoping that through the meritorious death and passion of our Savior and Redeemer Jesus Christ to receive absolution and remission for all my sins."[24]

In the final copy of his will that was ultimately attested, Mason wrote, "My soul I resign into the hands of my Almighty Creator, Whose tender mercies are all over His works ... humbly hoping from His unbounded mercy and benevolence, through the merits of my blessed Savior, a remission of my sins."[25]

James McHenry signed the Constitution and fought as an officer in the American Revolution, he also served as Secretary of War under Presidents George Washington and John Adams. He said, "public utility pleads most forcibly for the general distribution of the Holy Scriptures. Without the Bible, in vain do we increase penal laws and draw entrenchments around our institutions."[26]

Gouverneur Morris was a member of the Continental Congress and signed the Constitution. He is widely credited with the wording in the Preamble and is referred to as the "Penman of the Constitution." He said, "There must be religion. When that ligament is torn, society is disjointed and its members perish ... [T]he most important of all lessons is the denunciation of ruin to every state that rejects the precepts of religion."[27]

James Otis was a leader of the Sons of Liberty. He was a lawyer who mentored John Hancock and Samuel Adams. He was outspoken against British rule and, though not the originator of the idea or phrase, was famous for often saying "taxation without representation is tyranny." He authored several pamphlets that contributed to and informed Revolutionary sentiment. In one such pamphlet, *The Rights of the British Colonies Asserted and Proved*, he wrote, "Has [government] any solid foundation? Any chief cornerstone? ... I think it has an

[22] Ibid.
[23] Ibid.
[24] Ibid.
[25] Ibid.
[26] Ibid.
[27] Ibid.

everlasting foundation in the unchangeable will of God ... The sum of my argument is that civil government is of God."[28]

Robert Treat Paine signed the Declaration of Independence and served as Attorney General of Massachusetts. In his own will he wrote, "I am constrained to express my adoration of the Supreme Being, the Author of my existence, in full belief of His Providential goodness and His forgiving mercy revealed to the world through Jesus Christ, through whom I hope for never ending happiness in a future state."[29]

Charles Cotesworth Pinckney signed the Constitution and helped to found The American Bible Society. In his will he wrote, "To the eternal and only true God be all honor and glory, now and forever. Amen!"[30]

Benjamin Rush signed the Declaration of Independence and helped to ratify the Constitution. He was the Surgeon General of the Continental Army and is considered by many as the father of American medicine. He was also a strong advocate for public schooling under the Constitution. He said that "The Gospel of Jesus Christ prescribes the wisest rules for just conduct in every situation of life."[31]

In an essay he wrote titled *A Defence of the Use of the Bible as a School Book*, Rush wrote "the only means of establishing and perpetuating our republican forms of government is the universal education of our youth in the principles of Christianity by means of the Bible." In the same essay, he also wrote that "the Bible ... should be read in our schools in preference to all other books because it contains the greatest portion of that kind of knowledge which is calculated to produce private and public happiness."[32]

He also wrote in a correspondence, "The great enemy of the salvation of man, in my opinion, never invented a more effective means of limiting Christianity from the world than by persuading mankind that it was improper to read the Bible at schools."[33]

In another letter to Elias Boudinot, Rush wrote, "I am satisfied that [the Constitution] is as much the work of a Divine Providence as any of the miracles recorded in the Old and New Testament."[34]

Roger Sherman signed both the Declaration of Independence and the Constitution and helped to frame the Bill of Rights. He said, "I believe that there

---

[28] Ibid.
[29] Ibid.
[30] Ibid.
[31] Ibid.
[32] Ibid.
[33] Ibid.
[34] Ibid.

is one only living and true God ... That the Scriptures of the Old and New Testaments are a revelation from God ... I believe that God ... did send His own Son to become man, die in the room and stead of sinners, and thus to lay a foundation for the offer of pardon and salvation to all mankind, so as all may be saved who are willing to accept the Gospel offer ... that at the end of this world there will be a resurrection of the dead, and a final judgement of all mankind, when the righteous shall be publicly acquitted by Christ the Judge and admitted to everlasting life and glory, and the wicked be sentenced to everlasting punishment."[35]

Richard Stockton signed the Declaration of Independence. He wrote in his will, "I think it proper here not only to subscribe to the entire belief of the great and leading doctrines of the Christian religion, such as the being of God; the universal defection and depravity of human nature; the Divinity of the person and the completeness of the redemption purchased by the blessed Savior; the necessity of the operations of the Divine Spirit; of Divine faith accompanied with an habitual virtuous life; and the universality of the Divine Providence: but also, in the bowels of a father's affection, to exhort and charge [my children] that the fear of God is the beginning of wisdom, that the way of life held up in the Christian system is calculated for the most complete happiness that can be enjoyed in this mortal state."[36]

Charles Thomson was the Secretary of the Continental Congress and designed the seal of the United States. He signed the first draft of the Declaration of Independence approved by Congress. He said "I am a Christian. I believe only in the Scriptures, and in Jesus Christ my Savior."[37]

Daniel Webster was a constitutional lawyer immediately after the Founding and played a critical role in many landmark constitutional cases during the early 19th century, earning himself the title Great Expounder of the Constitution. Many cases he argued continue to serve as constitutional precedents today. In a speech delivered in the U.S. Supreme Court, Webster said, "the Christian religion—its general principles—must ever be regarded among us as the foundation of civil society."[38]

On another occasion, he said that "Whatever makes men good Christians, makes them good citizens."[39]

Lastly, in another address he gave, he stated, "to the free and universal reading of the Bible ... men [are] much indebted for right views of civil liberty."[40]

---

[35] Ibid.
[36] Ibid.
[37] Ibid.
[38] Ibid.
[39] Ibid.

Noah Webster fought in the Revolution and served as both judge and legislator. He is credited with pioneering scholarship and education in America, partly because of his enormous contribution to the English language through various publications of dictionaries. He said "the religion which has introduced civil liberty is the religion of Christ and His apostles ... This is genuine Christianity and to this we owe our free constitutions of government."[41]

He also said that "The moral principles and precepts found in the Scriptures ought to form the basis of all our civil constitutions and laws" and that "our citizens should early understand that the genuine source of correct republican principles is the Bible, particularly the New Testament, or the Christian religion."[42]

When discussing the appropriate curriculum to be undertaken by students, he said "the Christian religion is the most important and one of the first things in which all children under a free government ought to be instructed. No truth is more evident than that the Christian religion must be the basis of any government intended to secure the rights and privileges of a free people."[43]

In a letter to James Madison, Webster wrote "the Christian religion ... is the basis, or rather the source, of all genuine freedom in government ... I am persuaded that no civil government of a republican form can exist and be durable in which the principles of Christianity have not a controlling influence."[44]

John Witherspoon signed the Declaration of Independence and played a role in attaining ratification of the Constitution. He said "there is no salvation in any other than in Jesus Christ of Nazareth."[45] He also, like so many others of the Founding era, closely associated Christianity with freedom, he stated, "he is the best friend to American liberty who is the most sincere and active in promoting true and undefiled religion, and who sets himself with the greatest firmness to bear down profanity and immorality of every kind. Whoever is an avowed enemy of God, I scruple not to call him an enemy to his country."[46]

As noted above, there are a great number more of similar quotes and writings that could be included and this sampling is by no means an exhaustive list. When considered as a group, it is more than evident that the Founders were not atheists, deists, nor agnostics. They were Christians. They believed in the Bible and the Savior that it preaches, namely Jesus Christ. They spoke and wrote of

---

[40] Ibid.

[41] Ibid.

[42] Ibid.

[43] Ibid.

[44] Ibid.

[45] Ibid.

[46] Ibid.

Jesus Christ often and with reverence. This is true of an overwhelming majority of the men who were instrumental in the Founding of the American nation.

Moreover, they did not hesitate to speak of Jesus Christ or their Christianity in public settings and official government capacities. Those that were influential in the Founding of America frequently issued proclamations, resolutions, and recommendations for days of fasting, prayer, and thanksgiving. This was done most often at the state level but is far from unheard of at the national level. Often these days were intended as expressions of gratitude towards God, and often that gratitude was for the freedoms, rights, and privileges that the Colonists and early Americans enjoyed. They saw God as the source of their liberty. They considered the Christian religion and its precepts as the only true source of free government and society. They frequently acknowledged God's miraculous hand in the Founding and formation of the American nation, from their success in the Revolutionary War to the wording of the Declaration of Independence and the genius and remarkable structure of the Constitution. They overwhelmingly considered it beneficial to teach Christianity in schools and never intended for schooling, education, or public discourse to exclude God or religion.

In summary, the Founding Fathers were Christian. Nevertheless, it is necessary to examine a few individuals in greater detail because of the attention they receive both for the significant contributions they made to America's Founding and for the amount of attention they receive from those who profess a much more secular heritage for America.

George Washington

George Washington is for many the first individual who comes to mind in conjunction with the title Founding Father. He is often referred to as the "indispensable man" of America's Revolution and Founding, and as the father of the American nation.

Washington's religion has been a subject of some debate since around the middle of the twentieth century. Many are painting him with the brush of Deism, which is to say largely agnostic, believing in the existence of a supreme being but one who is distant, unknowable, and impersonal. The Deist God is one who created the universe like a clock, wound it up, and then went away, leaving the universe, and any life within it, to its own devices. The Deist God does not hear nor answer prayers and is not concerned with the affairs of mankind, does not communicate with man, and therefore has no revealed religion on the earth. Deism denies that scripture is revealed by God and consequently the divinity of Jesus Christ as professed in the Bible.

Washington has Deism ascribed to him on evidence that is usually scanty and often logically unsound. Moreover, one can only arrive at this conclusion regarding Washington by crediting some historical data and facts while conspicuously ignoring others.

One accusation made of George Washington as evidence of his Deism is that he avoided using the names God, and Jesus Christ. Washington was indeed fond of alternative titles and appellations for God. Among these honorary designations are titles such as the "Great Author of the Universe", the "Great Disposer of Human Events", and his favorite and most commonly used "Providence" and "Divine Providence."

Peter Lillback and Jerry Newcombe authored a book titled *George Washington's Sacred Fire*, comprising fifteen years of research and a veritable mountain of historical evidence attesting to George Washington's Christianity. Lillback and Newcombe point out that "[w]hen George Washington used his multitude of respectful titles for God, he was simply employing a Baroque style popular among many of the ministers at the time."[47] They likewise show that Washington did indeed also use the specific names God, and Jesus Christ many times in his writings and speeches.

The subject of Washington's preferred manner in which to refer to deity is merely an example of the arguments made against his religiosity. The present work will not address all of the allegations made. Lillback and Newcombe do just that, however. They address the myriad arguments made against Washington's spirituality. In the introduction to their book, they write, "*George Washington's Sacred Fire* intends to convince you that when all the available evidence is considered, the only viable conclusion is that George Washington was a Christian and not a Deist."[48] They use that evidence to show the following truths regarding George Washington: "He was clearly and deeply biblically literate"; "He was a committed churchman"; "There are numerous accounts from family and military associates—too numerous to be dismissed—of people coming across Washington in earnest, private prayer"; He "called on the nation's leaders to follow Christ's example."[49]

William Johnson authored a biography titled *George Washington The Christian*. In that book, Johnson writes:

> Sermons and orations by divines and statesmen were delivered all over the land at the death of Washington. A large volume of such was

[47] Peter A. Lillback, Jerry Newcombe, *George Washington's Sacred Fire*, 2006, p. 41
[48] Ibid., p. 35
[49] Ibid., pp. 34-35

> published. I have seen and read them, and the religious character of Washington was a most prominent feature in them; and for this there must have been some good cause. That Washington was regarded throughout America, both among our military and political men, as a sincere believer in Christianity, as then received among us, and a devout man, is as clear as any fact in our history.[50]

Johnson, in his biography, also compiled numerous testimonies of Washington's faith and his character as attested to by his peers and contemporaries. A sample of those testimonies follows.

Major-General Henry Lee was a member of the Virginia legislature and served under George Washington during the Revolutionary War. He spoke at Washington's funeral and said, "First in war, first in peace, and first in the hearts of his countrymen, he was second to none in the humble and endearing scenes of private life. Pious, just, humane, temperate, and sincere; uniform, dignified, and commanding, his example was edifying to all around him, as were the effects of that example lasting."[51]

John Mitchell Sewall, in his oration, stated that "[h]e was a firm believer in the Christian religion," and that "Washington, the great saviour of his country, did not disdain to acknowledge and adore a great Saviour."[52]

Jeremiah Smith delivered a similar oration of praise for Washington, saying:

> He had all the genuine mildness of Christianity with all its force. He was neither ostentatious, nor ashamed of his Christian profession. He pursued in this, as in everything else the happy mean between the extremes of levity and gloominess, indifference and austerity. His religion became him. He brought it with him into office, and he did not lose it there. His first and his last office acts (as did all the intermediate ones) contained an explicit acknowledgement of the overruling providence of the Supreme Being; and the most fervent supplication for His benediction on our government and nation.
>
> Without being charged with exaggeration, I may be permitted to say, that an accurate knowledge of his life, while it would confer on him the highest title to praise, would be productive of the most solid advantage to the cause of Christianity.[53]

Timothy Dwight, D.D., president of Yale College also delivered a discourse on Washington's character shortly after the latter's death. Dwight related:

---

[50] William Johnson, *George Washington The Christian*, 1919, p. 250

[51] Ibid., pp. 250-251

[52] Ibid., pp. 251-252

[53] Ibid., pp. 254-255

> For my own part, I have considered his numerous and uniform public and most solemn declarations of his high veneration for religion, his exemplary and edifying attention to public worship, and his constancy in secret devotion, as proofs, sufficient to satisfy every person, willing to be satisfied. I shall only add that if he was not a Christian, he was more like one than any man of the same description whose life has been hitherto recorded.[54]

In addition to the personal witnesses given to Washington's character above, a number of early historical biographers also drew the conclusions listed hereafter as results of studying the man and his life.

Mason L. Weems said, "[t]he noblest, the most efficient element of his character was that he was an humble, earnest Christian."[55]

Aaron Bancroft stated, "[i]n principle and practice he was a Christian."[56]

Cyrus R. Edmunds claimed that "[t]he elements of his greatness are chiefly to be discovered in the moral features of his character."[57]

Supreme Court Chief Justice John Marshall knew Washington personally and wrote a biography on him. In it, he wrote, "Without making ostentatious professions of religion, he was a sincere believer in the Christian faith, and a truly devout man."[58]

George Bancroft said, "Belief in God and trust in His overruling power, formed the essence of his character ... His whole being was one continued act of faith in the eternal, intelligent and moral order of the universe."[59]

Jared Sparks wrote of Washington:

> A Christian in faith and practice, he was habitually devout. His reverence for religion is seen in his example, his public communications, and his private writings...
>
> After a long and minute examination of the writings of Washington, public and private, in print and in manuscript, I can affirm that I have never seen a single hint or expression from which it could be inferred that he had any doubt of the Christian revelation, or that he thought with indifference or unconcern of that subject. On the contrary, whenever he approaches it, and indeed, whenever he alludes in any manner to religion, it is done with seriousness and reverence.[60]

---

[54] Ibid., p. 255
[55] Ibid.
[56] Ibid.
[57] Ibid.
[58] Ibid.
[59] Ibid.
[60] Ibid., p. 261

David Ramsay was a delegate to the Continental Congress from 1782 to 1786. In his biography, he wrote the following:

> There are few men of any kind, and still fewer of those the world calls great, who have not some of their virtues eclipsed by corresponding vices. But this was not the case with General Washington. He had religion without austerity, dignity without pride, modesty without diffidence, courage without rashness, politeness without affectation, affability without familiarity. His private character, as well as his public one, will bear the strictest scrutiny. He was punctual in all his engagements; upright and honest in his dealings; temperate in his enjoyments; liberal and hospitable to an eminent degree; a lover of order; systematical and methodical in his arrangements. He was a friend of morality and religion; steadily attended on public worship; encouraged and strengthened the hands of the clergy. In all his public acts he made the most respectful mention of Providence; and in a word, carried the spirit of piety with him both in his private life and public administration.[61]

Washington's family, friends, colleagues, acquaintances, and even enemies, all attested to the fact that he was devoutly religious, sincere and reverent, and a believer in the Christian religion, the Christian scriptures, and the Christian God. But surely the best judge of Washington's religious beliefs will be none other than Washington himself, so what follows is a series of things that he himself said and wrote. As mentioned briefly above, Washington was fond of referring to God with many diverse respectful titles. One of his favorites and most often used was "Providence." In a letter to a Hebrew congregation of Savannah, Georgia, Washington declares exactly who he is referring to when he uses this title.

> May the same wonder-working Deity, who long since delivering the Hebrews from their Egyptian Oppressors planted them in the promised land—whose Providential Agency has lately been conspicuous in establishing these United States as an independent Nation—still continue to water them with the dews of Heaven and to make the inhabitants of every denomination participate in the temporal and spiritual blessings of that people whose God is Jehovah.[62]

---

[61] Ibid., pp. 262-263

[62] Peter A. Lillback, Jerry Newcombe, *George Washington's Sacred Fire*, 2006, pp. 577-578

Here, Washington makes a clear connection between the Deity that delivered the Hebrews from Egypt and his oft-used designation of Providence or, in this case, a reference to that Deity's Providential Agency. He later explicitly identifies this Deity as Jehovah. Also note that Washington here states that this same Deity has been conspicuous or evident in the Founding of America.

Not only is it historically evident that Washington believed in the God spoken of and preached in the Bible, it is also found in his writings that he frequently had opportunity to observe God's hand in the Founding of America and was quick to acknowledge such as the case when it occurred. One example was shown above in his correspondence to a group of Hebrews. Another example is found in a letter to Connecticut Governor Jonathan Trumbull in July of 1788. In this letter, Washington speaks of God's influence in achieving the production and ratification of the Constitution. He wrote:

> Or at least we may, with a kind of grateful and pious exultation, trace the finger of Providence through those dark and mysterious events, which first induced the States to appoint a general Convention and then led them one after another (by such steps as were best calculated to effect the object) into an adoption of the system recommended by that general Convention...
>
> That the same good Providence may still continue to protect us and prevent us from dashing the cup of national felicity.[63]

During the winter of 1775-1776 the Colonial Army, under General George Washington, clandestinely laid siege to British occupied Boston by moving many tons of heavy artillery into position around the city. The artillery had been captured previously at Fort Ticonderoga. Strategically key to the siege was the fortification of Dorchester Heights, which put American cannons within reach of both the city and the harbor of Boston, putting both British troops and their ships at risk. Additionally, the height advantage placed the American cannons out of range of the British cannons firing from the lower elevation in and near the city.

General William Howe, commanding officer of the British troops in Boston, knew that they could not continue to hold Boston unless they successfully dislodged the Colonial stronghold on Dorchester Heights and especially their artillery. An assault was planned to do just that. The planned assault, however, was forestalled and eventually abandoned due to a storm. When the weather cleared, a different decision had been reached, to abandon Boston to the Colonial force.

---

[63] Ibid., pp. 583-584

Had the British conducted the assault they had planned, certainly this event, and possibly the war would have turned out differently. This is one of many different occasions where Washington and others recognized and acknowledged God's Almighty Hand interceding on behalf of the American Colonies, both in the military confrontations to gain independence from Britain and in the intellectual and ideological struggles to frame and adopt a new form of free, self-government. Of this event, Washington wrote to his brother:

> Upon their [the British] discovery of the works [the artillery] next morning, great preparations were made for attacking them; but not being ready before the afternoon, and the weather getting very tempestuous, much blood was saved, and a very important blow, to one side or the other, was prevented. That this most remarkable Interposition of Providence is for some wise purpose, I have not a doubt.[64]

In 1777, the British troops evacuated New Jersey just before harvest and were forced to leave the crops behind untouched for Colonial use. In a letter Washington penned to General John Armstrong, he wrote that "[t]he evacuation of Jersey at this time, seems to be a peculiar mark of providence, as the Inhabitants have an Opportunity of Securing their Harvests of Hay and Grain."[65]

Later that same year, in a letter to General Israel Putnam, Washington wrote, "Should Providence be pleased to crown our arms in the course of the campaign with one more fortunate stroke ... I trust all will be well in His good time..."[66] And in another letter written around the same time to Landon Carter, Washington said that "Providence is ordering everything for the best, and that, in due time, all will end well."[67]

The historical evidence is abundant and only briefly sampled herein. George Washington believed in a personal God with whom man can commune and who would in return answer and provide. He believed in the God of the Bible and believed in God's ability and willingness to intervene in man's affairs for their benefit. More importantly for the purposes of this work, Washington believed that he saw God's intervening hand in the Founding of America and frequently acknowledged such. George Washington attained the glory that he himself spoke of when he said, "To the distinguished character of Patriot, it should be our highest glory to add the more distinguished character of Christian."[68]

---

[64] Ibid., p. 584
[65] Ibid., p. 585
[66] Ibid.
[67] Ibid.
[68] Ibid., p. 33

George Washington was a Christian man. Too many testimonies from those who knew him personally attest to that fact to allow for any other conclusion. Furthermore, his own writings and orations are replete with reverent references to God and Jesus Christ, to his own Christian beliefs, and to the Bible and its teachings. The reader is reminded that George Washington was among the great men that appeared to Wilford Woodruff in the St. George temple and requested his work be done. He was one of only three individuals at that time to also be ordained a High Priest. While that occurrence in and of itself may be anecdotal, it lends credence to the stature of his character and the openness of his mind to the true Gospel of Jesus Christ. Personal witnesses are near universal in that Washington was a good man, a moral man, and an honest man. He was a man of integrity, honor, and faith.

John Adams

John Adams is another individual often held as an example of the Founders' agnosticism and even hostility toward religion, specifically Christianity. He is credited with numerous quotes and statements that seemingly reflect his animosity toward religion, referring to it as superstition, fables, or fiction. One such quote was written in a letter to Thomas Jefferson where he wrote, "The question before the human race is, whether the God of nature shall govern the world by his own laws, or whether priests and kings shall rule it by fictitious miracles?"[69] These quotes, however, are often misunderstood or misconstrued to say or mean something that Adams himself does not seem to have intended.

Another supposed piece of evidence cited by secularists is that John Adams professed Unitarianism as his religion and attended Unitarian congregations. Though this, in fact, is true of Adams and a number of other Founders, it can easily be used to mislead about the nature of their religious beliefs by confusing Unitarianism of today with that of the 18th and early 19th centuries. While the Unitarianism of today acknowledges a supreme being as creator of the universe, it largely rejects many other points of Christian doctrine, most notably the divine parentage of Jesus Christ Himself and thereby also His own divinity and godhood.

History attests to a very different Unitarianism during the Founding era. A Theological Dictionary of 1823 contains an entry by a professing Unitarian that describes contemporary Unitarians as follows: "In common with other Christians, they confess that he is the Christ, the Son of the Living God; and in one word, they believe all that the writers of the New Testament, particularly the four Evangelists, have stated concerning him."[70] In a pamphlet the Unitarians

---

[69] John Adams, letter to Thomas Jefferson, June 20, 1815

[70] Charles Buck, *A Theological Dictionary*, 1823, p. 582

themselves published around 1840 titled An Answer to the Question, "Why Do You Attend a Unitarian Church?", they answer: "Because the Unitarians reject all human creeds and articles of faith, and strictly adhere to the great Protestant principle, 'the Bible - the Bible only;' admitting no standard of Christian truth nor any rule of Christian practice but the words of the Lord Jesus and His Apostles...Because at the Unitarian Church I hear Jesus of Nazareth who was crucified, preached as the Christ, the Son of the living God...Because there the crucified Jesus is exalted as having attained His high dignity and glory and His appointment to be the Saviour and Judge of the world..."[71] In short, Unitarians of the Founders' era were Christians plain and simple. They believed in Jesus Christ as the Son of God and the Savior of mankind. To ascribe the beliefs of today's Unitarians to Unitarian Founders like John Adams, Daniel Webster, John Marshall, John Quincy Adams, Joseph Story, James Kent and others is disingenuous and done with the intent of furthering the claim that the Founding Fathers were secularists who established a secular government to govern a secular society.

A close and fair examination of the Unitarianism professed by John Adams and a number of other Founders reveals a faith deeply rooted in the Gospel of the Bible and a profound reverence for Jesus Christ as the Son of God and Savior of the world. They were extremely skeptical, however, of varying philosophies and superstitions that had been added by men to that Gospel. Adams, and other Unitarians of the time, believed in and had faith in Jesus Christ and professed His Gospel but criticized what they had perceived as inventions of men added on top of that Gospel. This resulted in many statements critical of superstitions and falsehoods found in the religious sects of their day that have since been misunderstood or misconstrued by many to be critical of religion or Christianity itself.

From this perspective, it becomes a bit easier to reconcile Adams' seemingly anti-religious sentiments with those of his that are very clearly of a religious supporting and even Christian nature. Take, for example, the statement made in the letter to Thomas Jefferson quoted above: "The question before the human race is, whether the God of nature shall govern the world by his own laws, or whether priests and kings shall rule it by fictitious miracles?" In this new light, it is easy to see that the derision in this statement is not directed at religion in general so much as at the priests and kings who invent false miracles to deceive. Note that the alternative to the false priests is to allow the "God of nature" to govern the world by His laws, which Adams clearly sees as the correct choice of

---

[71] David Barton, www.wallbuilders.com

the two given. The title "God of Nature" is one used frequently among some of the Founders, particularly Adams and Jefferson, and others of the time. It is a respectful title given to God and is important because of the association that several Founders frequently made between God and nature. Also of import in this reference is the allusion to some of the Founders' philosophies and intellectual foundations being rooted in Natural Law. This is discussed in greater detail later.

Another such quote is found in a letter he wrote to FA Van der Kamp, in the which he said, "As I understand the Christian religion, it was, and is, a revelation. But how has it happened that millions of fables, tales, legends, have been blended with both Jewish and Christian revelation...?"[72] Again, it is obvious to the observant reader that Adams is professing pure Christian religion to have been received by revelation and then criticizes all that man has done to add to or detract from it, but he is not critical of pure Christianity itself.

One more quote will serve to illustrate this point:

> If [the] empire of superstition and hypocrisy should be overthrown, happy indeed will it be for the world; but if all religion and all morality should be over-thrown with it, what advantage will be gained? The doctrine of human equality is founded entirely in the Christian doctrine that we are all children of the same Father, all accountable to Him for our conduct to one another, all equally bound to respect each other's self love.[73]

Once again it is evident that Adams' apprehension is not with religion or Christianity itself, which he praises as the foundation for civil society and the source of human equality, but with the superstition and hypocrisy of men that have too frequently grown out of some religious sects and organizations.

John Adams was no enemy to Christianity. In fact, on one occasion during the Continental Congress of 1776, a fast day was proposed and Thomas Jefferson opposed it. In his opposition, Jefferson appeared to be opposing Christianity in general though, as will be shown below, this would be out of character for Thomas Jefferson. Adams spoke in favor of the motion and against Jefferson's position. Years later, Benjamin Rush wrote to Adams of the incident.

> You rose and defended the motion, and in reply to Mr. Jefferson's objections to Christianity you said you were sorry to hear such sentiments from a gentleman whom you so highly respected and with whom you agreed upon so many subjects, and that it was the only

---

[72] John Adams, letter to FA Van der Kamp, December 27, 1816

[73] David McCullough, *John Adams*, 2001, p. 619

> instance you had ever known of a man of sound sense and real genius that was an enemy to Christianity.[74]

Adams was clearly no enemy to Christianity and, in fact, struggled to comprehend how a man of "sound sense and real genius" could ever be such. That Jefferson was an enemy to Christianity was a perception that Adams garnered from this specific incident. This perception, however, was mistaken. Jefferson was no more an enemy to Christianity than was Adams himself as will be shown in more detail below.

As was the case seen previously with George Washington, John Adams not only believed in and revered the Christian religion and Christ, but saw God's Hand in the Founding of America. He said on one occasion:

> The general principles on which the fathers achieved independence, were ... the general principles of Christianity ... Now I will avow, that I then believed and now believe that those general principles of Christianity are as eternal and immutable as the existence and attributes of God; and that those principles of liberty are as unalterable as human nature...[75]

Here Adams unequivocally expresses his own belief in the principles of Christianity and in the existence and immutable attributes of God. He similarly states without reservation that American independence was achieved on those same Christian principles. Adams clearly viewed America's struggle for independence as rooted in Christianity and is very direct in professing his own belief in Christian principles.

Adams also acknowledged God's direct influence in America's Founding and demonstrated remarkable foresight into her destiny. He said:

> I always consider the settlement of America with reverence and wonder, as the opening of a grand scene and design in Providence for the illumination of the ignorant, and the emancipation of the slavish part of mankind all over the earth.[76]

This statement is almost prophetic in nature and demonstrates a deep understanding of America's Founding that could scarcely be achieved without inspiration from above. Adams saw in America's Founding a plan being unfolded by God that would ultimately have effect on mankind all over the earth. Compare this statement with the detailed teachings in chapter 3 regarding

---

[74] Ibid., p. 113

[75] Kees de Mooy, *The Wisdom of John Adams*, 2003, p. 35

[76] Charles Francis Adams, *The Works of John Adams*, 1856, vol. 1, p. 66

America's prophetic destiny and the beneficiaries of the Constitution being intended as "all flesh"[77] or all mankind.

Finally, like so many of the other Founders as amply demonstrated above, Adams was far from averse to religious expression on a public scale. He said:

> The safety and prosperity of nations ultimately and essentially depend on the protection and the blessing of Almighty God, and the national acknowledgement of this truth is an indispensable duty which the people owe to Him.

Here Adams clearly considers it a duty of the nation and her citizenry to acknowledge the blessings of Almighty God in their safety and prosperity.

John Adams was not a Deist, nor hostile to religion, he was not a Unitarian by today's definition of the same. John Adams was a Christian, professing his own belief in Christianity and in the Christian heritage of the United States. Detractors from this truth misconstrue his skepticism and distrust of those that abused Christianity for their own personal gain as hostility towards religion or Christianity itself. Adams saw God's influence in the Founding of America and saw that Founding as only a part of a much larger design that God had for man. John Adams was also among the great individuals that appeared to Wilford Woodruff and requested that his temple work be performed.

Thomas Jefferson

Thomas Jefferson is one of the more hotly debated of all the Founders as to his religious inclinations. He is thought and preached by many to be Deist, Atheist, anti-Christian, and anti-religion. Much like Adams, Jefferson made numerous statements in speech and in writing that can seemingly be taken to be hostile to religion and, more specifically, Christianity. Also much like the statements of Adams, when close examination is made of these statements by Jefferson in their full context, a different picture emerges.

The first thing to note when examining things said or written by Thomas Jefferson is a particular characteristic of his correspondence. Jefferson was an intellectual man who, like many Founders and others of the era, held reason and logic in high regard. Many of today use this as evidence supporting the argument against Jefferson's religious convictions, but they do so by arguing from a false premise that reason and religious belief are mutually exclusive and cannot be both held by the same individual. The Founders clearly did not believe this except for maybe one notable exception, Thomas Paine, who is treated further

[77] D&C 101:77

below. As seen above, however, John Adams is one example of a Founder who failed to comprehend how a man of "sound sense and real genius" could ever be hostile to religion and particularly Christianity. When the Founders elevated reason and critical thinking, they did so in contrast to emotion and not to religion. The Founders emphasized thought and reason over emotion in conducting their own lives but especially when considering decisions that would impact society as a whole, as in those made within and regarding government. For example, one warning given by Alexander Hamilton is that "[n]othing is more common than for a free people, in times of heat and violence, to gratify momentary passions, by letting into the government, principles and precedents which afterwards prove fatal to themselves."[78]

As seen in a great number of quotes and writings used throughout the present work, the Founders were very religious. What more, they are often found to comment on the reasoning and thought processes they themselves used to arrive at their religious beliefs. To many of the Founders, sound reason and critical thought inevitably led to belief in Jesus Christ and the pure Christian religion.

Jefferson was very conversational in his letters and can often be found to be laying out his entire process of thought or reason on a particular matter when expounding on it to a friend. Jefferson frequently employed the written equivalent of what today is called thinking out loud. Because of this, it is often quite easy to take a small portion of a letter from Jefferson to ascribe to him a line of thinking that is actually completely opposite of that professed by Jefferson himself, often in the very same letter or text if only considered in its full context. Jefferson was particularly fond of corresponding in this manner with his lifelong friend, John Adams.

Another thing to note is that throughout his life, Jefferson continually worked to advance his own knowledge on a diverse array of subjects. He was extremely well read, fluent in several foreign languages, well versed in political theory, moral ideologies, history, and religion (among many other subjects). He constantly sought to increase his own knowledge and understanding. In the course of doing so, Jefferson was in a perpetual state of reshaping and refining his worldview and system of beliefs. As a result of this, he can be found to have given contradictory statements on certain matters at different stages of his life, including some doctrinal points of Christianity. It is important to note, however, that these changes in beliefs and understanding were always on specific points of

---

[78] Philip Kurland, Ralph Lerner, *The Founders' Constitution*, 1987, vol. 3, p. 346

doctrine within Christianity and not variations of his beliefs in the Christian religion as a whole.

This is an important distinction because many of the statements used by detractors from Jefferson's Christianity are used as being disparaging of Christianity in its entirety when in fact they are merely Jefferson's criticisms or expressions of disbelief in particular points of doctrine within the encompassing Christian religion.

Another common argument made by detractors from a religious Thomas Jefferson is that of the so called "Jefferson Bible." The story is oft repeated how Jefferson created his own bible by cutting out of the actual bible all references to miracles, anything supernatural, and anything considered to be mysticism or mythology. Many infer from this the removal of signs, healings, references to Jesus' divine parentage or the miraculous circumstances surrounding His birth, and the Resurrection.

There are varying opinions on which of Jefferson's works is to be considered his own version of the Bible but the "Jefferson Bible" label is most often placed on one of two. The first was compiled in 1804, while he was serving as President, and is titled *The Philosophy of Jesus of Nazareth*. The full title given to the work by Jefferson himself, however, includes a brief description and intent for the work:

> The Philosophy of Jesus of Nazareth, being Extracted from the Account of His Life and Doctrines Given by Matthew, Mark, Luke and John; Being an Abridgement of the New Testament for the Use of the Indians, Unembarrassed with Matters of Fact or Faith beyond the Level of their Comprehensions.[79]

Jefferson clearly states his intent for this work in the full, unedited title that he himself gave to it. It was not intended to be his own version of the Bible more congruent with his own beliefs but was an abridgement of the New Testament, particularly the four Gospels, for the use of preaching Christianity to the Native Americans. What more, a couple of years earlier, Jefferson signed into law the authorization of the Society of the United Brethren which made use of federal funds to establish churches, missionaries, and Christian schools among the Native Americans residing in the Northwest Territory.[80] This one executive action is completely contradictory to the ever growing modern misconstruction of the "separation of church and state" doctrine that was supposedly authored by Jefferson himself. This doctrine is treated in more detail separately.

---

[79] David Barton, *The Jefferson Lies*, 2012 p. 70

[80] Ibid.

The abridgment made by Jefferson was clearly intended for use to further Christian missionary work among the Native Americans. Jefferson wanted to scale back the overwhelming Bible to the core teachings of Jesus in an abridged form that would be more consumable for Native Americans. The abridgment was made for a specific audience and not with the intent of cutting out superstitions and myths. Included in this abridgement were many miracles, teachings of Jesus' divine parentage, His role as Savior, and His Resurrection.

The second work, and perhaps the one referred to more commonly as the "Jefferson Bible," was completed in 1820 and carries the title of *The Life and Morals of Jesus of Nazareth*. This one was for private use by Thomas Jefferson himself and was to be a concise and simple compilation of Jesus' major moral teachings for easy access and study. This work, similar to the one produced in 1804, contains teachings and references to healings and miracles, Heaven and Hell, angels and the Devil, the Holy Ghost, and the Second Coming or, in other words, all the things in the Bible that would be considered to be supernatural or mythical by religious critics today.

Jefferson's grandson, Thomas Jefferson Randolph, said of this work, "His codification of the Morals of Jesus was not known to his family before his death, and they learnt from a letter addressed to a friend that he was in the habit of reading nightly from it before going to bed."[81]

This codification by Jefferson was not widely known until 1900 when John Lacey, a U.S. Representative from Iowa, became aware of it and published a newspaper article that caught the attention of many people across the nation. In 1902 Lacey sponsored a congressional resolution to reprint the work for use by those elected to Congress. Lacey described the work to Congress as follows:

> [It] is a consolidation of the beautiful, pure teachings of the Savior in a compact form ... No greater practical test of the worth of the tenets of the Christian religion could be made than the publication of this condensation by Mr. Jefferson ... A verse of John is combined with a verse of Matthew with no interlineations, but is blended into a harmonious whole ... The work was intended to place the morals of Jesus in a form where, simple and alone, they could be contrasted with the teachings of the pagan philosophers. In doing this work, Mr. Jefferson has builded ... this beautiful little volume in a form to be accessible to the Christian world.[82]

---

[81] Ibid., p. 81

[82] Ibid., p. 82

Thomas Jefferson was a Christian. Undoubtedly, he had a very unique brand of Christianity all his own, but it was Christianity nonetheless. Thomas Jefferson believed in Jesus Christ and in His teachings. He believed in His role as the Savior and strived to live by His precepts. In a letter to Benjamin Rush he wrote:

> To the corruptions of Christianity I am indeed opposed; but not to the genuine precepts of Jesus Himself. I am a Christian in the only sense in which He wished any one to be: sincerely attached to His doctrines in preference to all others.[83]

Much like seen previously with John Adams, Jefferson was a friend to pure Christianity and saw the teachings of Jesus Christ as true religion. He was extremely skeptical and antagonistic, however, towards many contemporary Christian denominations—especially Catholicism—and the superstitions that they had added to that pure Christian religion.

Jefferson's own theology borrowed much from the restorationist worldview that looked forward toward a day when Christ's true Gospel and Church would be restored to the earth. In a letter to Francis A. Van Der Kemp, he wrote, "the genuine and simple religion of Jesus will one day be restored such as it was preached and practiced by Himself ... I hope that the day of restoration is to come."[84] The Latter-day Saint reader should see the evident similarities between Thomas Jefferson's beliefs and those taught by The Church of Jesus Christ of Latter-day Saints regarding the true and authentic religion of Jesus Christ. LDS theology teaches that shortly after Christ's mortal ministry, His religion was lost to apostasy and corruption, thereby necessitating a restoration in its original and pure form.

Thomas Jefferson had a clear enough understanding of the true Gospel of Jesus Christ to recognize many of the flaws found in contemporary denominations. This understanding seems unlikely to be achieved without frequent and longstanding aid from God's Holy Spirit. Jefferson anticipated the full restoration of Christ's true Gospel. He revered Jesus and His religion and did his best to emulate the Savior's example in his everyday living. Jefferson was also among those who appeared to Wilford Woodruff and requested his temple work be performed shortly after passing from mortality.

Benjamin Franklin

Benjamin Franklin is also very frequently held up by detractors and critics as an example of the Deism or Atheism of the Founders. Franklin, indeed, is one of the

---

[83] Ibid., p. 189
[84] Ibid., p. 178

less religious of the Founders and so the use of him as such an example is understandable and expected.

Franklin's religious beliefs are far more complex, however, than to permit ascribing to them a single philosophy such as Deism, Atheism, or Christianity. The best source for the religious beliefs of Benjamin Franklin is, of course, Benjamin Franklin himself. He said and wrote a number of things regarding his own religious beliefs, perhaps one of the more succinct descriptions of them was written in a letter to Ezra Stiles, President of Yale University at the time, who had written to Franklin inquiring about his beliefs on religion. He wrote:

> Here is my creed. I believe in one God, creator of the universe. That he governs it by his providence. That he ought to be worshipped. That the most acceptable service we render to him is doing good to his other children. That the soul of man is immortal, and will be treated with justice in another life respecting its conduct in this. These I take to be the fundamental principles of all sound religion, and I regard them as you do in whatever sect I meet with them.
>
> As to Jesus of Nazareth, my opinion of whom you particularly desire, I think the system of morals and his religion, as he left them to us, the best the world ever saw or is likely to see; but I apprehend it has received various corrupting changes, and I have, with most of the present dissenters in England, some doubts as to his divinity; though it is a question I do not dogmatize upon, having never studied it, and think it needless to busy myself with it now, when I expect soon an opportunity of knowing the truth with less trouble. I see no harm, however, in its being believed, if that belief has the good consequence, as probably it has, of making his doctrines more respected and better observed...[85]

Based on Franklin's own words here, it is difficult to deny that he was of a persuasion that at least leaned toward the Deistic. There remain, however, some key differences in Franklin's convictions when compared to pure Deism. First, and most importantly, Franklin believed that God governs the universe. But more than just the universe as a whole, Franklin believed that God governs on a more personal level as well. During the Constitutional Convention of 1787, Franklin at one point enjoined the entire convention to make use of prayer, stating:

> I have lived, Sir, a long time; and the longer I live, the more convincing proofs I see of this truth, that God governs in the affairs of men. And

[85] Andrew Allison, W. Cleon Skousen, M. Richard Maxfield, *The Real Benjamin Franklin*, 2008, pp. 472-473

> if a sparrow cannot fall to the ground without his notice, is it probable that an empire can rise without his aid? We have been assured, Sir, in the sacred writings that "except the Lord build the house, they labor in vain that build it." I firmly believe this; and I also believe that, without his concurring aid, we shall succeed in this political building no better than the builders of Babel...[86]

Notice the several references to the Bible and biblical concepts, including the reference to the Bible being comprised of "sacred writings." Also note that this statement was made as part of a plea to the Convention delegates to entreat God through prayer for his blessings and assistance in the proceedings. Franklin testified on a number of occasions of his personal observations that God had blessed him and assisted him throughout his own life.

Franklin did express doubts regarding the divinity of Jesus Christ, so he can't very well be considered to be a devout Christian. He was hardly hostile or antagonistic toward Christianity, however. If anything, he can be considered to be largely agnostic on this issue as he admitted to never having given the question its due consideration. He did, however, praise the Christian religion and it's important to note that he does so with the qualifier "as he left [it] to us" and then admitted the source of his apprehension toward contemporary Christianity stemmed largely from "various corrupting changes" that had been effected by men.

During the same Congress that produced the Declaration of Independence in 1776, Franklin, Adams, and Jefferson were commissioned to design a seal for the new, independent nation of America. Franklin's proposal for the new seal is described by him below:

> Moses in the Dress of High Priest standing on the Shore, and extending his Hand over the Sea, thereby causing the same to overwhelm Pharaoh who is sitting in an open Chariot, a Crown on his Head and Sword in his Hand. Rays from a Pillar of Fire in the Clouds reaching to Moses, to express that he acts by the Command of the Deity.[87]

Franklin desired to include a motto with this seal that would read: "Rebellion to Tyrants is Obedience to God."[88] An artist's rendering of this description can be seen in Bruce Feiler's work, *America's Prophet: Moses and the American Story*.

---

[86] Ibid., pp. 258-259
[87] Bruce Feiler, *America's Prophet*, 2009, p. 64
[88] Ibid.

Franklin clearly possessed a degree of reverence for the Bible and the stories and religion contained therein. He was also very skeptical of the corruptions, as he called them, introduced into that religion by men. Equally clear was Franklin's harboring of doubts regarding some of the teachings in the Bible itself, most notably, that of the divinity of Jesus Christ. His doubts regarding Christ's divinity, however, are not to be taken as hostility toward Christ or the Christian religion. He was not dogmatically opposed to Christ's divinity but rather, by his own admission, had merely not asked and addressed the question enough to satisfy himself one way or the other.

His spirituality tended him toward Christianity in the end. He believed in and professed the morals of the Christian religion throughout his life. And upon his passing into the next life, he indeed received his opportunity of knowing and accepting the truth.

As told previously, Benjamin Franklin was among the "great men" who appeared to Wilford Woodruff to petition their own temple work be performed. Among the approximately one hundred individuals who appeared and had their work performed at that time, Franklin was one of only three who were also ordained to be High Priests.

Ezra Taft Benson said of those men, "if they had not been God-fearing men, would they have come to the elders of Israel to seek their temple blessings? I think not."[89] Franklin was a God-fearing man. He certainly didn't have it all right, and did not have the fullness of the Gospel worked out but he appears to have believed and accepted it once it was presented to him in the next life, as is evidenced by what little we know of his actions since passing from this life.

Thomas Paine

Thomas Paine is arguably the least religious of all the Founders and is the one legitimate example proffered by critics of religion and detractors of America's religious roots. Paine achieved infamy with his pamphlet entitled *Age of Reason* in which he criticized organized religion and particularly Christianity.

Paine's writings and beliefs are interpreted by many to be atheistic and by some to be deistic. This section will not get into the details of Paine's religious beliefs or whether he was a true and full atheist or not. What is pretty unmistakable from Paine's works is that he was not the greatest friend or ally to Christianity. Many of the other Founders of his day interpreted his *Age of Reason* to be atheistic in nature or, at best, hostile toward Christianity and this

[89] Joseph Smith Foundation, *Eminent Spirits Appear to Wilford Woodruff*, www.josephsmithacademy.org

placed them at odds with Paine and his work, even those that have been considered to be less religious or of a Deistic bent themselves.

John Adams wrote of Thomas Paine:

> The Christian religion is, above all the religions that ever prevailed or existed in ancient or modern times, the religion of wisdom, virtue, equity, and humanity, let the Blackguard Paine say what he will.[90]

On another occasion, when asked about some of Paine's followers emigrating to America, Adams replied:

> The German letter proposing to introduce into this country a company of schoolmasters, painters, poets, &c., all of them disciples of Mr. Thomas Paine, will require no answer. I had rather countenance the introduction of Ariel and Caliban [mischievous Shakespearean spirits] with a troop of spirits.[91]

Samuel Adams wrote the following to Thomas Paine:

> [W]hen I heard you had turned your mind to a defence of infidelity, I felt myself much astonished and more grieved that you had attempted a measure so injurious to the feelings and so repugnant to the true interest of so great a part of the citizens of the United States. The people of New England, if you will allow me to use a Scripture phrase, are fast returning to their first love. Will you excite among them the spirit of angry controversy at a time when they are hastening to amity and peace? I am told that some of our newspapers have announced your intention to publish an additional pamphlet upon the principles of your *Age of Reason*. Do you think that your pen or the pen of any other man, can unchristianize the mass of our citizens, or have you hopes of converting a few of them to assist you in so bad a cause?[92]

Benjamin Rush wrote to John Dickinson that Paine's *Age of Reason* was "absurd and impious."[93] Charles Carroll described it as "blasphemous writings against the Christian religion."[94] John Witherspoon referred to Paine as "ignorant of human nature as well as an enemy to the Christian faith."[95] Elias Boudinot published a full length rebuttal to Paine's work titled the *Age of Revelation*. Patrick Henry

---

[90] David Barton, *Original Intent*, 2008, p. 137
[91] Ibid.
[92] Ibid., pp. 137-138
[93] Ibid., p. 138
[94] Ibid.
[95] Ibid.

referred to *Age of Reason* as "the puny efforts of Paine"[96] and penned his own refutation to it.[97]

William Paterson, who signed the U.S. Constitution and served as a Supreme Court Justice, upon learning that some Americans agreed with Paine's *Age of Reason* declared:

> Infatuated Americans, why renounce your country, your religion, and your God? Oh shame, where is thy blush? Is this the way to continue independent, and to render the 4th of July immortal in memory and song?[98]

John Jay stated:

> I have long been of the opinion that the evidence of the truth of Christianity requires only to be carefully examined to produce conviction in candid minds, and I think they who undertake that task will derive advantages ... As to The Age of Reason, it never appeared to me to have been written from a disinterested love of truth or of mankind.[99]

Whether Thomas Paine was Atheist or Deist is largely unimportant here. Whatever he was, he was no lover of Christianity. No attempt will be made to disabuse the reader of this notion. The more important thing to note about Thomas Paine and the one thing that needs to be stressed for this work is that he was clearly the exception and not the rule.

While Paine can well be considered to be either Atheist or Deist, it does not hold to reason to stand him up as representative of the entirety of the Founders' system of belief. It is disingenuous to cite Paine as an example of the Founders' religious beliefs as a whole.

Summary and Conclusions

The Founding Fathers of the United States of America were by and large Christian. They believed in the Bible and the gospel that it contained. They revered Jesus Christ as their Savior and advocated for His religion and His teachings. For an overwhelming majority of the individuals that could be considered Founders of America, the evidence is straightforward and direct.

For a small minority of those men, whom many consider to be the least religious of the group as a whole, their beliefs and statements on religion and

---

[96] Ibid.
[97] Ibid.
[98] Ibid., p. 139
[99] Ibid.

Christianity are more complex and require more detailed examination and analysis. Several of the more prominent of these few were considered here in detail. There is much dispute over the religious convictions of John Adams, Thomas Jefferson, George Washington, Benjamin Franklin, and even Thomas Paine to a degree.

Thomas Paine, in his now infamous work that attacked Christianity so fiercely, wrote "I believe in one God ... and I hope for happiness beyond this life."[100] This and other statements made in the very same work make it difficult to categorically ascribe Atheism even to Thomas Paine.

Regarding the other four aforementioned Founders, most people advocate or subscribe to one of two differing schools of thought. On the one hand, those who believe in and profess a very religious heritage for the United States tend toward the statements made in favor of Christianity and Christian principles and largely neglect or ignore the more uncomfortable writings and sayings that appear critical of the same. Admittedly, the statements made by these Founders in favor of Christ and His religion largely outnumber those that were made in seeming criticism. Nevertheless, the more contrary statements were made and should not be ignored.

On the other hand, those that would advocate for a more secular Founding and thereby a more secular government and society today, will tend to the opposite direction, considering only that minority of statements that can be interpreted as critical of religion or of Christianity. These most commonly arrive at the conclusion of Deism and ascribe that belief system to the entire body of Founders. The next step in the logical process leads many along this thought line to deduce that the Founders intended a secular society with religion, and especially Christianity, playing little to no part in it.

This deduction, however, carries with it an extremely major flaw. A very narrow definition of what constitutes a Founder must necessarily include at the very least the 56 men who signed the Declaration of Independence and the 55 men who attended the Constitutional Convention. Already, with over 100 Founders from this extremely narrow definition, it defies reason to claim that the religious beliefs of 5 of those men are representative of the body as a whole. The definition of a Founder here is so narrow that it fails to include the 90 members of the first United States Congress who framed the Bill of Rights, the several Continental Congresses that governed the Colonies during the interim between when independence was declared and when the United States was fully established through ratification of the Constitution, and all of those members of

---

[100] Ibid.

the various state governments (governors and legislators) who contributed to the ratifying of the Constitution. Ironically, the narrow definition used above excludes Thomas Paine, who participated very little in any government capacity and never in a legislative one or one that had him contributing to any of the chief Founding documents. Yet Paine is considered a Founder for his intellectual contribution to the Revolution, most notably through his publication of *Common Sense*.

Therefore, if it could be shown definitively that Adams, Jefferson, Washington, and Franklin were all Deists and that Paine was an Atheist, it is still unreasonable to then assign those beliefs to all the remaining Founders, even though some of these were larger contributors than many others of the Founders.

This chapter, however, has presented a sample of the evidence that exists on this matter and a different take on the supposed criticisms made by Founders regarding Christianity. First, Washington was a Christian. He was fond of using a wide variety of titles when referring to God, but these titles were always very respectful and always calculated to remind of all the various ways in which God acts. He was not avoiding the name and title of 'God' as an expression of disbelief. He also made many references directly to God and Jesus Christ. He knew and believed in the Bible and made reference to its scripture and precepts often. He frequently recognized and drew attention to God's hand in guiding the Revolution and protecting the Colonial army and strengthening them against the British. He was one who was very often found to be engaged in personal prayer with his Maker. All of those close to him describe him as pious, religious, and Christian.

Many statements made by Adams, Jefferson, and Franklin are interpreted to be hostile toward Christianity. A closer examination shows that their hostility was always directed not at the Christian religion or at Christ, but at the men who had usurped authority in Christ's name or who had manipulated the teachings to their own benefit. Adams and Jefferson both revered Christ and His religion, but often qualified their reverence by referring to the religion as it came directly from Christ. Franklin too favored the Christian religion although his favoring was more analytical than it was the reverence and devotion given by Adams, Jefferson, and Washington. Franklin also recognized and criticized the artifices of men that had creeped into Christ's religion.

The discerning LDS reader might begin to recognize an emerging pattern in the treatment of these, the "least religious" of the Founding Fathers. Adams, Jefferson, Franklin, and to a degree Washington were all largely disenchanted with the various Christian sects and denominations of their day, yet still held a profound reverence for Christ and His pure religion. Jefferson even awaited a restoration of Christ's true religion as He Himself preached it. This manner of thinking is very reminiscent of what Jesus Himself revealed to the Prophet Joseph Smith when He appeared to him in 1820. Speaking of those same Christian churches and denominations, Christ counseled Joseph Smith that "all their creeds were an abomination in his sight; that those professors were all corrupt; that: 'they draw near to me with their lips, but their hearts are far from me, they teach for doctrines the commandments of men, having a form of godliness, but they deny the power thereof.'"[101]

It has been shown that the Founders were "raised up" by God. It has also been shown that in order for that to have happened, they were necessarily blessed, led, and taught throughout their lives by God's Holy Spirit. It seems, then, a distinct possibility to Latter-day Saints that these men were in tune with God's Spirit enough that they saw clearly the "doctrines and commandments of men" that were being taught in the churches and sects of their day.

Some may see this as highly speculative and indeed so it may be. Regardless of whether this be the case, however, one thing cannot be denied: with the possible exceptions of Paine and Franklin, the Founding Fathers of the United States were deeply religious and, more specifically, devotedly Christian. When they spoke of God, they spoke of the Christian God, the Hebrew God, the God of the New Testament, the Almighty God, Jesus Christ, Jehovah and many other appellations that are hard to mistake. When the Founders spoke of God, they spoke of Him with reverence, adoration, and respect.

Furthermore, they spoke of the Christian God's influence in the Revolution and the creation of the United States of America. They credited Him with many miracles throughout their struggle for independence and notably with the miracle of the Constitution itself. They saw His hand in its principles and His influence in its production and ratification.

The Founders were Christian men who founded a government on Christian principles to protect the rights of a Christian people. History attests to this and any claim to the contrary is deliberate historical revisionism with the intent of driving religion and religious people out of public office and public discourse. This is contrary to who the Founders were and the type of society and government institutions that they intended. David Barton states it well that "[t]his is usually done to support a broad, separationist approach to religion and government, which is inconsistent with the words and deeds of those who created America's political system."[102]

---

[101] Joseph Smith – History 1:19

[102] David Barton, *Franklin's Appeal for Prayer at the Constitutional Convention*, www.wallbuilders.com

Chapter 5 – By Their Works Ye Shall Know Them

When preaching to the Nephite people after His resurrection, Jesus taught:

> Ye shall know them by their fruits. Do men gather grapes of thorns, or figs of thistles?
>
> Even so every good tree bringeth forth good fruit; but a corrupt tree bringeth forth evil fruit.
>
> A good tree cannot bring forth evil fruit, neither a corrupt tree bring forth good fruit.
>
> Every tree that bringeth not forth good fruit is hewn down, and cast into the fire.
>
> Wherefore, by their fruits ye shall know them.[1]

Mormon repeated this same principle, but translated "fruits" to "works" when he said, "For I remember the word of God which saith by their works ye shall know them; for if their works be good, then they are good also."[2] Good trees can only bring forth good fruit and bad trees can only bring forth bad fruit. Likewise, good men and women can only produce good works and bad men and women bad works. Applied to the Founders, this principle would seem to require an examination of their works to determine whether the Founders themselves were good or corrupt.

In the case of America's Founders, however, the examination of their works to determine how good they are is not necessary. This is because it has already been revealed by God that they are wise and that He justifies the work that they produced. Since the works produced by the Founders have already been thusly approved of by God, they are considered in the present work to be good without further proving.

This chapter will still conduct an examination of some of the works that were produced by America's Founders. This examination, however, will not be to determine whether they are good. Instead, this chapter is intended to merely highlight key, high level points and concepts of the works produced by the Founders and as a basis for the free government institutions that make up the

---

[1] 3 Nephi 14:16-20; Compare Matthew 7:16-20

[2] Moroni 7:5 (5-19)

United States of America. It should be noted that while these works were produced by the Founders, it was by God's own impetus that they did so, and so it is with God's desire that these works are had by America and the world. The examination of these works is only considered to be a cursory examination and the reader is strongly encouraged to pursue these subjects separately in greater depth and detail.

Principles of Civil Government

This section will give an overview of the philosophies and principles on which the Founders constructed the American form of free government. As with any group of thinking men, the Founding Fathers were not all in agreement on all things at all times. It is expected, therefore, that if one were to search hard enough, one might find statements, beliefs, or practices among the Founders that seem contrary to the general ideology laid out below. This ideology is not intended to be presented as a strict religious code among the Founders that was rigorously adhered to and consequently negated by the least bit of evidence to the contrary. Instead, the below ideology is considered to be the predominant system of beliefs subscribed to by the general body of the Founders, especially those who made substantial intellectual contributions to the principal Founding documents and original institutions. The ideology presented herein is the prevailing ideology that was imbued into America's original government institutions as intended by the Founders. It is the ideology that is reflected in the final product of what God Himself claims to have established as the form of government that He justifies.

The treatment of this ideology will remain at a high and summary level for two reasons. First, at a higher level, much more consensus is found among a larger majority of the Founders regarding these principles and philosophies. Where disagreements arose was in the more minute specifics and particularly in the application of these principles to the public institutions of government and society, not so much in the importance and relevance of these foundational principles themselves. Second, these philosophies and ideas constitute an extremely large body of work and so to treat them in any great detail would require a much larger work than the present one is intended to be.

Natural Law

An understanding of the Founders' thinking on government and law requires a brief introduction to the philosophy of Natural Law. Natural Law is predicated on the understanding that moral absolutes of right and wrong are universal and can be discovered through the observation of nature, particularly man's nature, and that sound moral law is based on these naturally observable absolutes.

One significant influence on the thinking of the Founders with respect to Natural Law is Marcus Cicero, a Roman philosopher and statesman who lived in the first century B.C. Cicero witnessed, and fought against, the slow degeneration of the Roman republic into tyranny. In his work, *On The State*, Cicero wrote:

> True law is Reason, right and natural, commanding people to fulfil their obligations and prohibiting and deterring them from doing wrong. Its validity is universal; it is immutable and eternal. Its commands and prohibitions apply effectively to good men, and those uninfluenced by them are bad. Any attempt to supersede this law, to repeal any part of it, is sinful; to cancel it entirely is impossible. Neither the Senate nor the Assembly can exempt us from its demands; we need no interpreter or expounder of it but ourselves. There will not be one law at Rome, one at Athens, or one now and one later, but all nations will be subject all the time to this one changeless and everlasting law.[3]

Cicero advocated that "Nature is the source of law."[4] The application of reason and the observation of nature inevitably lead to a universally valid, eternal law of right and wrong, good and bad. Good men submit to this law and bad men do not. This law is everlasting and cannot be altered by the activity of the state. In other words, state legislation cannot turn good into bad nor bad into good. Sound civil law will remain in accordance with the universal moral law observed in nature and legislative attempts to counter this Natural Law are "sinful."

A common intellectual exercise employed by philosophers of Natural Law is to make observations of man in his primitive and individual state to determine the rights and freedoms with which he is rightfully endowed. In his primitive state, man will spend much of his time and energy on the essential tasks of survival. He will hunt and forage for food, find or establish some sort of shelter, and construct tools and weapons to facilitate these activities. He will have an inventory of possessions that includes the land to which he lays claim. This land may be raw land, a cave, a field or fields of crops, a dwelling of some kind, or some combination of any or all of these. His inventory will also include the tools and weapons that he has constructed and stores on his land, and any stores or

---

[3] Michael Grant, *Cicero: Selected Works*, pp. 7-8

[4] Ibid., p. 186

sources of food that he has gathered and worked to preserve and maintain on his land.

A lone man in such a state of existence will be considered justified in preserving and protecting his life if threatened by another man, an animal, or whatever natural occurring event. In the case of his life being threatened by another man, or a group of men, he would be justified in using force or violence in defending and preserving his own life. He would be similarly justified in protecting himself from enslavement by other men so that he not be forced to provide his labor for the benefit of another instead of for the establishment and preservation of his own possessions and sustenance. Finally, this man would be justified in preserving and protecting those possessions that he has worked to acquire, whether he gathered, constructed, or merely claimed what was previously unclaimed. His possessions include the land that he claims, the tools, weapons, furniture, and dwellings that he has constructed, and any food that he has managed to preserve and store.

The observance of this man in a primitive state gives rise to the concept of Natural Rights. Natural Rights are those that are possessed by every individual and are observable through nature. The brief example above illustrates four specific Natural Rights possessed by the lone observed man. First, he possessed a right to his life, to work for its preservation and to protect it when threatened. Second, he had a right to his liberty, to be free to act for his own benefit and not be arbitrarily placed in bondage or slavery to another and forced to provide his labor for another's benefit. Third, he had a right to his property or possessions, that which his own labor had produced and which belonged to him and could not rightly be taken by another. Finally, he had a right to defend all of these and even employ violence to do so. These Natural Rights are treated in greater detail below.

It can be seen in this intellectual exercise that the observer will *naturally* distinguish between good and bad behavior and that the determinations are almost universally accepted. Attempts on another person's life are considered bad. Similarly, actions calculated to force an individual to do something against his own will or to manipulate him into actions or behavior desired by the perpetrator are also considered bad. Finally, any attempt to destroy or take another's property is universally considered bad behavior. In contrast, the individual man is considered to be acting well while simply working to maintain, preserve, and enrich his own life, his liberty, and his property, and is considered well justified in defending all of these from encroachments and threats by others.

This little experiment illustrates the concepts articulated by Cicero in the statement above. Law is natural and universally valid. Good people already consider themselves subject to it and those who do not are considered to be bad.

In a primitive state like the one observed above, it can be seen that a large amount of time and energy will be spent in protecting one's life, liberty, and property, or maintaining and preserving his Natural Rights. To facilitate this work, men will group together into societies and appoint some number of their group to specifically protect these things for them. To this group, the people delegate their power of protection to empower the appointed body to work for the protection of the people's lives, liberties, and properties. Thus is born the institution of government.

This is the way in which just government is formed. This formation of government is in accordance with that universal law that is observed through nature. Cicero's writings on Natural Law and republican government were highly influential to many Enlightenment thinkers and writers including Montesquieu, David Hume, and John Locke. Montesquieu was a French political philosopher and lawyer who lived during the first half of the 18th century. John Locke was a British philosopher who lived during the second half of the 17th century. He is considered the father of Classical Liberalism for his prolific writings on civil government as based in Natural Law. All of these men were highly influential in the thinking of the American Founding Fathers and consequently in American government principles. John Locke is famous for articulating sound and just civil government based on Natural Law in his work *Two Treatises on Government*. In the *Second Treatise*, Locke states the following:

> If Man in the State of Nature be so free, as has been said; If he be absolute Lord of his own Person and Possessions, equal to the greatest, and subject to no Body, why will he part with his Freedom? Why will he give up this Empire, and subject himself to the Dominion and Controul of any other Power? To which 'tis obvious to Answer, that though in the state of Nature he hath such a right, yet the Enjoyment of it is very uncertain, and constantly exposed to the Invasion of others. For all being Kings as much as he, every Man his Equal, and the greater part no strict Observers of Equity and Justice, the enjoyment of the property he has in this state is very unsafe, very unsecure. This makes him willing to quit this Condition, which however free, is full of fears and continual dangers: And 'tis not without reason, that he seeks out, and is willing to joyn in Society with others who are already united, or have a mind to unite for the mutual

> Preservation of their Lives, Liberties, and Estates, which I call by the general Name, Property.[5]

Locke writes that the reason that men enter into society and subject themselves to a governing body is the "mutual Preservation of their Lives, Liberties, and Estates [Property]." But they can only rightly do so through their own consent and willing delegation of their own power and authority to preserve their own lives, liberties, and property. This is the doctrine of delegated authority or consent of the governed, also advocated and articulated by John Locke in his *Second Treatise* on civil government.

There are a few very important things that need to be noted here before proceeding. First, man creates government. In the process of creating government, man must empower that government with a measure of his own power and authority. Man does this through delegation. Man creates and empowers government, government does not create nor empower man. Next, it is essential to note that man cannot give what he does not have or, in other words, he cannot delegate authority that he does not rightfully possess. Therefore, just government can only be empowered with the power that man, its creator, already possesses. Once government acts in a capacity that is outside the bounds in which man can rightfully act, then the government has become despotic, usurping more power and authority to itself than can rightfully be given to it by man. This is part of the doctrine of the consent of the governed. Man cannot consent to give authority that he does not have himself and therefore cannot delegate that authority to another, including to a government. Government acting outside of man's consented authority is unjust and despotic.

Additionally, the Founders subscribed to the legal philosophy known as the Rule of Law. The Rule of Law is the principle that all men are equal under the law and that for a government to be just and free, it must protect each citizen's rights equally and uniformly. A citizen whose rights are protected less than the rights of others is oppressed. Most importantly, this includes individuals of high status and wealth and those that are a part of the government itself.[6] Just laws will not apply to different groups differently, but will apply to all citizens uniformly, including those that participate in making the laws and those that possess a lot of material possessions or societal influence.

---

[5] Peter Laslett, *Locke: Two Treatises of Government*, 1960, pp. 350-351

[6] Compare Mosiah 29:32

Nature's God

Prevalent in America in the time preceding and during the Revolutionary and Founding Era was the marriage of the philosophy of Natural Law with the religion of Christianity. This union of ideologies was very common among those that are considered significant intellectual sources and influences over the American Revolution. It was likewise very common among many that participated in government at all levels from local to state to national.

This is not surprising since America was initially colonized by those that were fleeing religious persecution in Europe, persecution which came largely at the behest of the state. This led to an early American population that was overwhelmingly religious, especially Christian, while simultaneously very averse to state intrusions into their religious beliefs and practice. This naturally led to much interest in the Enlightenment philosophies of freer governments and increased tolerance of varying religions by governments.

The marriage of these two ideologies led to the philosophy of Natural Law being elevated to that of a more divine law. As devout Christians, early Revolutionary Americans, including the Founders, believed in God as the Creator. Therefore, to observe nature was to observe God's creations. So not only were moral absolutes of right and wrong observable through nature, but God's divine law and the moral right and wrong as decreed by Him could be discovered there, for He created nature!

The Latter-day Saint reader will find interesting parallels between this set of beliefs and the LDS doctrine often referred to as the Light of Christ or the Spirit of Christ. Moroni teaches that "the Spirit of Christ is given to every man, that he may know good from evil."[7] We enter this world already knowing good from evil. The observation of this universal knowledge leads the rational thinker to divine absolutes that have been given to us by God.

This manner of thinking led the Founders to often make references to natural and divine law, and their Author, in ways that may seem cryptic or obscure to modern readers of their works. Common titles employed to refer to God include the "God of nature" or "nature's God." Similarly, proposed legal provisions and measures were sometimes compared against the "laws of nature and nature's God" or the "laws of God and nature." One of the most notable examples of this language is found in the Declaration of Independence itself and will be discussed below.

---

[7] Moroni 7:16

Natural Rights

No real discussion on America's Founding can be had without a corresponding discussion on man's rights. The Founding of America was largely based on the rights of man and, unique to America's Founding, their source. The Founders expended much effort in studying, debating, and understanding man's rights. They were well read and deeply knowledgeable in political and moral theories and philosophies and they were well aware of all the different political philosophies that had been advocated or implemented throughout the centuries.

One of the most basic fundamentals on which America is founded and in which was rooted the thinking of the Founders is the concept of man's Natural Rights. It was previously shown how Natural Rights arise out of the philosophy of Natural Law. Certain rights can be seen to be possessed by man by observing man in a natural state of freedom. It was also shown how the Founders took concepts from Natural Law and advanced them further into the divine. God created nature and so anything that can be learned through the observation of nature is being taught by God. With this relationship between God and nature in mind, it is easy to see that when the Founders referred to Natural Rights, they were referring to rights given by God. Natural Rights are those that arise from man's nature as a creation of God. They come with man into the world and are not granted to him by other men or governments upon entering the world. In this way, they are inalienable or inseparable from each individual man and woman.

In the preamble to a bill he proposed on multiple occasions to the Virginia Legislature, Thomas Jefferson wrote:

> [C]ertain forms of government are better calculated than others to protect individuals in the free exercise of their natural rights, and are at the same time themselves better guarded against degeneracy, yet experience hath shown that, even under the best forms, those entrusted with power have, in time, and by slow operations, perverted it into tyranny.[8]

There is much in this statement from Thomas Jefferson worthy of consideration, but for now simply note the reference to Natural Rights.

Samuel Adams perhaps summed it up best when he wrote, "Among the natural rights of the Colonists are these: First, a right to life; Secondly to liberty; Thirdly to property; together with the right to support and defend them in the best manner they can."[9]

---

[8] Thomas Jefferson, *A Bill for the More General Diffusion of Knowledge*, 1778, Virginia State Legislature, Bill 79

[9] Samuel Adams, *The Rights of the Colonists*, 1772

Here Samuel Adams articulated very concisely the summation of the prevailing philosophy on man's rights as held by the Founders. Man has natural, God-given rights to life, liberty, property, and the right to defend them "in the best manner they can," which includes through the use of force or arms. When reading through the speeches and writings of the Founders, there are three principal Natural Rights that are referred to most often, they are life, liberty, and property, and they are most commonly listed in that order.

This philosophy was ardently advocated by John Locke who in his work, *Two Treatises of Government*, argued that governments exist to protect life, liberty, and property or life, liberty, and estate as he also put it. Each of these three chief Natural Rights is treated below, much of this treatment will focus on the right of property because that is the right that is the least understood. The right to defend oneself and one's rights is treated further below.

Life

The right to life is mostly self-explanatory and needs little in the form of clarification. Life is an obvious universal right acknowledged by most everyone. Most people see the wrongfulness in taking the life of another unless under extreme circumstances of self-defense, war, or as a consequence of a very grievous crime—usually involving the wrongful taking of another life. Even under such circumstances the question of justification for taking life is still frequently a very difficult and controversial one, this is because each of us is born into this life with an inherent reverence for that life and the life of others. Those few who do not carry such reverence for life are looked on by the rest of society as wrong, evil, or ill in some manner. As mentioned previously, the Latter-day Saint religion teaches this as the Light of Christ, possessed by everyone who enters this mortal world and a guiding light to recognize wrong from right.

Liberty

Liberty is freedom of the conscience together with the ability to act according to that conscience. In other words, the Founders saw that God had granted unto man the freedom to think and act as he pleases and that it therefore was wrong for one man to coerce or force certain thinking or behavior on another. Thomas Jefferson wrote to the Virginia delegates of the Continental Congress, "The God who gave us life gave us liberty at the same time."[10] Here Jefferson affirms that liberty is a natural, God-given right that each of us enters into this life already possessing.

[10] Thomas Jefferson, *A Summary View of the Rights of British America*, 1774

If liberty is a right given by God to every man, then it follows that it is unjust for one man to unduly deprive another of his liberty. In other words, "it is not right that any man should be in bondage one to another."[11]

The more influential of the Founders were unanimous in their reverence for liberty as a Natural Right that every individual enters this world endowed with. Liberty is not granted by governments or other men, liberty is a right inherent in man's existence and so cannot be infringed upon without offending the God that gave it to man. Liberty is the overarching principle that dominated the Founding of America and the thinking of those men who fought for its independence and established its form of free government.

Property

Private property is likely the least understood of the Natural Rights advocated by the Founders. Many find it challenging to consider property as a sacred right from God, especially in the present world with so much discussion around wealth distribution. Increasingly it is seen as evil or wrong to merely have a lot of money or possessions.

A detailed discussion on the merits versus the evils of wealth will not be included here, but one question must be asked of the reader. Many today find it distasteful or obscene to see the amount of wealth accumulated by relatively few people. But, no matter the feelings about another's wealth accumulation, under what circumstances is it justifiable to forcefully deprive an individual of his or her property? Some might say that it is right to do so for the benefit of the public or the more needy. Another common justification that is made amounts to no more than the fact that they can afford it, they already have enough, or they have more than they need. The Founders would disagree.

Charles Montesquieu was a philosopher who had a substantial impact on the Founding of America as he significantly influenced a number of the Founders including James Madison, John Adams, and Alexander Hamilton. He said, "Let us, therefore, lay down a certain maxim, that whenever the public good happens to be the matter in question, it is not for the advantage of the public to deprive an individual of his property, or even to retrench the least part of it by a law, or a political regulation."[12]

William Blackstone also contributed considerably to the Founding of America with the writing of his *Commentaries on the Laws of England*. This work by Blackstone, a British judge, was very heavily relied upon by the Founders and most legal professionals of the era. Indeed, Blackstone's *Commentaries* could be

---

[11] D&C 101:79

[12] Charles Montesquieu, *Spirit of Laws*, 1900, vol. 2, p. 73

considered the backbone of American legal thought throughout much of America's early history. In *Commentaries*, Blackstone wrote, "So great moreover is the regard of the law for private property, that it will not authorize the least violation of it; no, not even for the general good of the whole community."[13]

John Locke wrote in *Two Treatises on Government*, "the preservation of Property being the end of Government, and that for which Men enter into Society"[14] and that "Government ... can never have a Power to take to themselves the whole or any part of the Subject's Property, without their own consent. For this would be in effect to leave them no Property at all."[15]

All of the philosophers and thinkers that had significant influence on the thinking of the Founders viewed property as a Natural Right, and liberty as inextricably tied to that right. Their thinking and writing did not just treat property as important or nice to have, but rather as an essential ingredient in the recipe of freedom. Liberty cannot exist without the ability to own and control property and to be absolutely secure in the ownership of that property, never being able to be divested of it arbitrarily or without due process of law (having first committed a crime). With these philosophers and their ideas as their intellectual sources, it is expected that similar statements can be found to be made by the Founders themselves. Below is a small sample of statements made by various Founders on the subject of property.

John Adams, while defending U.S. constitutional government, stated, "Property is surely a right of mankind as really as liberty."[16] On another occasion he wrote that "Property must be secured, or liberty cannot exist."[17] Further down in the same aforementioned defense, Adams says:

> The moment the idea is admitted into society, that property is not as sacred as the laws of God, and that there is not a force of law and public justice to protect it, anarchy and tyranny commence. If "THOU SHALT NOT COVET," and "THOU SHALT NOT STEAL," were not commandments of Heaven, they must be made inviolable precepts in every society, before it can be civilized or made free.[18]

Adams is particularly forceful in that he elevates property to a level equal with and as sacred as God's own laws. Again, note that the comparison to God's law and to the Ten Commandments comes from one of the Founders that is often

---

13 Philip Kurland, Ralph Lerner, *The Founders' Constitution*, 1987, vol. 1, p. 586

14 Peter Laslett, *Locke: Two Treatises of Government*, 1960, p. 360

15 Ibid., p. 361

16 Philip Kurland, Ralph Lerner, *The Founders' Constitution*, 1987, vol. 1, p. 591

17 John Adams, *Discourses on Davila*, 1790, no. 13

18 Philip Kurland, Ralph Lerner, *The Founders' Constitution*, 1987, vol. 1, p. 591

cited as being hostile toward Christianity or even religion in general. Also note how Adams associates the violation of private property rights with breaking the commandments "Thou shalt not covet" and "Thou shalt not steal." Additionally, private property rights and these commandments must be made "inviolable" in order for a society to be civilized or free.

John Jay wrote, "It is the undoubted Right and unalienable Priviledge of a Freeman not to be divested, or interrupted in the innocent use, of Life, Liberty or *Property* ... This is the Corner Stone of every free Constitution..."[19] Jay reiterates the point made by Adams above, that property is a necessary corner stone of a free constitution.

James Madison states:

> Government is instituted to protect property of every sort; ... This being the end of government, that alone is a just government, which *impartially* secures to every man, whatever is his *own*. ...
>
> That is not a just government, nor is property secure under it, where the property which a man has in his personal safety and personal liberty, is violated by arbitrary seizures of one class of citizens for the service of the rest. ...
>
> That is not a just government, nor is property secure under it, where arbitrary restrictions, exemptions, and monopolies deny to part of its citizens that free use of their faculties..."[20]

Madison states unequivocally that a government is not a just government where citizens under it are denied the free and unrestricted use of their own property, or have their property arbitrarily seized for the benefit of others.

Fisher Ames, who contributed greatly to the framing of the Bill of Rights, said that "The chief duty and care of all governments is to protect the rights of property."[21]

Finally, John Dickinson, who signed the Constitution, said, "Let these truths be indelibly impressed on our minds—that we cannot be happy, without being free—that we cannot be free, without being secure in our property—that we cannot be secure in our property, if, without our consent, others may, as by right, take it away—that taxes ... do thus take it away..."[22]

It is clear from these and many other statements made by the American Founders that private property was more than just a passing fancy in their minds. It was with more than just a little thought on the matter that they constructed

---

[19] Ibid., vol. 5, p. 312 (emphasis added)
[20] Ibid., vol. 1, p. 598
[21] Henry Ewbank, *The Influences of Democracy on Liberty, Property*, 1835, p. 136
[22] John Dickinson, *Letters from a Farmer, in Pennsylvania, to the Inhabitants of the British Colonies.*, Letter XII

the Constitution and its resulting government in such a way as to protect property as a sacred right from God. Private property rights are discussed at great length by many of the philosophers who influenced the Founders, men whose writings the Founders had thoroughly studied, considered, and debated. The Founders themselves are found to have discussed and written much on the matter. They considered property as a sacred and Natural Right granted by God to man and instituted a government whereby that right was intended to be protected and held inviolate.

Compare these teachings by the Founders with the following verse in Doctrine & Covenants that reads: "We believe that no government can exist in peace, except such laws are framed and held *inviolate* as will secure to each individual the free exercise of conscience, *the right and control of property*, and the protection of life."[23]

"Inviolate" is similar to the language used by Blackstone when he said that just law would not allow the "least violation" of private property rights. "Inviolate" clearly does not suggest that private property should be respected only unless a better or more worthy use can be found for it by society at large. Nor does it suggest that property be respected only to a certain degree, and that once it is determined that an individual or group has enough of it or can afford to part with some then it becomes justified to deprive them of it. "Inviolate" means in no way infringed upon, unbroken, pure, untouched.

This verse in the Doctrine & Covenants is consistent with the thinking and teachings of the Founders. They expressly denied the national government the ability to deprive citizens of their private property for arbitrary purposes. In fact, under the Constitution as originally framed and signed by the Founders, the national or federal government did not have the power to tax individuals directly. That power was left to the various states and the federal government collected taxes from the states.

There is a simple reason why the right of private property is to be held sacred and why redistributive government policies are unlawful and unjust under the Constitution and the laws of nature and nature's God. The reason stems from the philosophies of Natural Law and government by consent.

The reader will recall that just government under Natural Law is created by man, by man consenting to join into a community and then delegating his own authority to a governing body to facilitate the protection and security of his Natural Rights. Man creates government, government does not create man, and part of that creation process is to delegate some of his own authority to that

---

[23] D&C 134:2 (emphasis added)

government. This process produces two logical outcomes. First, man is the source of the government's power and, as the creator of government, must retain power over the government that he creates. Second, man can only delegate authority, or power, that he already has and nothing more. One man cannot lawfully take the property of another, be it through force or by stealth, either way it is considered theft. If the individual man does not have this power, then he cannot delegate the power to another man, group of men, or government. Therefore, when government deprives a citizen of his property for the sole purpose of giving it to another, it has acted in a capacity outside of the bounds in which the individual man, its creator, is justified in acting. It has usurped a power to itself that is not possessed by man, who created it. This is an unjust and illegitimate power because it cannot be derived from the governed by their consent as the governed do not rightly possess this power themselves.

So, when government redistributes possessions and wealth, it acts outside of the authority that was given to it by man. Therefore, redistributive government is a usurpation of power because it is expanding its actions outside of the legitimate and just capacity in which its creator, and source of power, can rightly act. At this point, the government has become despotic, usurping illegitimate power that it does not derive from the people by consent.

The Declaration of Independence

On July 4th, 1776 the Continental Congress of the United States of America adopted the Declaration of Independence and declared to the world that they would no longer submit to the tyrannical government of Great Britain and the injustices that the British government was wont to impose on its colonies across the Atlantic.

A detailed and thoroughly historical analysis of the Declaration of Independence could fill an entire book by itself and so will not be conducted here. Nevertheless, some key points need to be elucidated for the purposes of the present work.

Before analyzing the Declaration itself there is one point that needs to be made. There is much disputation over how much legal weight the Declaration of Independence carries. For the Constitution to be accurately applied to society today, it needs to be understood within its appropriate historical context. This concept is treated in more detail later. At the very least the Declaration should be thoroughly understood and utilized as a significant contributor to that historical context and the spirit in which the Founders were framing the Constitution. Even if one considers the Declaration of Independence of no legal relevance, it is still produced by the same minds and stems from the same intellectual and moral foundations as the Constitution. Therefore, it at least informs the spirit in which the Constitution was written.

After listing and examining much evidence (that is not included here) in support of this notion and the Founders' affirmation of it, David Barton concludes:

> The Constitution cannot be properly interpreted nor correctly applied apart from the principles set forth in the Declaration; the two documents must be used together. Furthermore, under America's government as originally established, a violation of the principles of the Declaration was just as serious as a violation of the provisions of the Constitution.[24]

One of the pieces of evidence cited is a declaration made by the U.S. Supreme Court in 1897 that states of the Declaration and Constitution respectively: "The latter is but the body and the letter of which the former is the thought and the spirit, and it is always safe to read the letter of the Constitution in the spirit of the Declaration of Independence."[25] The use of the Declaration of Independence as a basis of interpretation for the U.S. Constitution was commonplace in the courts, as high up as the U.S. Supreme Court, and as late as the turn of the twentieth century. Since that time, efforts have been undertaken to divorce the one from the other by those who seek to remove religion and spirituality from America's heritage.

But merely as companion to the Constitution is not the position to which the Declaration of Independence ought to be relegated. It is a significant and substantial document in its own right. It establishes the foundational principles on which the American form of government is constructed. It declares the reasoning behind the separation of the American Colonies from Great Britain and, by so doing, lists a large number of items considered by the Founders to be tyrannical. The Declaration of Independence continues to be cited today by elected officials, sometimes out of sincere respect, but too often misconstrued for political expediency.

The first paragraph of the Declaration of Independence reads:

> When in the Course of human events, it becomes necessary for one people to dissolve the political bands which have connected them with another, and to assume among the powers of the earth, the separate and equal station to which the Laws of Nature and of Nature's God entitle them, a decent respect to the opinions of mankind requires

[24] David Barton, *Original Intent*, 2008, p. 257

[25] Ibid.

> that they should declare the causes which impel them to the separation.[26]

Key in this first paragraph is that one people is deciding to separate itself from another and that they are entitled to do so by the "Laws of Nature and of Nature's God." Note the influence of Natural Law and Christianity in the opening paragraph. It is interesting that in the opening statement of the Declaration of Independence reference is made to God and nature. It is also interesting to note that among the five individuals that were commissioned by the Continental Congress to draft the Declaration were John Adams, Thomas Jefferson, and Benjamin Franklin, who are considered by many to be among the least religious of the Founding Fathers. It was shown previously in chapter 4 that this is not the case, here the opening to the Declaration of Independence adds further evidence to that argument.

The Declaration of Independence is the first formal step taken towards the creation of the nation of America. How interesting then it is that the first thing the document endeavors to do is appeal to the laws of God, as observable through nature. This opening paragraph to the Declaration of Independence firmly roots America in natural and divine law, and firmly establishes that law as the basis for the coming nation and its governing institutions. It also reveals insight into the minds of those Founders who built them.

The remainder of this first paragraph presents that God's laws and nature's laws are such that no one people should feel obligated to exist in subjugation to another and that they are entitled by God and His laws to separate if they so choose.[27] Note the elevation of God's and nature's laws above those that are created by men, the "political bands" referred to early in the paragraph. Political ties are inventions of men and can only carry so much weight. Mankind is by nature subject to a higher law that entitles them to certain rights and privileges, including the willing dissolution of political bands established by other men.

The rest merely states that such being the case, it is polite and courteous to inform the world of their intent to conduct such a separation and the reasons as to why.

The second paragraph begins:

> WE hold these Truths to be self-evident, that all Men are created equal, that they are endowed by their Creator with certain unalienable Rights, that among these are Life, Liberty, and the Pursuit of Happiness—That to secure these Rights, Governments are instituted

[26] U.S. Declaration of Independence
[27] Compare D&C 101:79

> among Men, deriving their just Powers from the Consent of the Governed...[28]

Never before or since have more sublime and eloquent words served as the stated foundation for a nation's government. Since their adoption, these words have resonated across the centuries as the standard by which good government is measured. Contained within this statement is a series of fundamental truths, as seen by the Founders, that was prevalent in their political thinking and that they inculcated into the fabric of the government that they formed.

First and foremost is that "all Men are created equal." The first thing to note about this phrase is that men are created, which implies the existence of a Creator. The implication is subsequently made into a direct statement when specific reference is made to that Creator.

In addition to being created by a Creator, men are created equal to one another. This phrase has been largely misunderstood by many of recent and current generations. Many attempt to use this phrase in the Declaration to justify government forced equalization of wealth, wages, materials, or circumstances but this is contrary to the spirit in which the Founders intended it.

Benjamin Franklin, who was on the committee to draft the Declaration, said:

> An equal dispensation of protection, rights, privileges, and advantages is what every part is entitled to, and ought to enjoy; it being a matter of no moment to the state whether a subject grows rich and flourishing on the Thames or the Ohio, in Edinburgh or Dublin. These measures never fail to create great and violent jealousies and animosities between the people favored and the people oppressed; whence a total separation of affections, interests, political obligations, and all manner of connections necessarily ensue, by which the whole state is weakened, and perhaps ruined forever![29]

Franklin is clear in his assessment that each individual and group is entitled to an equal protection of rights and privileges. He does not include an equal distribution of property or possessions in this entitlement. He finishes this statement by declaring that legislation calculated to favor one group at the expense of oppressing another weakens the entire state and will perhaps lead to its ultimate ruin.

James Madison wrote in *The Federalist*:

---

[28] U.S. Declaration of Independence

[29] Allison, Andrew; Skousen, W. Cleon; Maxfield, M. Richard, *The Real Benjamin Franklin*, 2008, pp. 362-363

> Theoretic politicians ... have erroneously supposed that by reducing mankind to a perfect equality in their political rights, they would, at the same time, be perfectly equalized and assimilated in their possessions, their opinions, and their passions.[30]

Madison considers it erroneous to suppose that political equality necessarily equates to a similar equalization of possessions, opinions, and passions. Therefore, the political equality referred to in the Declaration of Independence is only erroneously taken to mean a similar equality in possessions, opinions, or passions.

John Adams, who also was on the committee that drafted the Declaration, wrote the following in a letter to one John Taylor of Caroline, Virginia:

> Inequalities are a part of the natural history of man ...
>
> That all men are born to equal rights is true. Every being has a right to his own, as clear, as moral, as sacred as any other being has. This is as indubitable as a moral government in the universe. But to teach that all men are born with equal powers and faculties, to equal influence in society, to equal property and advantages through life, is as gross a fraud, as glaring an imposition on the credulity of the people, as ever was practised by monks, by Druids, by Brahmins, by priests of the immortal Lama, or by the self-styled philosophers of the French Revolution. For honor's sake, Mr. Taylor, for truth and virtue's sake, let American philosophers and politicians despise it..[31]

Adams here is unequivocal. The equality of man of which the Founders spoke and wrote is a political equality, an equality to rights, and an equality in entitlement to the protection of those rights. Adams states that this equality in rights is as "indubitable as a moral government in the universe." To teach that this same equality is applicable to property, advantages, or societal influence, is, according to Adams, a gross fraud and he admonishes "American philosophers and politicians [to] despise it."

Also of note in this passage is Adams' reference to the "self-styled philosophers of the French Revolution." The French revolution is out of the intended scope of the present work, however, it is noteworthy to point out that many today make attempts to equate the American Revolution with that of the French. The American Founders disagreed vehemently with much of the ideology behind the French Revolution (which ideology was not equivalent to that of the American Revolution) and the manner in which it was conducted. While it is outside the

---

[30] James Madison, *The Federalist*, 1787-1788, No. 10

[31] George W. Carey, *The Political Writings of John Adams*, 2000, pp. 373-375

present scope, the reader is encouraged to study this subject. Americans, and especially Christians, should know the differences between the American and the French Revolutions.

Thomas Paine said:

> Rights are not gifts from one man to another, nor from one class of men to another ... It is impossible to discover any origin of rights otherwise than in the origin of man, it consequently follows, that rights appertain to man in right of his existence only, and must therefore be equal to every man.[32]

When the Founders spoke of the equality of man, they spoke of each individual being equal in his rights and privileges under Natural Law. Each individual is born into this life with an equal set of Natural Rights and an equal entitlement to protect himself and those rights whether individually or by participating in a society with a corresponding government.

The phraseology and ideas found in the Declaration of Independence regarding Natural Rights were unique as the basis for a national government at the time, but they were not unique to that document and they were not expressed for the first time in that Declaration. For example, the Virginia Declaration of Rights adopted a mere month prior to the Declaration of Independence, and authored by George Mason, reads:

> That all men are by nature equally free and independent, and have certain inherent rights, of which, when they enter into a state of society, they cannot, by any compact, deprive or divest their posterity, namely, the enjoyment of life and liberty, with the means of acquiring and possessing property, and pursuing and obtaining happiness and safety.[33]

History makes it clear that when the Founders spoke of men being created equal, they were in no way advocating for government to forcefully equalize men in their possessions or circumstances but rather that every man enters into this life with an equal endowment of rights and privileges, chief among those being life, liberty, and property. This is further clarified in the very next phrase of the text, which states "that they are endowed by their Creator with certain unalienable rights." This statement should not be interpreted as a wholly separate truth but as a further qualification of the first truth. All men are created equal. How? By each being endowed with the same set of unalienable rights.

---

[32] Thomas Paine, *Dissertation on First-Principles of Government*, 1795

[33] The Virginia Declaration of Rights, Adopted June 12, 1776 by the Virginia Constitutional Convention, Section I

A Natural Right is one that arises with each individual upon entering this life. These rights are granted to mankind by God and cannot be separated in any way from an individual. In this way they are unalienable, or unable to be separated from each individual. Among the Natural Rights of man are "life, liberty and the pursuit of happiness." Note that these three are rights listed "among" the Natural Rights of man and are not to be considered a comprehensive list of the same.

The Natural Right of life was discussed previously and the concept of liberty is treated in detail throughout this entire work. The right to a pursuit of happiness, however, is more ambiguous and deserves further consideration. There is much debate over the meaning of the phrase "pursuit of happiness" in the Declaration of Independence, some arguing that it is intended to mean private property while others aver that it was intended to mean autonomy, or self-rule. The debate will not be detailed here as it is a finer point that doesn't bear much meaning on the present subject.

When all of the writings and philosophies of Jefferson, who produced the initial draft of the Declaration, and the four others on the committee are considered, the phrase "pursuit of happiness" can appropriately be taken as meaning either property or autonomy or both. All members of the committee were advocates of the Natural Rights of life, liberty, and property, and all were for a limited government that would largely leave people to themselves to conduct their own lives. Jefferson himself gave a summary of sound government as follows:

> A wise and frugal government, which shall restrain men from injuring one another, shall leave them otherwise free to regulate their own pursuits of industry and improvement, and shall not take from the mouth of labor the bread it has earned. This is the sum of good government...[34]

In his *Notes on the State of Virginia*, Jefferson wrote that "The legitimate powers of government extend to such acts only as are injurious to others."[35] Jefferson, along with many of his contemporaries, was of the opinion that good, sound, just government largely left its citizenry alone and only interfered in affairs which involved citizens injuring one another, whether in their person or their property. Powers exercised outside of this scope were considered by them to be illegitimate.

Furthermore, when one studies the philosophies and thinking of the Founders and those who drafted and adopted the Declaration of Independence, it is

---

[34] Thomas Jefferson, First Inaugural Address, Delivered March 4, 1801

[35] Philip Kurland, Ralph Lerner, *The Founders' Constitution*, 1987, vol. 5, p. 79

evident that those men believed that the rights of property and autonomy are not entirely independent of one another. An individual cannot be granted full autonomy without the right and control of his property and cannot fully enjoy his right to private property without being granted the autonomy to control that property. In short, either of these interpretations is appropriate enough for the present discussion. Government should not take the property of its citizens and should leave them alone to pursue their happiness how they desire, provided those pursuits don't infringe on the rights of others. What is also very clear based on the thinking of the Founders is that it is a gross error to interpret this phrase as placing obligations on government to make efforts to increase the happiness of its citizens, especially through redistribution of materials, goods, and wealth. This is an erroneous argument commonly made today and must necessarily lead to the violation of private property rights.

Next, it is declared that it is the protection of these Natural Rights that is the purpose of instituting governments among men. Note the distinction here that governments are instituted to protect these rights and not to grant nor create them. Here again the language reveals the Founders' tendency toward Natural Law. Natural Rights accompany each individual into the world. Government is an institution where people have gathered together collectively to coordinate an effective defense for these rights. Government is in no way to be considered as the source or overseer of these rights but solely as a protector of them. Good, just, and sound government does only this, protects Natural Rights, and no more.

Finally, instituted governments are to derive their "just powers from the consent of the governed." Government by consent was articulated and heavily advocated by John Locke and this phrase, together with the declaration of man's Natural Rights, reveals significant influence from Locke on those who produced the Declaration of Independence. Government can only act with the moral authority that has been consensually delegated to it by the people forming it, the governed. This is how government derives its "just powers." Powers exercised by government that are not delegated by consent are usurpations of power and are not just. This includes those powers that are not rightly possessed by man to begin with, as man cannot consent to delegate powers that he himself does not already possess.

After stating the basic principles on which sound government is based, The Declaration proceeds to enumerate all the ways in which Great Britain has violated those principles. Below is a list of the "repeated injuries and usurpations,"[36] executed by King George III of Britain, that are "all having in

[36] U.S. Declaration of Independence

direct object the establishment of an absolute tyranny"[37] over the American Colonies. This list is important because it lists many acts of government that the Founders considered to be tyrannical in nature.[38]

1. He has refused his Assent to Laws, the most wholesome and necessary for the public good.
2. He has forbidden his Governors to pass Laws of immediate and pressing importance, unless suspended in their operation till his Assent should be obtained; and when so suspended, he has utterly neglected to attend to them.
3. He has refused to pass other Laws for the accommodation of large districts of people, unless those people would relinquish the right of Representation in the Legislature, a right inestimable to them and formidable to tyrants only.
4. He has called together legislative bodies at places unusual, uncomfortable, and distant from the depository of their public Records, for the sole purpose of fatiguing them into compliance with his measures.
5. He has dissolved Representative Houses repeatedly, for opposing with manly firmness his invasions on the rights of the people.
6. He has refused for a long time, after such dissolutions, to cause others to be elected; whereby the Legislative powers, incapable of Annihilation, have returned to the People at large for their exercise; the State remaining in the mean time exposed to all the dangers of invasion from without, and convulsions within.
7. He has endeavoured to prevent the population of these States; for that purpose obstructing the Laws for Naturalization of Foreigners; refusing to pass others to encourage their migrations hither, and raising the conditions of new Appropriations of Lands.
8. He has obstructed the Administration of Justice, by refusing his Assent to Laws for establishing Judiciary powers.
9. He has made Judges dependent on his Will alone, for the tenure of their offices, and the amount and payment of their salaries.
10. He has erected a multitude of New Offices, and sent hither swarms of Officers to harrass our people, and eat out their substance.

---

[37] Ibid.

[38] The numbering in this list is added for convenience in referencing by the author and not found in the Declaration of Independence itself

11. He has kept among us, in times of peace, Standing Armies without the Consent of our legislatures.
12. He has affected to render the Military independent of and superior to the Civil power.
13. He has combined with others to subject us to a jurisdiction foreign to our constitution, and unacknowledged by our laws; giving his Assent to their Acts of pretended Legislation:
    a. For Quartering large bodies of armed troops among us:
    b. For protecting them, by a mock Trial, from punishment for any Murders which they should commit on the Inhabitants of these States:
    c. For cutting off our Trade with all parts of the world:
    d. For imposing Taxes on us without our Consent:
    e. For depriving us in many cases, of the benefits of Trial by Jury:
    f. For transporting us beyond Seas to be tried for pretended offences
    g. For abolishing the free System of English Laws in a neighbouring Province, establishing therein an Arbitrary government, and enlarging its Boundaries so as to render it at once an example and fit instrument for introducing the same absolute rule into these Colonies:
    h. For taking away our Charters, abolishing our most valuable Laws, and altering fundamentally the Forms of our Governments:
    i. For suspending our own Legislatures, and declaring themselves invested with power to legislate for us in all cases whatsoever.
14. He has abdicated Government here, by declaring us out of his Protection and waging War against us.
15. He has plundered our seas, ravaged our Coasts, burnt our towns, and destroyed the lives of our people.
16. He is at this time transporting large Armies of foreign Mercenaries to compleat the works of death, desolation and tyranny, already begun with circumstances of Cruelty & perfidy scarcely paralleled in the most barbarous ages, and totally unworthy the Head of a civilized nation.
17. He has constrained our fellow Citizens taken Captive on the high Seas to bear Arms against their Country, to become the executioners of their friends and Brethren, or to fall themselves by their Hands.
18. He has excited domestic insurrections amongst us, and has endeavoured to bring on the inhabitants of our frontiers, the merciless

> Indian Savages, whose known rule of warfare, is an undistinguished destruction of all ages, sexes and conditions.

A brief analysis is given below of this list of tyrannical government actions as considered by the Founders. With each item under number 13 being considered separately and 13 itself also a separate item, the list is 27 items long.

Before presenting the analysis, some very wise counsel given by James Madison is applicable to the discussion. He said:

> It is proper to take alarm at the first experiment on our liberties. We hold this prudent jealousy to be the first duty of Citizens, and one of the noblest characteristics of the late Revolution. The free men of America did not wait till usurped power had strengthened itself by exercise, and entangled the question in precedents. They saw all the consequences in the principle, and they avoided the consequences by denying the principle.[39]

Far too many in present day America make the mistake of associating tyranny only with large displays of military force or actual violence perpetrated by a government against its citizenry. It is often very easy to ignore anything less or to consider it as not too problematic. Similarly, too many find it of little concern when illegitimate powers are granted to the government, or taken by the government to itself, as long as the power is used for a perceived good. These are the "principles" referred to by Madison. He extolls the American Revolutionaries for recognizing the dangers in the principles and not waiting until the resulting consequences of usurped power arose. How much better is it to recognize the slow descent into tyranny and arrest that progress before the problems and consequences become large, and often bloody, to resolve.

The enumeration of usurpations in the Declaration of Independence serves as a useful reference to the types of "experiments on our liberties" at which alarm should be taken. The list illustrates what the Founders considered to be usurped power by government. It also lists examples of the types of powers that Madison would have considered it the duty of citizens to deny to government in principle.

Interestingly, analysis of this list reveals that much of it consists of items that amount to little more than parliamentary tricks and political gaming to block the passage of undesirable legislation or merely to stand in the way of things desired by political opponents. This type of gaming of the political institutions and processes is all too commonplace in America's government today.

---

[39] Philip Kurland, Ralph Lerner, *The Founders' Constitution*, 1987, vol. 5, p. 82

Items 1 – 10, and 13, 13d, 13g, 13h, and 13i are all items that involve this sort of political game play. That is over half of the items in the list. As an example, item number 1 is analogous to today's American government as abuse of the executive veto power to block legislation passed by an elected Congress but disagreed with by the President, not because the legislation is unconstitutional but because it is of a differing political ideology than that of he who holds the veto power.

Items 11 and 12 mention the military but do not refer to it as being used in force against the Colonists. Item 13 is very similar to current trends among elected officials in all three branches of the federal government toward rendering American law and America's Constitution as subservient to the will of foreign and international bodies such as the United Nations. There is a similar idea gaining popularity that suggests when decisions are made in American courts, consideration should be given to international laws and those of other countries in addition to what is contained in the U.S. Constitution.

Items 14 – 18 are ones that are more obvious and would hopefully be easily recognized by most citizens as government overreach. About a third of all the items listed above make mention of the king's use of his military.

The two paragraphs following this list detail the peaceful ways in which the Colonies had sought resolution to these matters. These two paragraphs leave the reader with the impression that what they are saying is that they've tried every other course and are now left with no choice but to separate from the tyranny of Britain's monarchy.

In the final paragraph, two more references are made to God. The first mention is the act of "appealing to the Supreme Judge of the World for the Rectitude of [their] Intentions."[40] After the appeal, independence from Great Britain is claimed and all the powers and freedoms associated therewith. The closing to the Declaration of Independence reads as follows:

> And for the support of this Declaration, with a firm Reliance on the Protection of divine Providence, we mutually pledge to each other our Lives, our Fortunes, and our sacred Honor.[41]

It should not be discounted that these men were committing treason against the British Crown and were risking everything they had. It was with courage that they pledged their lives, their fortunes, and their sacred honor. Some of them indeed lost their lives as a result of signing this document. All of them knew it was a risk they were taking. They had confidence in what they were doing and

[40] U.S. Declaration of Independence

[41] Ibid.

risked their lives to do it, and they did it "with a firm Reliance on the Protection of divine Providence."

The U.S. Constitution

The Constitution of the United States was drafted in 1787 and fully ratified and operational in all 13 states by 1790. God stated by revelation that He established it, that it is based on just and holy principles (central of which is agency), and that He justifies man in befriending it. He also stated by revelation that it is for the benefit of all mankind, that it should be maintained, and that anything more or less than it, with respect to civil law or the law of man, comes from evil. These items have all been treated at great length elsewhere in the present work and will not be treated again here.

Joseph Smith wrote from Liberty Jail to the body of the Church that "the Constitution of the United States is a glorious standard; it is founded in the wisdom of God. It is a heavenly banner..."[42] William Gladstone said "the American Constitution is, so far as I can see, the most wonderful work ever struck off at a given time by the brain and purpose of man."[43] Thomas Jefferson declared it "unquestionably the wisest ever yet presented to men."[44]

Much like with the Declaration of Independence, a complete and comprehensive examination of the U.S. Constitution is a substantial work in itself and so a full and complete analysis will not be conducted here. There are, instead, certain key principles highlighted below that are considered pertinent to the present work and discussion and of interest to the intended audience of this work.

The original Constitution, as signed by its Framers, consisted of a preamble and seven articles. The seven articles of the Constitution are organized as follows:

Article I:	Legislature
Article II:	Executive
Article III:	Judiciary
Article IV:	Federalist relationship between the states and the Union
Article V:	Amendment process
Article VI:	Supreme Law of the Land
Article VII:	Ratification and Unanimous Consent

Before treating the Constitution in detail, it is necessary to make a couple of points. The first point is on the importance of possessing and enforcing a written

[42] Richard C. Galbraith, *Scriptural Teachings of the Prophet Joseph Smith*, 1993, p. 168
[43] Suzy Platt, *Respectfully Quoted*, 1989
[44] Andrew Allison, *The Real Thomas Jefferson*, 2008, p. 142

Constitution. The second point is on the standard by which "constitutional" can be measured.

A Written Constitution

When two or more parties unite together in a business venture, the first thing they will do is to establish and agree to a contract binding each of the interested parties to an agreement. If later any of the parties are suspected of violating the agreement, then all parties have the written contract to refer to in order to prove the offense. Likewise, a mediator will have access to the agreement in the case of independent arbitration.

Without a written agreement or contract, such proving of an offense becomes enormously more difficult and independent arbitration near impossible. Memories are feigned or forgotten, discrepancies inevitably arise in the memories of each party regarding the terms agreed to, and nothing exists to prove the original agreement and resolve the dispute.

Having a written Constitution is similar to the business contract in the hypothetical scenario above. It is a written and established contract between the people and their established government. In the case of the U.S. Constitution, it says, in effect, that the people of the United States agree to delegate certain powers and authority to the national government while that government is restrained in the use of that power so as never to infringe on the rights of the people.

Without a written Constitution, the people have no standard or agreement to which to hold their government, and the government inevitably grows at the expense of the people's liberty. Likewise, if the people don't enforce what is written in the Constitution, be it through apathy, ignorance, or willingness, then it is as if there is no written Constitution and the government similarly grows at the expense of the people's liberty.

To this effect, Thomas Jefferson admonished, "Our peculiar security is in the possession of a written Constitution. Let us not make it a blank paper by construction."[45] Jefferson understood that there is great security in a written Constitution, a contract between the people and their government, as long as government is restrained by it. The security he refers to is the security of the people in their liberties as a written, and effective, Constitution retains the appropriate restraints on government to prevent it from encroaching on the Natural Rights of its citizens.

---

[45] Thomas Jefferson, Letter to William C. Nicholas, September 7, 1803

James Madison said, "If men were angels, no government would be necessary. If angels were to govern men, neither external nor internal controls on government would be necessary. In framing a government which is to be administered by men over men, ... you must first enable the government to control the governed; and in the next place oblige it to control itself."[46] The security had in possessing the U.S. Constitution in written form is that it obliges government to control itself, fulfilling Madison's latter requirement for any government of men over men.

The people, however, must retain ultimate authority over that government and the people must be the enforcers of the contract between themselves and that government. This can only occur if the people are aware of the substance of that contract, the U.S. Constitution. It is not enough to know the text, it is requisite that the underlying principles, the spirit, and the intents of its authors be understood as well.

The people of the United States have a peculiar security in their possession of a written Constitution. The judiciary, as an arbitrating body, has a written contract to refer to when ruling on government actions and measures. This is a must for the existence of liberty. There must be a contract between the people and the government and it must be enforced. If not, then the government becomes arbitrary, exercising arbitrary powers at its own discretion. Jefferson warns to not make the Constitution into blank paper or, in other words, render it meaningless by interpreting it too loosely or by not obliging government to adhere to its precepts.

What is the U.S. Constitution?

Another clarification that needs to be made before continuing the discussion on the Constitution is what it is and what it is not. The U.S. Constitution defines the federal, or national, government of the United States of America. It defines the functions of the separate branches of that government. It also defines qualifications for office, the lengths of terms, and various procedures to address exceptional circumstances that arise from time to time in the government. The Constitution describes the processes by which laws are to be made. Together with the Bill of Rights and the Declaration of Independence, it articulates the principles on which those laws should be founded.

What the Constitution is not is an exhaustive set of all the laws, statutes, and regulations that were meant to govern all of society at the time of its adoption.

---

[46] James Madison, *The Federalist*, 1787-1788, No. 51 (compare Mosiah 29:12-13,16)

It contains the principles on which sound laws are based and not all of the laws themselves.

This is an important distinction because it is easily blurred by those who advocate government breaking through the restraints imposed on it by the Constitution in order to achieve expedient political objectives. One of the first arguments made by those friendly to this position was that the Constitution had become outdated. This argument is still made by many today. The claim is that the Constitution was created for an agrarian society that existed over 200 years ago and that it is unsuited for the complex, technological society we live in today.

The argument sounds appealing on the surface but only holds if the Constitution indeed actually regulated that agrarian society, which it did not. A common and somewhat comical example that is often used is to point out that the Constitution was produced in a time where the mode of transportation was with horse and carriage and so it couldn't possibly be suited for today when use is made of cars, subways, and airplanes. The Constitution, however, makes no mention of either horse or carriage and makes no law or regulation applicable to either one. Instead of endeavoring to be that comprehensive set of laws and regulations that govern American society, the Constitution defines a set of unchanging principles on which laws and regulations should be made. The complexity and nature of a society notwithstanding, these principles do not change.

This concept is addressed further in chapter 7.

Constitutionality

The terms "constitutional" and "unconstitutional" are presently invoked often in efforts to support or criticize legislation and measures either proposed or implemented by government. They are often used with little regard for their actual meaning and often by individuals or groups who know little of, or have little respect for, the Constitution and its authors. Unfortunately, "constitutional" has become pretext for "what I want" and "unconstitutional" for "what I oppose." Additionally, "constitutional" is often confused with the term "legal." It is essential to recognize that legislation, programs, court decisions, and government actions may be considered legal according to present laws and statutes, established precedent, or merely by widely accepted practice, while simultaneously being unconstitutional. Measures may be technically legal while still violating constitutional principles.

One tactic used to confuse constitutionality is to refer to the text of the Constitution, without any regard for historical context or intent, and extract politically expedient interpretations or meanings from that text. This can only serve to weaken the constitutional bounds placed on government as those bounds are reduced from firm constitutional restraints, as placed there by the Framers, to merely the limitations of imagination and ingenuity in extracting any desired meaning from the text.

Another tactic employed is to refer to a measure or law as constitutional, but then refer only to court decisions and other past interpretations of the Constitution for supporting evidence, all the while ignoring the original intent of those who authored and established it. This is referred to as legal precedent and is the legal or political equivalent of saying, "somebody else has done this before or interpreted the law in this manner before, so it is justifiable to do it again now." This too weakens the restraints placed on government by the Constitution by allowing anything that violates those restraints to be considered only one time. Once somebody has successfully implemented or interpreted a law in a way that circumvents or breaks constitutional restraints, that case becomes a precedent and the constitutionality of the action, and similar subsequent actions, is rarely if ever revisited. Instead, that precedent is then referred to as justification for future decisions to violate the same principle or, more commonly, to violate the same original principle in addition to a new or further violation of it or another related principle. In this manner, government scope and influence creeps ever so slightly at the expense of the people's freedom.

It is this slow process, of establishing precedents that are by small degrees further and further away from the originally intended constitutional principles, of which James Madison cautioned when he said, "I believe there are more instances of the abridgement of freedom of the people by gradual and silent encroachments by those in power than by violent and sudden usurpations."[47]

On the matter of constitutionality, Elder Dallin H. Oaks of the Quorum of the Twelve Apostles counseled:

> Some of the things said by various persons in recent public discourse cause me to urge that we be more careful in the way we throw around the idea that something is unconstitutional. A constitution should not be used as a weapon to end debate. A public policy or a proposed law that is unwise is not necessarily unconstitutional. Even if it is a stupid proposal, it is not necessarily unconstitutional. A constitution gives the people and their elected leaders the opportunity to make many decisions that are unwise or even reckless. When that happens—when the government or one of its officials engages in some kind of action that we consider to be wrong—we should engage in vigorous public debate about it. But we should not use up a constitution by

[47] James Madison, Speech in the Virginia Ratifying Convention, June 16, 1788

> attempting to strike down every ill-conceived act of government or to discredit every unwise official. A constitution is the ultimate weapon, and we preserve that weapon best by using it sparingly and carefully. If we call some action unconstitutional, we should be prepared to explain what provision or principle of a constitution it violates. In this way, a constitution can be used to stimulate discussion and to seek unity.[48]

The only way to know whether a proposed law or measure is constitutional is to understand the Constitution in its historical context and as intended by those who authored it.

Thomas Jefferson, while serving as President, admonished Justice William Johnson of the Supreme Court, "On every question of construction, carry ourselves back to the time when the Constitution was adopted, recollect the spirit manifested in the debates, and instead of trying what meaning may be squeezed out of the text, or invented against it, conform to the probable one in which it was passed."[49] Jefferson advocated for interpreting the Constitution in the manner and with the meaning in which it was originally established by its authors.

Madison wrote in a letter to Henry Lee in 1824:

> I entirely concur in the propriety of resorting to the sense in which the Constitution was accepted and ratified by the nation. In that sense alone it is the legitimate Constitution. And if that be not the guide in expounding it, there can be no security for a consistent and stable, more than for a faithful, exercise of its powers. If the meaning of the text be sought in the changeable meaning of the words composing it, it is evident that the shape and attributes of the government must partake of the changes to which the words and phrases of all living languages are constantly subject. What a metamorphosis would be produced in the code of law if all its ancient phraseology were to be taken in its modern sense![50]

Madison, much like Jefferson, was in agreement that the only legitimate interpretation of the Constitution is that interpretation that preserves its original meaning when it was produced and ratified by the nation. If the meaning of the text changes with time, like all languages do, then the exercise of government powers must also necessarily change. This produces an illegitimate government, inconsistent, unstable, and invariably tending toward the despotic. If the

---

[48] Dallin H. Oaks, *Fundamentals of Our Constitutions*, September 17, 2010

[49] M. Richard Maxfield, K. DeLynn Cook, W. Cleon Skousen, *The Real Thomas Jefferson*, 2008, p. 382

[50] James Madison, *Letters and Other Writings of James Madison*, 1884, vol. 3, p. 442

meaning of the Constitution can be altered through reinterpretation, then the security of possessing a written Constitution is lost or greatly diminished as the text of it arbitrarily varies in meaning and therefore is rendered without meaning at all.

Noah Webster further expounded on the potential for serious error in the interpretation of language. Webster made this statement as to the reason why he saw fit to produce a new translation of the Bible. So, while he was not specifically speaking of the Constitution, his assessment of the way language changes and how those changes can lead to serious interpretive errors is correct. He said:

> [I]n the lapse of two or three centuries, changes have taken place, which, ... obscure the sense, of the original languages. Some words have fallen into disuse; and the signification of others in current popular use, is not the same now as it was when they were introduced into the version. The effect of these changes is, that some words are ... now used in a sense different from that which they had ... [and so] present a wrong signification or false ideas. Whenever words are understood in a sense different from that which they had when introduced ... mistakes may be very injurious.[51]

The same injurious mistakes can be made in interpreting the Constitution, or any law, with meaning that is different than originally intended. Webster was referring to injurious mistakes that could be made in interpreting religion from sacred text, but the same mistakes will be made and result in as much injury if meanings in the Constitution are interpreted in a manner other than how intended by its Framers.

James Wilson, who sat on the first U.S. Supreme Court, proclaimed, "The first and governing maxim in the interpretations of a statute is, to discover the meaning of those, who made it."[52] This, of course, is the only way to sensibly interpret laws and statutes. They cannot be correctly applied without the originally intended spirit and meaning being sought first. The same holds true for the entire Constitution, on which all American law should be based.

Joseph Story, who was appointed to the Supreme Court by James Madison, similarly stated of the Constitution specifically:

> The instrument [the Constitution] furnishes essentially the means of its own interpretation. The first and fundamental rule in the interpretation of all instruments is to construe them according to the

---

[51] John Wright, *Early Bibles of America*, 1894, p. 141

[52] Bird Wilson, *The Works of the Honourable James Wilson, L.L.D.*, 1804, p. 14

> sense of the terms and the intention of the parties. The intention of a law is to be gathered from the words, the context, the subject-matter, the effects and consequence, or the reason and spirit of the law.[53]

Story, like many others among his contemporaries, understood that it is a fundamental rule of interpreting all instruments, that the intent of the producing parties be considered as well as the spirit in which they produced it.

The only valid and legitimate interpretation of the Constitution is in the manner intended by its Framers. To understand whether a proposed law, regulation, or provision of a law is constitutional, one must refer to the Constitution in its historical context and in the context of the minds and philosophies of its Framers. Unfortunately, this exercise is conducted far too seldom today. Sometimes it is by mere intellectual laziness, but all too often it is with real mal-intent that the true meaning and intent of the Founders is ignored, concealed, or misconstrued. Instead, what occurs too often today is what Jefferson referred to as starting with a desired meaning and then having that meaning "squeezed out of the text, or invented against it."[54]

Because of LDS religious beliefs regarding the source of the Constitution and constitutional principles, it is the opinion of the author that Latter-day Saints are uniquely responsible and duty-bound to understand those principles and be able to articulate when something is constitutional or unconstitutional. All Americans, however, if they are to be successful in preserving their freedom, also have a need to better understand when proposed legislation is truly constitutional or not and discontinue the use of constitutionality as a hyperbolic weapon to support desired legislation and criticize undesired legislation.

For a much more thorough treatment of the importance, value, and legitimacy of a written constitution and a more detailed justification of interpreting the U.S. Constitution according to its original meaning, the reader is encouraged to refer to *Restoring the Lost Constitution* by Randy E. Barnett.

Preamble

The Preamble to the Constitution is a brief paragraph stating the intent of the document. It is hopefully familiar to the reader. It reads:

> We the people of the United States, in order to form a more perfect Union, establish justice, insure domestic tranquility, provide for the common defence, promote the general welfare, and secure the

[53] U.S. Dept. of State, *Foreign Relations of the United States*, 1889, p. 1034

[54] M. Richard Maxfield, K. DeLynn Cook, W. Cleon Skousen, *The Real Thomas Jefferson*, 2008, p. 382

> blessings of liberty to ourselves and our posterity, do ordain and establish this Constitution for the United States of America.[55]

The first phrase, "We the people of the United States," declares that the Constitution is to be ordained and established by the people of the United States and so embodies the principle of popular sovereignty into the document and the government that it forms.

What follows is a short list of intents and purposes for undertaking to establish the Constitution. It is important to note here that this list is a list of objectives and not explicit delegations of powers or authority.

Many use the phrase "promote the general welfare" contained here in the preamble and a similar phrase in the eighth section of Article I as justification for the federal government to do just about anything that is deemed beneficial for all or part of the citizenry. This is erroneous and subversive to constitutional government and will be treated in detail below.

Articles I-V

The first three articles of the Constitution define the three separate branches of government, the legislative, executive, and judicial branches respectively. These three articles comprise what is commonly referred to as the principle of Separation of Powers.

Each article grants certain powers and authority to the respective branches of the federal government together with a system of checks and balances between those branches, allowing each branch of government certain abilities and powers to keep the other two branches in check and to continually balance the power between all three. Additionally, each article defines the qualifications for candidacy to their respective offices as well as term durations.

In addition to separating powers among the three separate branches of the federal government, the Constitution also separates powers between the national and state governments. This concept is known as federalism, because one way to view the nation as a whole, or the Union, is as a federation of its various states. Federalism provides for an additional layer of representation and self-government by having an influential governing body much closer and more accessible to the people than the national government.

This approach made many skeptical at first. The Constitution was replacing the Articles of Confederation which retained supreme authority to the states. In fact, one of the big criticisms of the Articles of Confederation that provided the impetus for the Constitution was that the national government under the Articles

---

[55] U.S. Constitution

of Confederation was too weak, lacking the power and authority to carry out functions that should've fallen under its purview, such as national defense. The weak national government under the Articles of Confederation made the Revolutionary War extremely challenging to fight, but this provided a proving ground where many of the Founders learned valuable lessons that aided them in knowing how to empower the new national government under the Constitution.

Articles IV and V of the U.S. Constitution, together with the Tenth Amendment treated in greater detail below, build this federalist structure by defining some of the relationships between the individual states and between the collective states and the federal government. Article V also defines the process by which the Constitution can be amended, a process that can be initiated by either the states or by the national Congress. In this manner, the Constitution also places a series of checks and balances between the state governments and the federal government.

An important part of the structure created by the Constitution and its Framers is the original makeup of the bicameral congress. The House of Representatives was to be the chamber representative of the American people with the number of Representatives determined by population in each state. The House was expected to be a bit more turbulent and emotional as a result of being directly elected by the people. It was also anticipated that members of the House of Representatives would have more frequent contact with the people they represent as they were elected for short terms in office. The House was to be the direct representation of the people of the United States in the federal Congress.

The Senate, on the other hand, as originally constructed, was to be made up of two Senators from each state that were appointed by the legislatures of each individual state. This provided for a representation of each state within the federal government. The risk of having a strong national government was that it would inevitably begin to usurp power and authority that it shouldn't have. The authority and power that the federal government could usurp could be at the expense of individual citizens, or the people, but also could be at the expense of the state governments, who were closer and more accessible to the people. This makeup of Congress provided for layered protection of the freedoms of the people.

The variation in structure between the two chambers of congress was not by accident but rather was the result of careful consideration and debate among the Framers. Where the House was intended to be closest to the people, the Senate was designed to be a more enduring and deliberative body. This struck an ingenious balance between heated, popular emotion and cool, reasoned debate.

Additionally, this structure provided for more layered representation, the House being direct representatives of the people and the Senate being representatives of the individual states. This proved effective to the retaining of government power within the states, whose government was closer and more accessible to the people.

In 1913, the seventeenth amendment to the Constitution was ratified. The seventeenth amendment altered the structure of the U.S. Senate and made it more like the House of Representatives. This amendment changed the appointment of Senators to a direct, popular election equivalent to the manner in which Representatives are elected to the House. It is the opinion of the author that this is one case where an amendment to the Constitution is contrary to the spirit of the Constitution and serves to weaken the overall constitutional structure. This amendment homogenizes the two separate chambers of Congress, eliminating an important distinction between them, and bringing the two separate and distinct bodies closer to being a single parliamentary body. It reverses the intent of the Founders with respect to the makeup of Congress.

Additionally, the seventeenth amendment removed all representation of the states in the national government. The effect of this has been the gradual expansion of the power, scope, and influence of the federal government at the expense of the same at the level of the state. Therefore, legislation, administration, and governance on matters of concern to the people have been slowly transferred away from the closer, more accessible state governments and up to the more remote and inaccessible federal government. This has taken away a measure of Americans' freedom, as envisioned and established by the Founders, by trading away the freedom associated with the self-government of a local and accessible governing body in exchange for the less desirable and less free governing influence of a remote ruling body.

Another effect of this change is that regulations necessarily become more cumbersome because they are now made by a governing body whose jurisdiction encompasses the whole nation. The inevitable result is the drafting of laws and regulations that make sense in one part of the country but not so much in others. This makes many regulations seem silly or overly bureaucratic since they are made to address situations in one portion of the country or to protect against rare and exceptional cases but have to apply to the entire country and everyone in it.

In a 1992 article in the *Ensign* magazine, Elder Dallin H. Oaks of the Quorum of the Twelve Apostles described America's federalism as a "[d]ivision of powers" (as opposed to the *separation* of powers which is between the various branches of the federal government). In that article, he wrote:

> Another inspired fundamental of the U.S. Constitution is its federal system, which divides government powers between the nation and the various states. Unlike the inspired adaptations mentioned earlier, this division of sovereignty was unprecedented in theory or practice. In a day when it is fashionable to assume that the government has the power and means to right every wrong, we should remember that the U.S. Constitution limits the national government to the exercise of powers expressly granted to it...
>
> This principle of limited national powers, with all residuary powers reserved to the people or to the state and local governments, which are most responsive to the people, is one of the great fundamentals of the U.S. Constitution.[56]

As stated previously, it is the opinion of the author that this great fundamental principle of the Constitution was substantially weakened by the Seventeenth Amendment. Elder Oaks does not explicitly say the same and one can only speculate as to his opinion. He does, however, clearly agree that federalism is one of the Constitution's great fundamentals and says that he does so because the state and local governments are "most responsive to the people." Unfortunately, many matters today are now addressed and regulated at the federal level that were originally intended by the Founders to be handled by the states.

Articles VI–VII

Article VI of the Constitution is a brief article proclaiming that the Constitution is the supreme law of the land regardless of any state law to the contrary. It also declares that the nation of the United States under the Constitution will assume all debts and contracted engagements made under the previous Confederation.

The final paragraph of Article VI requires an oath or affirmation by elected officials to support the Constitution and prohibits any religious test as a qualification for office.

Article VII prescribes that the Constitution will be in effect with the ratification of nine states, or a two thirds majority of the existing states at the time. It also declares that the Constitution was approved in convention by unanimous consent of all the states that were present by delegation (all except Rhode Island).

Noteworthy in the Seventh Article of the Constitution is the time reckoning given for the adoption of the Constitution by the convention. The year is given in

---

[56] Dallin H. Oaks, *The Divinely Inspired Constitution*, *Ensign*, February-1992

two different manners, both in the "Year of our Lord" and in the year "of the independence of the United States of America."

First, it is noteworthy that there is a direct reference to the Lord in the U.S. Constitution. This further reinforces the religiosity of its Framers as previously treated in detail.

The second reckoning makes reference to America's independence. Some interpret this to be a direct incorporation of the Declaration of Independence into the Constitution and thereby into American law. Whether this is the case is left to the reader to research and judge. But, what is noteworthy in this second reckoning, with respect to the present work, is the similarity to the Nephites' alteration of their timekeeping to be rooted in the event of the establishment of their free government in place of the monarchy to which they had been subject up to that point in their history. This similarity is interesting to note, but admittedly does not contribute much to the present discussion.

Article I. Section 2 – Three Fifths

Article I, section 2 of the original U.S. Constitution reads in part:

> Representatives and direct Taxes shall be apportioned among the several States which may be included within this Union, according to their respective Numbers, which shall be determined by adding to the whole Number of free Persons, including those bound to Service for a Term of Years, and excluding Indians not taxed, three fifths of all other Persons.[57]

There are many today who mistakenly, or disingenuously, charge the Founders with racism based on the last phrase in this clause that counts slaves as 3/5 of a free person. The charge is usually to the effect that the Founders of America considered a black person to be of 3/5 the value of a white person, that America was built on slavery, or that the Constitution institutionalized slavery.

There were indeed a few present in the Constitutional Convention that were of the opinion that Africans were of an inferior race. But these were not the major intellectual contributors to the final product of the Constitution nor are they the more well-known names of the Convention. They were some of those among the representation from the slave states of the south, more specifically North Carolina, South Carolina, and Georgia.

The debates around this clause were mostly around the taxation and representation of the states in the national congress, and did not focus on the worth or value of human beings. They consisted mostly of whether to consider

[57] U.S. Constitution, Article I. Section 2 (later altered by the Fourteenth Amendment)

slaves as people or property for the purposes of apportioning taxation and representation to the states, including those where slavery was practiced.

On the one hand, counting slaves as people equal to free persons disproportionately increased representation of the slave states in the national congress, giving those states more influence and control over national policy and law. This was, of course, objectionable to the northern non-slave states for a number of reasons. The slave states would benefit from increased representation but the slaves that were purportedly being represented—by virtue of having been counted for representation—would not be allowed to vote by the states that imposed their condition of slavery. So it would be the slaveholders that benefited from the increased representation and not the slaves themselves. Additionally, the increase in representation would provide incentive for the slave states to continue, or even expand, the practice of slavery. It was the slave holding states of the South that most wanted the slaves to be counted as full citizens for purposes of determining their representation in the federal congress. That increased representation would have made the eventual abolition of slavery much more difficult to achieve and all involved knew this.

While the Southern states, particularly South Carolina, were arguing for full representation of each slave, that is, considering slaves as equal to free men when calculating representation, Gouverneur Morris, from Pennsylvania, concisely summarized the position of most from the North as follows:

> Upon what principle is it that the slaves shall be computed in the representation? Are they men? Then make them Citizens and let them vote ... The admission of slaves into the Representation when fairly explained comes to this: that the inhabitant of Georgia and S.C. who goes to the Coast of Africa, and in defiance of the most sacred laws of humanity tears away his fellow creatures from their dearest connections and damns them to the most cruel bondages, shall have more votes in a Govt. instituted for protections of the rights of mankind, than the Citizen of Pa or N. Jersey who views with a laudable horror, so nefarious a practice.[58]

Morris continued with a rhetorical question regarding whether the Southern states would then be restrained in their importing of new slaves from Africa and then answered, "nay they are to be encouraged to it by an assurance of having their votes in the Natl Govt increased in proportion."[59]

---

[58] Philip Kurland, Ralph Lerner, *The Founders' Constitution*, 1987, vol. 2, p. 111

[59] Ibid.

On the other hand, it was argued that the slave states did indeed benefit economically from the labor performed by slaves. To count slaves purely as property, as many argued they were treated by their slave holders and the states that sanctioned slavery, would allow those states to benefit economically from the labor of slaves and not pay corresponding taxes on that economic benefit.

Neither side could have it both ways, considering slaves as people for one apportionment and as property for the other. Taxation and representation had to be apportioned equally to the same number of people. So a middle ground had to be agreed on and that middle ended up being what is appropriately referred to now as the 3/5 compromise.

It is important to note that the 3/5 compromise was applicable only to slaves and not to all people of a particular race or nationality. In other words, there were free black people in the United States at the time of authorship and ratification of the Constitution. Those people were counted as full citizens and allowed to vote. The Constitution makes no distinction between races, but only between the condition of free people and slaves.

While posing the question of whether slaves were to be considered as people or property by the national Constitution, *for the purposes of taxation and representation*, James Madison makes a detailed argument in *The Federalist* that their situation is peculiar in that they were treated as both under existing slavery laws, "being considered by our laws, in some respects, as persons, and in other respects, as property."[60] Madison writes that:

> The Foederal [*sic*] Constitution therefore, decides with great propriety on the case of our slaves, when it views them in the mixt character of persons and of property. This is in fact their true character. *It is the character bestowed on them by the laws under which they live...*
>
> Let the case of the slaves be considered as it is in truth a peculiar one. Let the compromising expedient of the Constitution be mutually adopted, which regards them as inhabitants, but as debased by servitude below the equal level of free inhabitants, which regards the slave as divested of two fifth of the man.[61]

Very importantly, Madison is not here advocating for the debasing treatment of slaves or for slavery at all. Madison is arguing that the state of the slaves was already one of debasement by existing laws under which they lived and that the federal Constitution was merely reflecting that reality when considering how to count them for purposes of taxation and representation. They should not be

---

[60] James Madison, *The Federalist*, No. 54

[61] Ibid. (emphasis added)

counted as full citizens because they weren't being treated as full citizens and as such would not themselves be represented in Congress had they been fully counted in the calculation for that representation.

The hard truth is that slavery was already a reality when the Constitution was being created and for the resulting Union to have its best chance at success, all of the Colonies had to join. This meant that it was necessary to come together on terms that would be agreeable to all parties, including the Southern states that already allowed and even promoted slavery. Complete abolition of slavery as a condition to join the Union was not a possibility at the time if the Southern states were going to be a part.

What's most notable about the 3/5 calculation is that it satisfied all parties involved. Furthermore, it goes largely unnoticed and unmentioned today that the 3/5 compromise was actually the first step along the road to abolition. It was the 3/5 compromise that was agreeable enough to the slave states that they joined the Union under the Constitution, the spirit of which, when interpreted correctly, did not allow slavery. It was the Constitution and Declaration of Independence that were used by Abraham Lincoln as the intellectual vehicles to abolish slavery in the Union overall and outright years later. Admittedly, this abolition came after too many years and too much bloodshed than would have been desired by the Founders, but it came nonetheless, and the Founders and the Constitution, with the 3/5 compromise, helped to initiate that process.

Article I. Section 8 – General Welfare and the Enumerated Powers

Article I, section 8 of the U.S. Constitution begins with the following preamble:

> The Congress shall have Power To lay and collect Taxes, Duties, Imposts and Excises, to pay the Debts and provide for the common Defence and general Welfare of the United States; but all Duties, Imposts and Excises shall be uniform throughout the United States;[62]

What follows for the remainder of this section is an enumeration of seventeen specific powers granted to congress and are referred to as the enumerated powers of the U.S. Constitution. The term "general welfare" in this section is used by many today as justification for enormously broad governmental powers. But this use is contrary to the meaning intended by those who framed the Constitution as will be shown below.

James Madison, known as the father of the Constitution, said that "If Congress can do whatever in their discretion can be done by money, and will promote the

---

[62] U.S. Constitution, Article I. Section 8

General Welfare, the Government is no longer a limited one, possessing enumerated powers, but an indefinite one, subject to particular exceptions."[63]

On another occasion, while debating a bill in the Virginia House of Representatives, Madison spoke from the House floor and gave substantial insight into his criticisms of interpreting the phrase "general welfare" too loosely. He said:

> If Congress can employ money indefinitely to the general welfare, and are the sole and supreme judges of the general welfare, they may take the care of religion into their own hands; they may appoint teachers in every state, county and parish and pay them out of their public treasury; they may take into their own hands the education of children, establishing in like manner schools throughout the Union; they may assume the provision for the poor; they may undertake the regulation of all roads other than post-roads; in short, every thing, from the highest object of state legislation down to the most minute object of police, would be thrown under the power of Congress.... were the power of Congress to be established in the latitude contended for, it would subvert the very foundations, and transmute the very nature of the limited Government established by the people of America.[64]

It is interesting to note how many of the items in Madison's list above are today assumed to be under the purview of Congressional authority with little to no question or discussion to the contrary. Even more interesting is Madison's description of a Congress so authorized, that "it would subvert the very foundations, and transmute the very nature of the limited Government established by the people of America." This is quite a statement from the father of the Constitution and is something that deserves ample consideration by Americans today.

Thomas Jefferson shared Madison's interpretation of the "general welfare clause" as it is popularly known today. He said:

> I suppose its meaning to be that Congress may collect taxes for the purpose of providing for the general welfare, in those cases wherein the Constitution empowers them to act for the general welfare. To suppose that it was meant to give them a distinct, substantive power

---

[63] James Madison, Letter to Edmund Pendleton, January 21, 1792

[64] Jonathan Elliot, *The Debates in the Several State Conventions*, 1888, p. 129

> to do any act which might tend to the general welfare is to render all the enumerations useless, and to make their powers unlimited.[65]

On another occasion, Jefferson said:

> Congress had not unlimited powers to provide for the general welfare, but were restrained to those specifically enumerated; and that, as it was never meant they should provide for that welfare but by the exercise of the enumerated powers, so it could not have been meant they should raise money for purposes which the enumeration did not place under their action; consequently, that the specification of powers is a limitation of the purposes for which they may raise money.[66]

Jefferson, like Madison, was very direct and clear in stating that the phrase "general welfare" used in the Constitution was not meant to empower the federal government to do anything it considered beneficial to the public at large. Nor was it a justification for public welfare programs. Jefferson further argues that by extension, Congress is also limited in what they can raise money for and are not empowered to raise money for anything and everything that they consider to tend toward the public good.

Jefferson commented on this subject on a number of different occasions. The quote below is comprehensive in illustrating Jefferson's mindset regarding the general welfare clause.

> For the laying of taxes is the power, and the general welfare the purpose for which the power is to be exercised. They are not to lay taxes ad libitum for any purpose they please; but only to pay the debts or provide for the welfare of the Union. In like manner, they are not to do anything they please to provide for the general welfare, but only to lay taxes for that purpose. To consider the latter phrase, not as describing the purpose of the first, but as giving a distinct and independent power to do any act they please which might be for the good of the Union, would render all the preceding and subsequent enumerations useless. It would reduce the whole instrument [the Constitution] to a single phrase, that of instituting a Congress with power to do whatever would be for the good of the United States.[67]

Jefferson argues that providing for the general welfare is the purpose of the exercise of legitimate government powers and not an independent power in

---

[65] M. Richard Maxfield, K. DeLynn Cook, W. Cleon Skousen, *The Real Thomas Jefferson*, 2008, p. 453
[66] Ibid., p. 454
[67] Ibid., p. 452

itself. This is fairly clear in the eighth section of Article I, which reads, "The Congress shall have Power To lay and collect Taxes … to pay the Debts and provide for the common Defence and general Welfare of the United States." He further reinforces this interpretation by pointing out that to interpret this any other way would effectively render the rest of the entire document meaningless.

Similarly, James Madison, who was present during every session of the Constitutional Convention and kept exhaustive notes on each of them, offers the following clarification of the entire section in *The Federalist*, number 41:

> For what purpose could the enumeration of particular powers be inserted, if these and all others were meant to be included in the preceding general power? Nothing is more natural nor common than first to use a general phrase, and then to explain and qualify it by a recital of particulars. But the idea of an enumeration of particulars which neither explain nor qualify the general meaning, and can have no other effect than to confound and mislead, is an absurdity…[68]

The Constitution, in Article I, Section 8, explicitly enumerates powers that are granted to the federal government and, in the Tenth Amendment of the Bill of Rights, explicitly prohibits any that are not so granted. The use of those enumerated powers is intended for the general welfare of the nation. In both cases where "general welfare" is used in the Constitution, it is stated as an end of government use of power and not as being associated with those powers itself. Furthermore, the thinking and statements made by the very authors of the Constitution reinforce that the government was not being empowered by these clauses to do anything and everything that tended towards the general welfare, but that it was one of the stated ends of the appropriate use of explicitly granted powers.

Another common mistake made is to assign the present-day definition of the term welfare to the phrase used in the Constitution. In today's terminology, the word "welfare" is associated with government funded and run social and charity programs. Often the mere use of the word "welfare" in the Constitution is used as justification for these programs, erroneously assuming the same meaning across over 200 years of the word's use. The Constitution uses the word in its more traditional definition of simply referring to well-being.

Additionally, the word "general" is often ignored in this clause. The word "general" is here employed by the Constitution and its Framers as meaning applicable to the whole body or the entire citizenry. The Founders often used the word "general" in this way. For example, they referred to the federal or

[68] James Madison, *The Federalist*, No. 41

national government as the "general government," general as in its jurisdiction was the whole nation.

With the historical meaning of these words restored, and with Jefferson's interpretation of it as being the objective of the use of explicitly enumerated powers and not as part of the enumeration itself, it is a more accurate interpretation of the "general welfare" clause to say that the end of government's use of its just and enumerated powers is to benefit society as a whole and they should not be used for the benefit of particular groups or factions at the expense of others.

This is how the general welfare clause was understood and interpreted for nearly 150 years after ratification of the Constitution. This traditional interpretation was reversed In 1935 when the Social Security Act was passed and later challenged on the grounds that it entailed the spending of money for purposes outside of the enumerated powers of the Constitution. The Supreme Court ruled in *Helvering v. Davis* that the Social Security Act was indeed constitutional per the general welfare clause. The majority opinion, written by Progressive Justice Benjamin Cardozo, states:

> Congress may spend money in aid of the "general welfare." There have been great statesmen in our history who have stood for other views. We will not resurrect the contest. It is now settled by decision.[69]

Cardozo does not equivocate, he acknowledges outright that many have stood for other views, surely aware that "great statesmen" includes the very authors of the clause themselves. But, he nevertheless takes it upon himself to settle the debate "by decision" and reinterpretation by the court.[70] This sort of audacious and expansive reinterpretation of the Constitution and America's Founding is characteristic of the Progressive Era, which is treated in greater detail in chapter 7. The reader is invited to research how government spending has trended since this decision by the Supreme Court reinterpreted the Constitution to mean something that was not intended by its authors.

The Bill of Rights

In 1789, the First United States Congress approved twelve amendments to the Constitution and submitted them to the states for ratification. By 1791, ten of

---

[69] Charles Murray, *By The People*, 2015, p. 19

[70] For a detailed treatment of *Helvering v. Davis* and other significant Supreme Court cases that contributed substantially to reinterpreting the Constitution, please see *The Dirty Dozen* by Robert A. Levy and William Mellor.

those amendments were ratified by the states and are now referred to as the Bill of Rights. James Madison was the principal author of the Bill of Rights.

Some of the Framers of the Constitution greatly desired a Bill of Rights and withheld their full support of the Constitution without one. Likewise, many among the states who were opposed to ratification of the Constitution cited their opposition to the lack of a Bill of Rights and many only approved on condition of a Bill of Rights being created. People desired to be assured that they possessed explicit rights that the federal government would be legally barred from violating.

This section will not treat the Bill of Rights in comprehensive detail but will highlight some important aspects of these Amendments as they pertain to the present discussion. Most amendments are treated only briefly, but the first two will be treated in some detail.

Amendment I

The First Amendment to the Constitution reads:

> Congress shall make no law respecting an establishment of religion or prohibiting the free exercise thereof; or abridging the freedom of speech, or of the press; or the right of the people peaceably to assemble and to petition the government for a redress of grievances.[71]

The First Amendment is among the most well-known, but is still often abused or misconstrued to mean less than, or in some cases the opposite of, what was intended by the Founders. It is from the First Amendment that is extracted the so called "Separation of Church and State" doctrine that is increasingly used to remove any semblance of religious awareness from public view and discourse, and to perpetuate the falsehood that the Founders intended a secular society.

Upon being elected president, Thomas Jefferson received a letter from the Baptist Association of Danbury, Connecticut. The letter congratulated Jefferson on his election to the presidency but also expressed some concerns regarding their religious liberty. The letter in part reads:

> Our sentiments are uniformly on the side of religious liberty: that religion is at all times and places a matter between God and individuals, that no man ought to suffer in name, person, or effects on account of his religious opinions, [and] that the legitimate power of civil government extends no further than to punish the man who works ill to his neighbor. But sir, our constitution of government is not specific ... [T]herefore what religious privileges we enjoy (as a minor

[71] U.S. Constitution: Amendment I

> part of the State) we enjoy as favors granted, and not as inalienable rights.[72]

The Baptists of Danbury, Connecticut, feared that the First Amendment to the Constitution was an act of government granting a right or privilege of religious freedom and so consequently, that privilege could later be revoked or regulated. This interpretation was erroneous since the intended purpose of the First Amendment and entire Bill of Rights was to place restrictions on the government and thereby retain rights for the people. Jefferson's response included the following:

> Believing with you that religion is a matter which lies solely between man and his God; that he owes account to none other for his faith or his worship; that the legislative powers of government reach actions only and not opinions, I contemplate with sovereign reverence that act of the whole American people which declared that their legislature should "make no law respecting an establishment of religion or prohibiting the free exercise thereof," thus building a wall of separation between Church and State. Adhering to this expression of the supreme will of the nation in behalf of the rights of conscience, I shall see with sincere satisfaction the progress of those sentiments which tend to restore to man all his natural rights...[73]

From this letter penned by Thomas Jefferson to the Danbury Baptists originates the modern doctrine of "separation of church and state" and Jefferson's supposed authorship of it. Jefferson included the phrase, however, as an assurance to the Baptists of Danbury that religion is protected from intrusion by government by virtue of the First Amendment, and not that government is to be shielded from all religious influence or that it should eschew all religious expression and awareness.

Ironically, Jefferson is widely credited with originating and advocating the doctrine of a secular society free from religious influence and with placing that doctrine into the Constitution through the First Amendment. But, Jefferson's interpretation of the First Amendment and use of the phrase "separation between Church and State" clearly favors protections for the church from the state and not the other way around. This truth is further clarified and enforced by numerous other statements he made on the subject. Among those statements are these he made below:

---

[72] David Barton, *Original Intent*, 2008, pp. 49-50 (compare Alma 30:7-11)
[73] Ibid., pp. 51-52

> [N]o power over the freedom of religion ... [is] delegated to the United States by the Constitution.[74]
>
> In matters of religion I have considered that its free exercise is placed by the Constitution independent of the powers of the general [federal] government.[75]
>
> [O]ur excellent Constitution ... has not placed our religious rights under the power of any public functionary.[76]
>
> I consider the government of the United States as interdicted [prohibited] by the Constitution from intermeddling with religious institutions ... or exercises.[77]

Acting as Secretary of State under George Washington, Jefferson oversaw the layout and construction of Washington , DC. Jefferson approved the plan for the city in 1791 and construction of permanent federal buildings such as the White House and the U.S. Capitol building was underway by 1793. In 1795, before the Capitol was fully completed, Jefferson approved of it being used on Sundays as a church. Before it was used for the convening of Congress, the U.S. Capitol was used as a church! This activity in the U.S. Capitol building was approved by and participated in by several Founders themselves. It is ironic to note that much of the behavior that is presently being ruled as unconstitutional is behavior that the Framers of the Constitution themselves engaged in, or allowed and advocated for the government to engage in, themselves.

After Congress moved into the new Capitol building in 1800, they approved a plan to hold Christian church services in the Hall of the House of Representatives each Sunday. At the time, Jefferson was serving as Vice President to John Adams and so was presiding over the U.S. Senate. Jefferson himself attended church services at the U.S. Capitol building throughout his vice presidency and later tenure as President. While serving as President and speaking of this activity, he said, "No nation has ever yet existed or been governed without religion—nor can be. The Christian religion is the best religion that has been given to man and I, as Chief Magistrate [President] of this nation, am bound to give it the sanction of my example."[78] By 1867, the U.S. Capitol was still being used as a church on Sundays and had grown to be the largest congregation in Washington, DC.

---

[74] Ibid., p. 50
[75] Ibid.
[76] Ibid.
[77] Ibid.
[78] David Barton, *The Jefferson Lies*, 2012, pp. 134-135

Other actions taken by Thomas Jefferson while President of the United States further reinforce that he in no way intended or advocated a secular society wholly divorced from religion. He signed federal acts to set aside government lands for missionary use in "propagating the Gospel" among the Indians.[79] He directed the Secretary of War to appropriate federal money to a religious school established for the Cherokees in Tennessee.[80] He used federal money to fund Christian missionaries to the Kaskaskia Indians and to build a church building among them.[81]

Thomas Jefferson, the supposed author of the Separation of Church and State doctrine, clearly did not agree with a purely secular society devoid of all religious and pious expressions. But, what of the other Founders? Schools are a popular place where the separation doctrine is often applied today, so it's worthwhile to examine things said by the Founders regarding education.

William Samuel Johnson, who signed the Constitution, addressed an individual who had received education in public schools as follows, " You have ... received a public education, the purpose whereof hath been to qualify you the better to serve your Creator and your country ... Your first great duties, you are sensible, are those you owe to Heaven, to your Creator and Redeemer."[82]

Samuel Adams stated:

> As piety, religion and morality have a happy influence on the minds of men, in their public as well as private transactions, you will not think it unseasonable, although I have frequently done it, to bring to your remembrance the great importance of encouraging our University, town schools, and other seminaries of education, that our children and youth while they are engaged in the pursuit of useful science, may have their minds impressed with a strong sense of the duties they owe to their God. If we continue to be a happy people, that happiness must be assured by the enacting and executing of the reasonable and wise laws expressed in the plainest language and by establishing such modes of education as tend to inculcate in the minds of youth the feelings and habits of piety, religion and morality.[83]

Gouverneur Morris, who signed the Constitution, said, "Religion is the only solid basis of good morals; therefore education should teach the precepts of religion and the duties of man towards God."[84]

---

[79] Ibid., p. 135
[80] Ibid.
[81] Ibid.
[82] David Barton, *Original Intent*, 2008, pp. 158-159
[83] Ibid., p. 159
[84] Ibid.

Benjamin Rush, who signed the Declaration of Independence, stated that "the only foundation for a useful education in a republic is to be laid in religion. Without this there can be no virtue, and without virtue there can be no liberty, and liberty is the object and life of all republican governments. Without religion, I believe that learning does real mischief to the morals and principles of mankind."[85]

Noah Webster argued, "In my view, the Christian religion is the most important and one of the first things in which all children, under a free government, ought to be instructed ... No truth is more evident to my mind than that the Christian religion must be the basis of any government intended to secure the rights and privileges of a free people."[86]

It was shown previously that the only correct interpretation of the Constitution is in the manner in which it was intended by those who influenced, authored, signed, and ratified it. The first clause of the First Amendment uses language that is very specific, "Congress shall make no law respecting an establishment of religion." This is clearly intended, and is attested to over and over by those who produced, advocated, and fought for the Constitution, to prevent the federal government from creating an established state religion, or preferring or favoring one denomination over the others. No one sect was to get special treatment from the federal government.

More specifically, Congress is prohibited from passing a law that serves to establish a sanctioned religion. This does not prohibit the federal government from supporting, or even funding, religious activities. It does not prohibit the federal government from generally promoting religious and moral values. It certainly does not prohibit any religious expression of any kind in any setting that can be even remotely related to government (e.g. public schools). To say that it is unconstitutional to allow students to pray or study scriptures in schools is counter to what the authors of the Constitution and the First Amendment intended.

The Founders clearly did not intend a secular society, but a religious one. They themselves were religious and saw no problem with expressing that religiosity in their public capacities. What more, some went so far as to see it their duty as public servants to pay sincere devotions to God. They repeatedly professed their Christianity both in private and public capacities, and repeatedly referred to it as the only sure foundation for a free nation. They saw religion, and particularly Christianity, as the only sound foundation for stable and free government. They saw Christian values as necessary for a peaceful, just, and free society. They used

---

[85] Ibid.

[86] Ibid., pp. 159-160

federal buildings for church services. They made use of federal funds and resources to promote Christianity and even to preach it to Native Americans. They frequently proposed and passed resolutions calling for state and national days of prayer, fasting, repentance, thanksgiving, and acknowledgement of a benevolent God who had so conspicuously aided the fledgling nation through its period of founding and formation.

The view of the Founders is accurately summarized in a statement made by Supreme Court Justice Joseph Story, who was appointed to the court by James Madison. He said of the First Amendment as it was being debated:

> We are not to attribute this prohibition of a national religious establishment to an indifference to religion in general, and especially to Christianity (which none could hold in more reverence, than the framers of the Constitution) ... Probably, at the time of the adoption of the Constitution, and of the Amendment to it now under consideration, the general, if not the universal, sentiment in America was that Christianity ought to receive encouragement from the State...[87]

Another very important detail of the First Amendment is the next restraint placed on Congress and the federal government that they "shall make no law ... prohibiting the free *exercise*"[88] of religion. The free exercise of religion is more than mere belief, but the ability to choose how to put those beliefs into practice. This is an essential distinction because many today are making attempts to diminish the Natural Right guaranteed under this amendment by claiming that this amendment only guarantees the freedom to one's religious *beliefs* or guarantees the freedom to *worship* in any manner chosen by an individual. But the First Amendment guarantees the Natural Right to *exercise* one's religion however he sees fit, with the obvious qualification that the exercise of it does not injure nor violate any other individual or their Natural Rights.

In 2011, Elder Dallin H. Oaks addressed the Chapman University School of Law in Orange, California. In this speech, Elder Oaks expressed dismay at the shifting language regarding the First Amendment and concern with the specific shift to "the words *freedom of worship* instead of *free exercise of religion*"[89] as it was intended. In this speech, Elder Oaks also states, "[i]t was apparent twenty-five years ago, and it is undeniable today, that the significance of religious freedom is

---

[87] Ibid., pp. 35-36

[88] U.S. Constitution: Amendment I (emphasis added)

[89] Dallin H. Oaks, *Preserving Religious Freedom*, February 4, 2011

diminishing."[90] The reader is referred to this address for a detailed treatment of how religious liberty is being diminished today.

It is crucial that religious people in America, and particularly Latter-day Saints, understand the rights and protections that are guaranteed under the First Amendment. If these protections are not understood, and fought for, they will inevitably be lost.

Amendment II

The Second Amendment is one of the more controversial and the subject of many constitutional debates. There is much disagreement on the interpretation of this amendment as to the right defined and who is the possessor of that right. Some argue that the right to bear arms is only reserved for bodies such as law enforcement and military and not for the general citizenry. Others argue that private citizens have the right to possess firearms, but only those that are used for shooting sports such as hunting and target shooting.

The Second Amendment reads:

> A well regulated militia being necessary to the security of a free State, the right of the people to keep and bear arms shall not be infringed.[91]

The purpose of the Bill of Rights is to serve as an enumeration of rights that are retained by the people, the people being the general citizenry of the nation. It is intended as a charter of rights of the people, protected by the Constitution, from infringement by the national government. The Second Amendment explicitly identifies the general citizenry in stating that "the right of the *people* to keep and bear arms shall not be infringed."

The claim that this particular right is guaranteed only to certain groups of people and not the citizenry as a whole requires the interpretation of an implicit exception in the reference to "the people" for which there is no justification. Why would "people" here refer to specific groups when every other case has it referring to the citizenry as a whole?

Moreover, the only correct interpretation of the Second Amendment can be found in the minds of those who authored and approved it.

Fisher Ames was a member of the First United States Congress and contributed greatly to the final wording of the Bill of Rights. He is considered one of the Framers of the Bill of Rights. He said, "the right ... of bearing arms ... is declared to be inherent in the people."[92]

---

[90] Ibid.

[91] U.S. Constitution: Amendment II

[92] David Barton, *The Second Amendment*, 2000, p. 25

Richard Henry Lee was also a member of the First Congress and helped to frame the Bill of Rights. He said, "To preserve liberty, it is essential that the whole body of the people always possess arms."[93]

Thomas Jefferson stated, "what country can preserve its liberties if its rulers are not warned from time to time that this people preserve the spirit of resistance? Let them take arms."[94]

Edmund Randolph said "A people who mean to continue free must be prepared to meet danger in person, not to rely upon the fallacious protection of ... armies."[95]

George Washington said, "[a] free people ought ... to be armed."[96]

John Adams said, "Resistance to sudden violence for the preservation not only of my person, my limbs, and life, but of my property, is an indisputable right of nature which I never surrendered to the public by the compact of society and which, perhaps, I could not surrender if I would ... the maxims of the law and the precepts of Christianity are precisely coincident in relation to this subject."[97]

George Mason pointed out that "when the resolution of enslaving America was formed in Great-Britain, the British parliament was advised ... to disarm the people. That it was the best and most effectual way to enslave them. But that they should not do it openly; but to weaken them and let them sink gradually."[98]

Noah Webster taught, "Before a standing army can rule, the people must be disarmed—as they are in almost every kingdom in Europe. The supreme power in America cannot enforce unjust laws by the sword because the whole body of the people are armed."[99]

This is a mere sampling of quotations from various Founders on the right of bearing arms. It is clear from these, and many others, that the Founders included the Second Amendment to the Constitution for the express purpose of preserving liberty and as a defense against tyrannical government. It strains credulity to suggest that this amendment was in any way associated with a protection for citizens to merely enjoy shooting for sport or for hunting as has been suggested by some in the present. Every citizen retains the Natural Right to bear arms and to use those arms in the protection of his other Natural Rights—including life, liberty, and property—be it from another individual, a government, or a foreign invading force.

---

[93] Ibid., p. 26
[94] Ibid.
[95] Ibid., p. 28
[96] Ibid., p. 29
[97] Ibid., p. 24
[98] Ibid., p. 27
[99] Ibid., p. 29

The right to bear arms is considered by the Founders to be a hallmark characteristic of a free people. For this reason, they included it as a Natural Right and preeminently within the Bill of Rights. This right is listed as second only to the freedoms related to conscience. This ordering gives an idea of how prominent it was in the minds of the Founders. Also evident in their speech and writing is that they considered this right a necessity to preserve freedom, both for protection of each individual's life, liberty, and property, and also for a defense from a government that would encroach on these rights.

Amendment IV

> The right of the people to be secure in their persons, houses, papers, and effects, against unreasonable searches and seizures shall not be violated, and no warrants shall issue but upon probable cause supported by oath or affirmation, and particularly describing the place to be searched and the persons or things to be seized.[100]

This amendment protects against general warrants or the process of "fishing" for criminal activity. It stipulates that the government cannot search a citizens property, person, or effects unless a warrant is obtained that specifically identifies what is to be searched and what there is a reasonable expectation of finding. Furthermore, the warrant can only be obtained with probable cause.

In other words, there has to be reasonable suspicion of a crime being or having been committed in order for the government to search a citizen or his property. A warrant needs to be obtained and the warrant has to specifically describe where the search will be conducted and what property will be seized upon being found. Presumably, the searched and seized property has to be related to the suspected crime.

The intent of this amendment is to protect against arbitrary searches of people that are disliked by those in authority in hopes of finding criminal activity. The stipulation is that reasonable suspicion of criminal activity must be present first, and then searches may be conducted.

Amendment V

The Fifth Amendment contains a number of different freedoms and rights, but this writing will focus on the phrase below:

---

[100] U.S. Constitution: Amendment IV

> No person shall be ... deprived of life, liberty, or property, without due process of law...[101]

In the Fifth Amendment, the principal Natural Rights to life, liberty, and private property again make an appearance. In this clause of the Fifth Amendment, these rights are reinforced as the chief rights retained by the people and respected by just and free governments. It is unlawful for the government to deprive any citizen of life, liberty, or property without due process of law. A crime must have been committed and proven in court for any citizen to be deprived of any of these Natural Rights. Any other deprivation of life, liberty, or property is unlawful.

This principle likely sounds more than reasonable to most readers. There is, however, a corollary and that is that no law should be established unless the violation of that law would rightly and justly require a corresponding deprivation of life, liberty, or property. Ezra Taft Benson sums this up in his speech *The Proper Role of Government*:

> An important test I use in passing judgement upon an act of government is this: If it were up to me as an individual to punish my neighbor for violating a given law, would it offend my conscience to do so? Since my conscience will never permit me to physically punish my fellow man unless he has done something evil, or unless he has failed to do something which I have a moral right to require of him to do, I will never knowingly authorize my agent, the government to do this on my behalf. I realize that when I give my consent to the adoption of a law, I specifically instruct police—the government—to take either the life, liberty, or property of anyone who disobeys that law.[102]

Benson admonishes that we take care in the laws and measures that we support and advocate. In consenting to laws, we authorize the government to deprive others of their rights for the violation of those laws and so need to be sure of a moral justification to do so. If no other source from this book is pursued by the reader, it is recommended that at the very least this speech, *The Proper Role of Government* by Ezra Taft Benson, be read.

Amendments IX and X

The Ninth and Tenth Amendments of the Bill of Rights are largely ignored today. The federal government has been violating these rights for so long now that one is perceived as naïve for making any reference to them at all.

---

[101] U.S. Constitution: Amendment V

[102] Ezra Taft Benson, *The Proper Role of Government*, www.latterdayconservative.com

The Ninth Amendment reads:

> The enumeration in the Constitution of certain rights shall not be construed to deny or disparage others retained by the people.[103]

The Tenth Amendment reads:

> The powers not delegated to the United States by the Constitution nor prohibited by it to the States are reserved to the States respectively or to the people.[104]

These two amendments taken together further reinforce the philosophy of the Founders that rights are inherent in the people by nature and by God. The government does not define nor grant rights. Instead, people naturally possessing their rights may delegate some of their power and authority to a government body.

These two amendments are clear that any perceived enumeration in the Constitution of rights retained by the people is not intended to limit that set of rights. In other words, merely making the case that a right is not defined in the Constitution is not case enough to limit that right from the people, or refuse to protect it.

Conversely, it is also clearly stated that a set of specific powers has been enumerated throughout the Constitution as being delegated to the federal government. Any power not explicitly delegated by the Constitution is not considered to fall under the purview of federal authority. Many try to get around this amendment by claiming broad authority under the "general welfare" clause and other clauses, but this does not do either as was demonstrated previously.

It is clear that the Bill of Rights, and especially Amendments IX and X, were drafted for the protection of the rights of the people, the general citizenry. Any ambiguity should be interpreted in favor of the people's rights and not government powers. The intent of these final two Amendments is to make that clear. The government is to act only with the powers expressly enumerated to it in the Constitution and with no others. Any power not explicitly enumerated is not considered a just federal power, and makes that government that exercises it despotic and unconstitutional.

The rights guaranteed and retained by the people are many and not all listed. Just because it is not listed in the Constitution does not negate it as a right. Clearly, the Founders were favoring individual rights over government authority.

---

[103] U.S. Constitution: Amendment IX

[104] U.S. Constitution: Amendment X

America – A Christian Nation

Much has been made in recent years over whether the United States of America is a Christian nation. The trend is away from this being the case, but this trend is at odds with the nation's heritage and Founding.

One of the principal arguments against this notion is that the First Amendment prohibits the federal government from any religious expression or promotion. It was demonstrated at length earlier in this chapter that the Founders did not intend the First Amendment this way. For a much more detailed treatment of this subject, the reader is referred to David Barton's *Original Intent: The Courts, the Constitution, & Religion*.

As has been shown, Jefferson's metaphoric "wall of separation between Church and State" is a wall protecting the church from the state and not the other way around.

Another commonly used example is a treaty agreed to between America and the then nation of Tripoli in 1797. The treaty in part reads, "the government of the United States of America is not in any sense founded on the Christian religion."[105] Many use this treaty as the sole evidence that the Founders did not intend a Christian or religious society, but a secular one, or that the Founders did not see America as a Christian nation.

This conclusion is fallacious for several reasons. First, this is a single statement that was not made by the Founders themselves but by emissaries sent to negotiate peaceful relations with a foreign power. Next, this single statement cannot be considered in isolation but must be considered as part of the entire body of statements, quotes, and writings of the Founders. As hopefully demonstrated throughout the present work, this extant body of known writings from the Founders is large and replete with sentiments attesting to the belief that America is indeed a Christian nation. Finally, this statement is not an untrue statement but is instead misused by those who wish to rewrite America's history.

The statement in question clearly refers to the *government* of the United States and not the nation of the United States. The government of the United States is indeed not founded on the Christian religion in the same way that most European governments of the time were. It was those more theocratic governments of Europe with which the Islamic states of the Barbary Coast had had much experience and conflict. This statement in the treaty was meant to distinguish the American government from those governments and to assure the Muslim powers of those states that America was not interested in a holy war or crusade against Muslim nations. This is made a bit more clear when the entire

---

[105] David Barton, *Original Intent*, 2008, p. 133

section of the treaty is considered as a whole. The section in question is shown below.

> As the government of the United States of America is not in any sense founded on the Christian religion as it has in itself no character of enmity against the laws, religion or tranquility of Musselmen and as the said States have never entered into any war or act of hostility against any Mahometan nation, it is declared by the parties that no pretext arising from religious opinions shall ever produce an interruption of the harmony between the two countries.[106]

The statement in question, perhaps worded poorly, is merely declaring that the U.S. government is not based on an established religion of Christianity, which is completely congruent with the Constitution and its First Amendment. The Constitution expressly forbids religious tests for office and a state-established religion. In this sense, the government indeed is not founded on any religion. The U.S. government was not and is not married to a specific religion or denomination the way most European governments of the time were.

It has been illustrated throughout this work, however, that the nation of America was founded on Christian principles, as were its government institutions. This is attested to in scripture, in revelation, and in the words of the Founders themselves. America's Christian heritage is undeniable. America is a Christian nation in the sense that it was founded on Christian principles by a body of men who were overwhelmingly Christian and still today has a population that is a majority Christian.

Summary and Conclusions

It was pointed out briefly in the opening of this chapter that the works of the Founders are considered good and that revelation provides evidence that God Himself approves of them and participated in producing them. He called the Founders wise and He said the works they produced are justifiable before Him and that He justifies mankind in befriending them.[107] He also said that anything more or less than what the Founders produced, with respect to civil law and civil government, comes from evil.[108]

The Founders were God fearing men who, to varying degrees, believed they were about the work of God in establishing a just and free government based on Natural Rights and natural and divine law. What they likely didn't realize to its full extent is that they had been called, foreordained, and prepared for that very

---

[106] Ibid.

[107] See Alma 41:5

[108] D&C 98:5-7; 101:77-80

work. They had been taught by God's Spirit the things they needed to know in order to produce a basis for a civil government that was justifiable before God Himself.

The principles so eloquently articulated in the Declaration of Independence are that all men are created with an equal set of natural, God-given rights. Among these rights are life, liberty, property, autonomy, and the defense of each of these. Each individual enters this life already possessing these rights. They are not created nor granted by man and therefore cannot be abolished, revoked, nor diminished by man without giving offense to the God of nature who endowed mankind with them. These rights are unalienable, meaning they cannot be justly separated from an individual. The principal and just purpose of civil government is to effectively maintain and protect these rights equally and uniformly among its citizenry. Sound and just government is formed by the consent of those to be governed with an accompanying delegation of authority from them. The just and legitimate powers of government must be derived from the people creating it and therefore can only extend as far as the powers that the people themselves already possess. Therefore, the legitimate powers of government extend only to actions where one individual or group injures another individual or group, in their persons or their property, or infringes on their Natural Rights.

The Constitution of the United States is the embodiment of the Spirit of these principles, forming a government that is empowered only with the powers that the people already possess and only so far as is necessary to protect these rights equally among the people. The powers granted to the federal government by the people are expressly enumerated in the Constitution. Explicit clauses are included to prohibit any power not so enumerated. Furthermore, the Constitution, mainly through the Bill of Rights, explicitly enumerates a set of restraints on the federal government to prevent the same government from infringing on these rights of the people. The U.S. Constitution, by divine inspiration from Almighty God, is an instrument intended to jealously guard the Natural Rights of the individual citizen, and to grant to the government that it creates the least possible set of powers necessary to function for the protection of these same rights equally among all of the citizens that it governs. In this manner it is "for the rights and protection of all flesh."[109]

This is liberty. This is the liberty understood by the Founders and inculcated into the fabric of American government and society. These are the "just and holy principles"[110] on which the United States of America was founded by wise men who were instructed in them by Almighty God. This is the law that man is

---

[109] D&C 101:77

[110] D&C 101:77

justified by God in befriending and supporting. This is the law that God commanded be "maintained for the rights and protection of all flesh."[111] This is the law that serves as the dividing line between good and evil with respect to civil government among men.[112] This is the law of the Constitution of the United States of America.

---

[111] D&C 101:77

[112] See D&C 98:7

Chapter 6 – Modern Revelation and Prophets

This chapter will not have much of a narrative. The reason for including this chapter is to have a place where a number of scriptures, quotes, and teachings from Restoration Prophets, Apostles, and General Authorities of the Church can be included.

In some cases, some of these items are already utilized elsewhere in the book, but are still included here either in greater context or more detail. In other cases, quotes are considered valuable to the subject of this writing but challenging for one reason or another to fit into the overall narrative of the book and so have been included here.

One of the intents of this chapter is to impress the reader with the amount of scripture and prophetic teachings that can be found on the present subject. The information included in this chapter is only a sampling, however, and much more can be found. Resources are included in the attached appendices to get the reader started in pursuing further research on the subject.

Scriptures

Some of the scriptures included in this section are used quite extensively elsewhere in this book, but are included again here for the sake of completeness. This is the body of scripture considered to be both relevant to the subject and easily understood. There are, obviously, many other passages and stories from the scriptures that teach the principles pertinent to the present discussion (i.e. Mosiah chapter 29), but require deeper analysis or discussion. The scriptures included below are considered those that contain and express a particular principle that is readily accessible with even a relatively casual reading. Taken all together, they support the argument of this book.

Each scripture is followed by a brief explanation of the important principles that are being used for this book.

> 34 Behold, there are many called, but few are chosen. And why are they not chosen?
> 35 Because their hearts are set so much upon the things of this world, and aspire to the honors of men, that they do not learn this one lesson—

> 36 That the rights of the priesthood are inseparably connected with the powers of heaven, and that the powers of heaven cannot be controlled nor handled only upon the principles of righteousness.
> 37 That they may be conferred upon us, it is true; but when we undertake to cover our sins, or to gratify our pride, our vain ambition, ***or to exercise control or dominion or compulsion upon the souls of the children of men***, in any degree of unrighteousness, behold, the heavens withdraw themselves; the Spirit of the Lord is grieved; and when it is withdrawn, Amen to the priesthood or the authority of that man.
> 38 Behold, ere he is aware, he is left unto himself, to kick against the pricks, to persecute the saints, and to fight against God.
> 39 We have learned by sad experience that it is the ***nature and disposition of almost all men, as soon as they get a little authority, as they suppose, they will immediately begin to exercise unrighteous dominion***.
> 40 Hence many are called, but few are chosen.
> 41 No power or influence can or ought to be maintained by virtue of the priesthood, only by persuasion, by long-suffering, by gentleness and meekness, and by love unfeigned;
> 42 By kindness, and pure knowledge, which shall greatly enlarge the soul without hypocrisy, and without guile—
> ...
> 46 The Holy Ghost shall be thy constant companion, and thy scepter an unchanging scepter of righteousness and truth; and thy dominion shall be an everlasting dominion, and ***without compulsory means*** it shall flow unto thee forever and ever.[1]

The above verses are fairly well known among Latter-day Saints. They describe the principles of righteousness on which the Priesthood and the powers of Heaven are based. Though it is not stated directly here, one central principle of Heaven and righteousness being referred to is the principle of agency. Note in verses 37 and 39 that it is offensive to the Spirit of God for an individual to exercise control, dominion, or compulsion, on another. Doing so results in a withdrawal of the Spirit and the associated powers of Heaven. Note also the negativity associated with the disposition of most men to exercise unrighteous dominion on others, or to take any little bit of authority and thereby usurp further dominion and control. This passage alone should lead readers to a healthy distrust of any person granted authority over another.

---

[1] D&C 121:34-42,46 (emphasis added)

> 16 And behold, I am sent to command thee that thou return to the city of Ammonihah, and preach again unto the people of the city; yea, preach unto them. Yea, say unto them, except they repent the Lord God will destroy them.
> 17 For behold, they do study at this time that they may destroy the liberty of thy people, (for thus saith the Lord) which is contrary to the statutes, and judgments, and commandments which he has given unto his people.[2]

An angel appears to Alma and commands him to return to the city of Ammonihah and to preach to them that they need to repent or they will be destroyed by the Lord. But why do they need to repent? Because they were studying how to destroy the liberty of the Nephite people. This is one of several examples of the Lord taking an active role in the liberty of His people and even calling a people to repentance, with severe consequences otherwise, for working against that liberty.

> 26 And he caused that all the people in that quarter of the land should gather themselves together to battle against the Lamanites, to defend their lands and their country, their rights and their liberties; therefore they were prepared against the time of the coming of the Lamanites.[3]

> 47 And again, the Lord has said that: Ye shall defend your families even unto bloodshed. Therefore for this cause were the Nephites contending with the Lamanites, to defend themselves, and their families, and their lands, their country, and their rights, and their religion.[4]

> 20 Behold, whosoever will maintain this title upon the land, let them come forth in the strength of the Lord, and enter into a covenant that they will maintain their rights, and their religion, that the Lord God may bless them.[5]

In these verses above, the Nephites, under the command of Captain Moroni, were fighting against the Lamanites and the reasons behind their fighting were repeatedly stated as being to defend their rights and their liberty. This further

[2] Alma 8:16-17
[3] Alma 43:26
[4] Alma 43:47
[5] Alma 46:20

strengthens the importance of liberty and rights in the minds of the authors of The Book of Mormon who were Prophets of God.

> 35 And it came to pass that whomsoever of the Amalickiahites that
> would not enter into a covenant to support the cause of freedom, that
> they might maintain a free government, he caused to be put to death;
> and there were but few who denied the covenant of freedom.[6]

Here Captain Moroni executed those who would not covenant to support the cause of freedom and fight to maintain the Nephites' free government. Captain Moroni understood the gravity of liberty and took it as seriously as God does. He defended liberty even unto bloodshed.

> 11 And Moroni was a strong and a mighty man; he was a man of a
> perfect understanding; yea, a man that did not delight in bloodshed; a
> man whose soul did joy in the liberty and the freedom of his country,
> and his brethren from bondage and slavery;
> 12 Yea, a man whose heart did swell with thanksgiving to his God, for
> the many privileges and blessings which he bestowed upon his people;
> a man who did labor exceedingly for the welfare and safety of his
> people.
> 13 Yea, and he was a man who was firm in the faith of Christ, and he
> had sworn with an oath to defend his people, his rights, and his
> country, and his religion, even to the loss of his blood.[7]

The above is a description of Captain Moroni as penned by Mormon. Note the repeated mention of liberty, rights, and privileges as clarifying additions to being "a man of a perfect understanding."

> 13 And it came to pass that Moroni was angry with the government,
> because of their indifference concerning the freedom of their
> country.[8]

> 18 But why should I say much concerning this matter? For we know
> not but what ye yourselves are seeking for authority. We know not
> but what ye are also traitors to your country.[9]

> 1 AND now it came to pass that when Moroni had received this
> epistle his heart did take courage, and was filled with exceedingly

[6] Alma 46:35
[7] Alma 48:11-13 (see also Alma 60:36)
[8] Alma 59:13
[9] Alma 60:18 (see entire chapter)

> great joy because of the faithfulness of Pahoran, that he was not also a traitor to the freedom and cause of his country.[10]

In these verses above, Captain Moroni is angry with the government of the Nephites for being indifferent concerning freedom. He writes a very strongly worded letter to the leader of that government, Pahoran. Notice his accusation of being a traitor for seeking one's own authority as opposed to the freedom of his country. The entire 60th chapter of the Book of Alma is this letter from Moroni to Pahoran in which he threatens to turn his army back on his own government to purge them of traitors that won't fight for freedom before resuming the war for that freedom against the Lamanites. In the end, Moroni's fears regarding Pahoran prove to be unfounded and he was given cause to rejoice at Pahoran's response.

> 37 Now it came to pass that when Lehi and Moroni knew that Teancum was dead they were exceedingly sorrowful; for behold, he had been a man who had fought valiantly for his country, yea, a true friend to liberty; and he had suffered very many exceedingly sore afflictions. But behold, he was dead, and had gone the way of all the earth.[11]

Here one of Moroni's generals, Teancum, had been killed in an ongoing conflict with the Lamanites. Moroni and Lehi mourn for him and the praise that they direct to him, as paraphrased by Mormon who is abridging and inserting this passage, is that he fought valiantly for his country and that he was a true friend to liberty. For these reasons they mourned his loss so greatly.

> 7 ... [T]he Lord God will raise up a mighty nation among the Gentiles, yea, even upon the face of this land[12]

The nation referred to above is now known to be the United States of America and it was raised up by God.

> 2 And behold, this is the thing which I will give unto you for a sign—for verily I say unto you that when these things which I declare unto you, and which I shall declare unto you hereafter of myself, and by the power of the Holy Ghost which shall be given unto you of the Father, shall be made known unto the Gentiles that they may know

[10] Alma 62:1
[11] Alma 62:37
[12] 1 Nephi 22:7

concerning this people who are a remnant of the house of Jacob, and
concerning this my people who shall be scattered by them;
3 Verily, verily, I say unto you, when these things shall be made
known unto them of the Father, and shall come forth of the Father,
from them unto you;
4 For it is wisdom in the Father that they should be established in this
land, and be set up as a free people by the power of the Father, that
these things might come forth from them unto a remnant of your
seed, that the covenant of the Father may be fulfilled which he hath
covenanted with his people, O house of Israel;
5 Therefore, when these works and the works which shall be wrought
among you hereafter shall come forth from the Gentiles, unto your
seed which shall dwindle in unbelief because of iniquity;
6 For thus it behooveth the Father that it should come forth from the
Gentiles, that he may show forth his power unto the Gentiles, for this
cause that the Gentiles, if they will not harden their hearts, that they
may repent and come unto me and be baptized in my name and know
of the true points of my doctrine, that they may be numbered among
my people, O house of Israel;
7 And when these things come to pass that thy seed shall begin to
know these things—it shall be a sign unto them, that they may know
that the work of the Father hath already commenced unto the
fulfilling of the covenant which he hath made unto the people who are
of the house of Israel.[13]

God the Father, in His wisdom and by His power, established the United States of America and set up the Gentiles who inhabit her as a free people. It was done partly so that The Church of Jesus Christ could be restored and then spread throughout the world. It is considered here, by the Savior, as being part of the work of fulfilling the Father's covenants with the House of Israel. Note the references to a specific group of Gentiles, namely those of the United States who would receive the Gospel and carry it to the descendants of Lehi, as opposed to a blanket reference to all the Gentiles throughout the world.

10 But behold, this land, said God, shall be a land of thine inheritance,
and the Gentiles shall be blessed upon the land.
11 And this land shall be a land of liberty unto the Gentiles, and there
shall be no kings upon the land, who shall raise up unto the Gentiles.
12 And I will fortify this land against all other nations.
13 And he that fighteth against Zion shall perish, saith God.

[13] 3 Nephi 21:2-7

> 14 For he that raiseth up a king against me shall perish, for I, the Lord, the king of heaven, will be their king, and I will be a light unto them forever, that hear my words.
> 15 Wherefore, for this cause, that my covenants may be fulfilled which I have made unto the children of men, that I will do unto them while they are in the flesh, I must needs destroy the secret works of darkness, and of murders, and of abominations.
> 16 Wherefore, he that fighteth against Zion, both Jew and Gentile, both bond and free, both male and female, shall perish; for they are they who are the whore of all the earth; for they who are not for me are against me, saith our God.
> 17 For I will fulfil my promises which I have made unto the children of men, that I will do unto them while they are in the flesh—
> 18 Wherefore, my beloved brethren, thus saith our God: I will afflict thy seed by the hand of the Gentiles; nevertheless, I will soften the hearts of the Gentiles, that they shall be like unto a father to them; wherefore, the Gentiles shall be blessed and numbered among the house of Israel.
> 19 Wherefore, I will consecrate this land unto thy seed, and them who shall be numbered among thy seed, forever, for the land of their inheritance; for it is a choice land, saith God unto me, above all other lands, wherefore I will have all men that dwell thereon that they shall worship me, saith God.[14]

This land is a land of liberty as designated by God. That liberty is established and defended by God Himself. This land is consecrated to be inherited by Lehi's posterity and Gentiles that accept the Gospel. That the Lord will fight against those that would establish kings or fight against Zion is considered by Him to be fulfillment of His promises. Presumably, these blessings are like other blessings in that they are contingent on our faithfulness. He will fulfill His promises, but we too must be faithful to what He has revealed. The U.S. Constitution is the instrument He has revealed to protect against kings and secret works.

"This land" is an ambiguous identifier at best, and it does not serve the present argument to get into all the possible interpretations of it. It is necessary, however, to point out that the narrowest interpretation of "this land" must, at a minimum, include the rough area that is now the United States of America. This is evidenced in prophecies and teachings found elsewhere in The Book of Mormon itself. For one, Nephi prophesies of the colonization of America and subsequent revolution.[15] In this prophecy there is clear reference to "the seed of

---

[14] 2 Nephi 10:10-19 (see also 2 Nephi 1:7)

[15] 1 Nephi 13:1-19

[Nephi's] brethren, who were in the promised land,"[16] and "multitudes of the Gentiles upon the land of promise."[17] The Gentiles scatter and smite the seed of Nephi's brethren and then fight a war against their "mother"[18] nation from whom they are delivered by God. Additionally, multiple references are made to the prophesied city of New Jerusalem being built upon "this land"[19] and it is known from modern day revelation that the city spoken of will be built in and around what is now Independence, Missouri.[20] So, at a minimum, references to "this land," the "promised land," and the "land of promise" must include at least the Eastern half of the United States of America (from Western Missouri to the East Coast where the nation was established, natives were "scattered", and the Revolution was fought). Additionally, there is sufficient basis to extend this area West to the Rocky Mountains since Salt Lake City and its surroundings contain the main body of the Gentiles who were given the Gospel in the latter days and are bringing it to the seed of Nephi's brethren and to the world as prophesied.[21] Furthermore, it seems unreasonable to interpret "this land" to be referring to two thirds of the United States and not the remaining land out to the West Coast of the country. Still further, for obvious reasons, "this land" must include the lands where The Book of Mormon took place, though we do not know with certainty where that is. Finally, because of the nature of the way The Book of Mormon authors used the term land, the actual content of their descriptions and prophecies regarding "this land" and "the promised land," and their general lack of insight into modern political boundaries, the area and land referred to by these statements likely includes the encompassing continent(s), although this last extension is not required by the argument being presented in this book.

So, in summary, Lehi prophecies that "this land"—referring *at least* to the modern day United States of America—"shall be a land of liberty." It is noteworthy that Nephi, while documenting his father's teachings prior to his death, includes this detailed teaching of the Promised Land being a land of liberty.

> 77 According to the laws and constitution of the people, which I have suffered to be established, and should be maintained for the rights and protection of all flesh, according to just and holy principles;
> 78 That every man may act in doctrine and principle pertaining to futurity, according to the moral agency which I have given unto him,

[16] 1 Nephi 13:12
[17] 1 Nephi 13:14
[18] 1 Nephi 13:17
[19] 3 Nephi 20:22, 21:4, 21:23; Ether 13:4, 13:6
[20] D&C 57:3, 84:3
[21] 3 Nephi 21:1-6

> that every man may be accountable for his own sins in the day of judgment.
> 79 Therefore, it is not right that any man should be in bondage one to another.
> 80 And for this purpose have I established the Constitution of this land, by the hands of wise men whom I raised up unto this very purpose, and redeemed the land by the shedding of blood.[22]

This passage was treated in great detail previously. In short, the Constitution was established by God for the protection of man's liberty to exercise his agency. He did so through the Founders, whom He called wise and whom He raised up for that very purpose. It is for the protection of the rights and privileges of all mankind.

> 4 And now, verily I say unto you concerning the laws of the land, it is my will that my people should observe to do all things whatsoever I command them.
> 5 And that law of the land which is constitutional, supporting that principle of freedom in maintaining rights and privileges, belongs to all mankind, and is justifiable before me.
> 6 Therefore, I, the Lord, justify you, and your brethren of my church, in befriending that law which is the constitutional law of the land;
> 7 And as pertaining to law of man, whatsoever is more or less than this, cometh of evil.[23]

This passage was also treated in great detail previously. To summarize, God justifies civil law that is based on constitutional principles and supports freedom, preserving the rights and privileges of individuals. Any civil law not rooted in those principles is authored by the Adversary. Again, constitutional law belongs to all mankind. It should be noted that civil law based on the U.S. Constitution is the only civil law on the earth today that God has personally justified.

> 1 We believe that governments were instituted of God for the benefit of man; and that he holds men accountable for their acts in relation to them, both in making laws and administering them, for the good and safety of society.
> 2 We believe that no government can exist in peace, except such laws are framed and held inviolate as will secure to each individual the free

---

[22] D&C 101:77-80
[23] D&C 98:4-7

> exercise of conscience, the right and control of property, and the protection of life.[24]

Mankind will someday be required to give an accounting of how they understood and acted in relation to governments. This is especially significant for American Latter-day Saints who are recipients of a benevolent and just form of government revealed by God Himself and informed of that revelatory source of it. Governments can only exist in peace as they protect, and don't violate themselves, the natural, God-given rights of life, liberty, and property.

> Prayer offered at the dedication of the temple at Kirtland, Ohio, March 27, 1836. HC 2:420–426. According to the Prophet's written statement, **this prayer was given to him by revelation**.[25]
>
> 54 Have mercy, O Lord, upon all the nations of the earth; have mercy upon the rulers of our land; may those principles, which were so honorably and nobly defended, namely, the Constitution of our land, by our fathers, be established forever.[26]

In a prayer received by revelation from God, the Prophet Joseph Smith prays that constitutional principles be established forever. This speaks to a purpose for the Constitution that's more eternal and far reaching in nature than to merely be used to govern an infant nation for a few decades until it is supplanted by something better or more progressed, as determined by the minds of men. Also note that by revelation from God came the statement that those principles were honorably and nobly defended.

> Wilt Thou, O our Father, bless the Chief Executive of this land that his heart and will may be to preserve for us and our posterity the free institutions Thy Constitution has provided. Wilt Thou too bless the Legislative and Judicial branches of our government as well as the Executive, that all may function fully and courageously in their respective branches completely independent of each other to the preservation of our Constitutional form of government forever.
>
> We pray that kings and rulers and the peoples of all nations under heaven may be persuaded of the blessings enjoyed by the people of this land by reason of their freedom under Thy guidance and be constrained to adopt similar governmental systems, thus to fulfill the

[24] D&C 134:1-2 (see entire section)

[25] D&C 109:Heading (emphasis added)

[26] D&C 109:54 (emphasis added)

> ancient prophecy of Isaiah that "out of Zion shall go forth the law and the word of the Lord from Jerusalem."[27]

President George Albert Smith, while dedicating the Idaho Falls temple in 1945, prayed for the "preservation of our Constitutional form of government forever." He also states that the influence of the U.S. Constitution on other nations and their governments is fulfillment of the prophecy that "out of Zion shall go forth the law"[28] and prays for that influence to be increased to "all nations under heaven." Similar veneration for the Constitution and its principles continues to be found in the dedicatory prayers of temples today.

> 17 Wo unto you poor men, whose hearts are not broken, whose spirits are not contrite, and whose bellies are not satisfied, and whose hands are not stayed from laying hold upon other men's goods, whose eyes are full of greediness, and who will not labor with your own hands![29]

This verse strongly warns against covetousness, greed, and theft, depriving others of their property instead of working to produce and improve one's own. It is too easy for too many to feel a moral detachment when government is sent to do the depriving instead of those advocating for the policies having to do it themselves. Because government is delegated representation and authority, if one advocates and votes for representatives, or government, to take another's property for his own benefit or the benefit of others, it is the same as if he takes it from the other himself. It is imperative to not detach morally merely for being removed from the physical act of taking.

Teachings of Church Leaders

This section consists of teachings and statements made by Prophets, Apostles, and other authorities of The Church of Jesus Christ of Latter-day Saints. Most are taken from official Church forums such as General Conference or official publications like the *Ensign* and *Improvement Era* magazines. A few are taken from settings outside of official Church purview, however. In these cases it is individuals who have also taught the same principles in official Church capacities and are considered to still be teaching principles understood by the Holy Spirit of God.

Just as in the scriptures section above, some cases will include brief analyses and explanations of the principles pertinent to the argument made throughout

---

[27] www.lds.org
[28] Isaiah 2:3; 2 Nephi 12:3
[29] D&C 56:17

this book. Other quotations will be left without commentary by the present author because the quotation itself is detailed commentary on the subject at hand. An attempt is made to group the following teachings together roughly by the subject being taught, but in some cases the quotation spans multiple subjects and a strict categorization is not possible.

Agency and Liberty

In a devotional address delivered to a BYU audience, Elder D. Todd Christofferson said, "We recognize the gift of agency as a central aspect of the plan of salvation proposed by the Father in the great premortal council, and that 'there was war in heaven' to defend and preserve it ... Satan has not ceased his effort 'to destroy the agency of man.'"[30]

Elder Christofferson affirms agency as central to the Plan of Salvation and that Satan continues in his efforts to destroy it.

In 1974, Daniel H. Ludlow delivered a devotional address at Brigham Young University. In it, he said:

> But Lucifer is trying to run up as high a score as he can, and he does this by trying to keep us individually from achieving the great divine purposes for which we came here upon this earth, including the exercise of our free agency. He can do it by denying us any one of the four essential qualities of moral free agency. He can do it by denying us the opportunity of choice, and he tries to do this through certain types of governments, dictatorships, through the lack of governments (anarchy), and so on.[31]

Later in the same address, Ludlow states:

> To achieve his devilish aims, Lucifer can and does work through many means: business combines, governments on all levels, military forces, educational institutions, secret combinations of all kinds, and even families, teachers, and churches. Wherever and whenever you find a person or an institution that seeks to destroy the free agency of man, there you will find the influence of Lucifer.[32]

Daniel H. Ludlow teaches that Satan employs a variety of vehicles to interfere with the unrestricted exercise of man's agency, including governments. His statement regarding the destruction of man's agency is in disagreement with the definition of agency used in this book. This is a minor technicality in the context

---

[30] D. Todd Christofferson, *Moral Agency*, BYU, January-2006
[31] Daniel H. Ludlow, *Moral Free Agency*, BYU, July-1974
[32] Ibid.

of his statement, however, and it seems likely that Ludlow would fully agree with a more accurate—within the context of this writing—statement saying that wherever any effort is found to limit or restrict the full exercise of man's agency or to destroy man's liberty, there Satan's influence will be found behind the effort.

Elder Dallin H. Oaks also taught the concept that government is one avenue through which freedom is lost. In a BYU devotional address given in 1987, Elder Oaks said, "Many losses of freedom are imposed by others. The science of government is a consideration of the procedures by which and the extent to which the official representatives of one group of citizens can impose restrictions on the freedom of others."[33]

In a 1962 issue of the *Improvement Era* magazine, President David O. McKay wrote:

> Next to the bestowal of life itself, the right to direct that life is God's greatest gift to man. One of the most urgent needs today is the preservation of individual liberty. Freedom of choice is more to be treasured than any possession earth can give. It is inherent in the spirit of man. It is a divine gift to every normal being. Whether born in abject poverty or shackled at birth by inherited riches, everyone has this most precious of all life's endowments—the gift of free agency—man's inherited and inalienable right.
>
> Free agency is the impelling source of the soul's progress. It is the purpose of the Lord that man become like him. In order for man to achieve this it was necessary for the Creator first to make him free. "Personal liberty," says Bulwer-Lytton, "is the paramount essential to human dignity and human happiness."
>
> References in the scriptures show that this principle of free agency is essential to man's salvation; and may become a measuring rod by which the actions of men, of organizations, and of nations may be judged.
>
> I do not know that there was ever a time in the history of mankind when the evil one seemed so determined to strike at this fundamental virtue of free agency. ...
>
> Freedom of the will and the responsibility associated with it are fundamental aspects of Jesus' teachings. Throughout his ministry he emphasized the worth of the individual and exemplified what is now expressed in modern revelation as "his work and his glory." (see Moses 1:39) Only through the divine gift of soul freedom is such progress possible.

---

[33] Dallin H. Oaks, *Free Agency and Freedom*, BYU, October-1987

> Force, on the other hand, emanates from Lucifer himself. Even in man's pre-existent state, Satan sought power to compel the human family to do his will by suggesting that the free agency of man be inoperative. If his plan had been accepted, human beings would have become mere puppets in the hands of a dictator, and the purpose of man's coming to earth would have been frustrated. Satan's proposed system of government, therefore, was rejected, and the principle of free agency established in its place. ...
>
> Force rules the world today. Individual freedom is threatened by international rivalries and false political ideals. Unwise legislation, too often prompted by political expediency, if enacted, will seductively undermine man's right of free agency, rob him of his rightful liberties, and make him but a cog in the crushing wheel of regimentation.
>
> It is well ever to keep in mind the fact that the state exists for the individual; not the individual for the state. Any form of government that destroys or undermines the free exercise of free agency is wrong. Liberty becomes then license, and the man a transgressor. It is the function of the state to curtail the violator and to protect the violated. ...
>
> The power of choice is within you—the roads are clearly marked. In making the choice, may God give you clear-seeing, strong wills, courageous hearts![34]

President McKay reinforces the importance of agency in God's eternal plan and of the close relationship that individual liberty on earth holds with that supernal and eternal principle. He notes how determined Satan is to undermine man's agency and declares with some force how his attacks make him appear more determined than at any other "time in the history of mankind." This was in 1962. After stating that Satan is behind the attacks, President McKay then goes on to describe how the attacks are undertaken and includes governments and their legislation as primary vehicles. President McKay emphasizes that force is of the Adversary. It is Satan who subjects individuals by force, it was Satan's plan to use force from the beginning. Of particular note is the unequivocal declaration that "[a]ny form of government that destroys or undermines the free exercise of free agency is wrong." It is also noteworthy that these forms of government will "*seductively* undermine man's rights." The use of the word "seductively" implies that the false political ideals and unwise legislation he mentions are enticing in nature and would therefore be easy to misidentify as beneficial, good, or otherwise appealing. If we are not rooted in constitutional principles of freedom,

---

[34] Jerreld L. Newquist, *Prophets, Principles and National Survival*, 1964, pp. 135-137

we will fall for seductive and enticing legislation and ideals that appear sound on the surface but are actually calculated to undermine our liberty.

On another occasion, in the October General Conference of 1951, President McKay taught, "Free agency is a divine gift more precious than peace, more to be desired even than life. Any nation, any organized group of individuals that would deprive man of this heritage should be denounced by all liberty-loving persons."[35] Of particular import in this statement is that agency is more precious than peace. Compare this statement from President McKay with that of Benjamin Franklin when he said, "They who can give up essential liberty to obtain a little temporary safety deserve neither liberty nor safety."[36]

President David O. McKay was an outspoken advocate of individual liberty as protected by America's constitutional form of government. In the April General Conference of 1950, he said:

> Let us, by exercising our privileges under the Constitution (1) Preserve our right to worship God according to the dictates of our conscience, (2) Preserve the right to work when and where we choose ... (3) Feel free to plan and to reap without the handicap of bureaucratic interference. (4) Devote our time, means, and life if necessary, to hold inviolate those laws which will secure to each individual the free exercise of conscience, the right and control of property, and the protection of life.[37]

Elder Marion G. Romney also spoke on the matter during the Priesthood session of the October, 1960 General Conference. He said:

> Free agency is the principle against which Satan waged his war in heaven. It is still the front on which he makes his most furious, devious, and persistent attacks. That this would be the case was foreshadowed by the Lord...
>
> You see, at the time he was cast out of heaven, his objective was (and still is) 'to deceive and to blind men, and to lead them captive at his will.' This he effectively does to as many as will not hearken unto the voice of God. His main attack is still on free agency. When he can get men to yield their agency, he has them well on the way to captivity.
>
> We who hold the Priesthood must beware concerning ourselves, that we do not fall into the traps he lays to rob us of our freedom. We must be careful that we are not led to accept or support in any way

[35] David O. McKay, General Conference, October-1951

[36] Andrew Allison, W. Cleon Skousen, M. Richard Maxfield, *The Real Benjamin Franklin*, 2008, p. 419

[37] David O. McKay, General Conference, April-1950

> any organization, cause or measure which, in its remotest effect, would jeopardize free agency, whether it be in politics, government, religion, employment, education, or any other field. It is not enough for us to be sincere in what we support. We must be right![38]

Elder Romney, as an apostle of the Lord, reiterates that which others have said: that Satan continues his war to undermine and fight against man's agency. He then gives the dire warning for holders of the Priesthood to not get caught by his traps, including those laid in government and politics.

In the October General Conference of 1963 Ezra Taft Benson, as a member of the Quorum of the Twelve Apostles, said, "It was the struggle over free agency that divided us before we came here; it may well be the struggle over the same principle which will deceive and divide us again."[39] Benson also acknowledges the ongoing struggle over man's agency and warns of the great potential to be deceived in it.

President Benson, in a devotional address delivered at Brigham Young University while serving as Prophet and President of the Church said:

> The first basic principle is agency. The central issue in the premortal council was: Shall the children of God have untrammeled agency to choose the course they should follow, whether good or evil, or shall they be coerced and forced to be obedient? Christ and all who followed him stood for the former proposition—freedom of choice; Satan stood for the latter—coercion and force. The war that began in heaven over this issue is not yet over. The conflict continues on the battlefield of mortality. And one of Lucifer's primary strategies has been to restrict our agency through the power of earthly governments.[40]

In General Conference, in 1961, then Elder Ezra Taft Benson declared:

> Although there is nothing more desirable to a Latter-day Saint than eternal security in God's presence, and although God knew, as did we, that some of us would not achieve this security if we were allowed our freedom—yet the very God of Heaven, who has more mercy than us all, still decreed no guaranteed security except by a man's own freedom of choice and individual initiative.
>
> Today the devil as a wolf in a supposedly new suit of sheep's clothing is enticing some men, both in and out of the Church, to parrot his line

---

[38] Marion G. Romney, General Conference, October-1960
[39] Ezra Taft Benson, General Conference, October-1963
[40] Ezra Taft Benson, *The Constitution – A Heavenly Banner*, BYU, September-1986

> by advocating planned government guaranteed security programs at the expense of our liberties. Latter-day Saints should be reminded how and why they voted as they did in heaven. If some have decided to change their vote they should repent—throw their support on the side of freedom—and cease promoting this subversion.
>
> No true Latter-day Saint and no true American can be a socialist or a communist or ***support programs leading in that direction***. These evil philosophies are incompatible with Mormonism, the true gospel of Jesus Christ.[41]

Note that per Elder Benson's counsel above, it is not enough to not be a socialist or a communist. To truly follow his counsel, it is necessary to understand Socialism and Communism, their underlying principles, and then be able to recognize when programs and measures lead in their direction, and then oppose such programs and measures.

Finally a statement from Elder J. Reuben Clark on the risk of losing liberty, who gave a dire warning in the April, 1944 General Conference when he said:

> Brethren, let us think about that, because I say unto you with all the soberness I can, that we stand in danger of losing our liberties, and that once lost, only blood will bring them back; and once lost, we of this Church will, in order to keep the Church going forward, have more sacrifices to make and more persecutions to endure than we have yet known, heavy as our sacrifices and grievous as our persecutions of the past have been.[42]

Elder Clark's warning is one that should be taken seriously. In all the history of mankind, freedom is a scarcity and has always taken bloodshed to achieve or, quite often, to even maintain. It will not do to recognize when freedom is lost. It is necessary to recognize the present risks and dangers of losing it and arrest the offending processes and programs before liberties are lost to that point where only bloodshed can offer any hope of regaining them.

Founders and Constitution

While incarcerated at Liberty Jail in Clay County, Missouri, the prophet Joseph Smith testified of the Constitution saying, "The Constitution of the United States is a glorious standard; it is founded in the wisdom of God. It is a heavenly banner."[43]

---

[41] Ezra Taft Benson, General Conference, October-1961 (emphasis added)

[42] J. Reuben Clark, General Conference, April-1944

[43] The Church of Jesus Christ, *History of the Church*, vol. 3, p. 304

In the Church News publication in 1952, J. Reuben Clark wrote, "But I declare to you, for what it may be worth, that [the Constitution] is what Gladstone said it was, the greatest document 'ever struck off at a given time by the brain and purpose of man,'" and "that the price of liberty is and always has been blood, human blood, and if our liberties are lost, we shall never regain them except at the price of blood. They must not be lost!"[44]

In the *Improvement Era* magazine, in 1940, J. Reuben Clark wrote, "This principle of allegiance to the Constitution is basic to our freedom. It is one of the great principles that distinguishes this 'land of liberty' from other countries."[45]

President John Taylor was unequivocal when he said:

> It is a duty that our families demand of us; it is a duty that the honest in this nation demand of us, and that God demands of us; and we will try and carry it out, God being our helper. And if other people can afford to trample under foot the sacred institutions of this country, we cannot. And if other people trample upon the Constitution and pull it to pieces, we will gather together the pieces and rally around the old flag, or what is left of it, and proclaim liberty to the world, as Joseph Smith said we would.[46]

President Taylor here iterates a part of the argument made throughout this book, that if God is the author of the Constitution, then God's people have an obligation to support and uphold it. In fact, according to John Taylor, Latter-day Saints cannot afford not to. The reference here made to Joseph Smith is a reference to an oft repeated prophecy of his regarding the Constitution that is not treated here in this work. For a detailed treatment of this prophecy and others regarding America in the last days, the reader is referred to *The Coming of the Lord* by Gerald N. Lund.

In the October, 1952 General Conference, Elder Harold B. Lee stated, "We alone know by revelation as to how the Constitution came into being, and we, alone, know by revelation the destiny of this nation. The preservation of 'life, liberty and the pursuit of happiness' can be guaranteed upon no other basis than upon a sincere faith and testimony of the divinity of these teachings."[47] Elder Lee reinforces the previous statement by President Taylor that it is a duty of Latter-day Saints, because of the knowledge revealed on the matter, to uphold and support the Constitution.

---

[44] Jerreld L. Newquist, *Prophets, Principles and National Survival*, 1964, p. 71
[45] Ibid., p. 198
[46] Ibid., pp. 156-157
[47] Harold B. Lee, General Conference, October-1952

In the April, 1948 General Conference of the Church, President George Albert Smith said the following:

> I am saying to you that to me the Constitution of the United States of America is just as much from my Heavenly Father as the Ten Commandments. When that is my feeling, I am not going to go very far away from the Constitution, and I am going to try to keep it where the Lord started it, and not let anti-Christs come into this country that began because people wanted to serve God.[48]

In this quote George Albert Smith, while he was the prophet of the Lord on the earth, declared in a General Conference session that the Constitution was as much from God as the Ten Commandments, and that therefore he would "try to keep it where the Lord started it." The seeming interpretation of this statement is that President Smith would avoid innovations on the Constitution's principles and continue to interpret the document in its proper historical context, advocating a form of government based on the original intent of the Constitution's authors and not on whatever "meaning may be squeezed out of the text, or invented against it."[49] Note that President Smith refers to those who would do the opposite of keeping the Constitution "where the Lord started it" as anti-Christs. This, presumably, is because they would be fighting against the Constitution, which is established by God and Christ.

In the *Improvement Era* magazine, in a 1950 issue, President Smith wrote:

> There are those who would destroy the Constitution of this land, and there are those who would rejoice if they could overthrow this nation. *No loyal member of this great Church will raise his voice against the constitutional law of the land*, but he will be found upholding it; ...
>
> Upon you men of Israel—to whom the priesthood of the Holy One has been given—there rests an obligation. You must serve the Lord and keep his commandments. It matters not what others may do, but for you there is only one course, and that is to *sustain the Constitution of this great land*...[50]

Again, President Smith shows his belief that it is an obligation and a duty of loyal members of the Latter-day Saint Church to uphold and sustain the Constitution.

President David O. McKay a few years later, in 1954, wrote in the *Church News* publication:

---

[48] George Albert Smith, General Conference, April-1948

[49] M. Richard Maxfield, K. DeLynn Cook, W. Cleon Skousen, *The Real Thomas Jefferson*, 2008, p. 382

[50] Jerreld L. Newquist, *Prophets, Principles and National Survival*, 1964, p. 100 (emphasis added)

> We owe at least the consideration to be loyal to this country and to spurn with all the soul that is within us the scheming disloyal citizens who would undermine our Constitution, or who would deprive the individual of his liberty vouchsafed by that great document ... Let every loyal member of the Church look down with scorn upon any man or woman who would undermine that Constitution.[51]

This is quite a forceful statement from a President of the Church. He clearly viewed the Constitution, "that great document," as essential for the protection of mankind's freedom, the ability to act according to his own God-given agency, and therefore saw it as reasonable to, and even encouraged Church members to, scorn any individual who would make attempts to undermine it.

In the Liahona in 1956, President McKay wrote that "Latter-day Saints should have nothing to do with secret combinations and groups antagonistic to the constitutional law of the land ... Next to being one in worshipping God, there is nothing in this world upon which this Church should be more united than in upholding and defending the Constitution of the United States!"[52]

In the October, 1951 General Conference, President McKay pleaded, "Oh, let us oppose any subversive influence that would deprive us of our individual freedom or make this government a dictator instead of a servant to the people."[53]

In the April, 1935 General Conference of the Church, Elder J. Reuben Clark, who was then serving as the First Counselor in the First Presidency, expressed a sentiment very similar to George Albert Smith's above:

> To me, that statement of the Lord, "I have established the Constitution of this land," puts the Constitution of the United States in the position in which it would be if it were written in this book of Doctrine and Covenants itself. This makes the Constitution the word of the Lord to us. That it was given, not by oral utterance, but by the operation of his mind and spirit upon the minds of men, inspiring them to the working out of this great document of human government, does not alter its authority.[54]

In the October, 1987 General Conference of the Church, President Ezra Taft Benson said, "I reverence the Constitution of the United States as a sacred document. To me its words are akin to the revelations of God, for God has placed His stamp of approval upon it. I testify that the God of heaven sent some

---

[51] Ibid., p. 90
[52] Ibid., pp. 100-101
[53] David O. McKay, General Conference, October-1951
[54] J. Reuben Clark, General Conference, April-1935

of His choicest spirits to lay the foundation of this government, and He has now sent other choice spirits to help preserve it."[55]

Elder J. Reuben Clark, while serving as Second Counselor in the First Presidency to President David O. McKay, in the April, 1957 General Conference of the Church said:

> Having in mind what the Lord has said about the Constitution and its Framers, that the Constitution should be "established, and should be maintained for the rights and protection of all flesh," that it was for the protection of the moral agency, free agency, God gave us, that its "principle of freedom in maintaining rights and privileges, belongs to all mankind," all of which point to the destiny of the free government our Constitution provides, unless thrown away by the nations—having in mind all this, with its implications, speaking for myself, I declare that the divine sanction thus repeatedly given by the Lord himself to the Constitution of the United States as it came from the hands of the Framers with its coterminous Bill of Rights, makes of the principles of that document an integral part of my religious faith. It is a revelation from the Lord. I believe and reverence its God-inspired provisions. My faith, my knowledge, my testimony of the Restored Gospel, based on the divine principle of continuous revelation, compel me so to believe. Thus has the Lord approved of our political system, an approval, so far as I know, such as he has given to no other political system of any other people in the world since the time of Jesus.
>
> The Constitution, as approved by the Lord, is still the same great vanguard of liberty and freedom in human government that it was the day it was written. No other human system of government, affording equal protection for human life, liberty, and the pursuit of happiness, has yet been devised or vouchsafed to man. Its great principles are as applicable, efficient, and sufficient to bring today the greatest good to the greatest number, as they were the day the Constitution was signed. Our Constitution and our Government under it, were designed by God as an instrumentality of righteousness through peace, not war.[56]

Elder Clark affirms with others that the Constitution is revealed of God and therefore a part of his religious faith and his testimony. Notice that Elder Clark, however, qualifies his reverence for the Constitution as being for it only "as it came from the hands of the Framers" and "as approved by the Lord." The intent of these qualifiers seems to serve to remind the listener and reader that Elder

[55] Ezra Taft Benson, *Our Divine Constitution*, General Conference, October-1987
[56] J. Reuben Clark, General Conference, April-1957

Clark does not approve of every innovation and interpretation of that document since its inception and signing. That is, the Constitution is most certainly inspired of the Lord, but not necessarily so for everything that has since been done in its name.

In the April, 1925 General Conference of the Church, Elder Charles Nibley was serving as the Presiding Bishop of the Church and was very shortly thereafter called to be a Counselor in the First Presidency. He stated in that Conference:

> Now, coming to our own land, our own Constitution, I think we hardly appreciate sufficiently, what this Constitution means to us and to the work of the Lord. It is my belief that this Constitution, which the Lord declared he established, is for the benefit of all mankind ... Certainly, the fundamental governing principles which the Lord has established on the earth under the name of the Constitution of the United States, were meant for all men, everywhere. These principles, with their accompanying freedom and liberty, are inseparably connected with our great latter-day work, it seems to me; for the Lord tells us that this freedom, this liberty, was brought about through the hands of wise men whom he raised up. Without this great Government of ours, this God-given Constitution, the gospel of Jesus Christ could never have found an abiding place in the earth. They are connected, correlated, interlocked one with the other; for the Constitution, like the gospel itself, is for the benefit of all flesh, for all mankind.[57]

Elder Nibley correctly reasons that the principles on which the Constitution is based are "inseparably connected with our great latter-day work," because "the Constitution, like the gospel itself, is for the benefit of all flesh, for all mankind." In addition to this connection, it has also been shown that those principles are the just and holy principles of Heaven on which God Himself based the Constitution.

In 1883, Elder Erastus Snow, while serving as an apostle in the Quorum of the Twelve Apostles delivered an address in the tabernacle in Salt Lake City. Below is a series of excerpts from that speech.

> In all these works and labors we discern an overruling providence, and manifestations of the mercy and loving kindness of God to His people, and the revelations of His Spirit imparted, to a greater or less degree, unto the wise and patriotic fathers of our country, who were thus enabled to unite upon the best form of government existing among men, or which, perhaps, ever has existed, unless it has been those

---

[57] Charles Nibley, General Conference, April-1925

which God himself directly revealed through the Patriarchs and Prophets of older times ... But we regard the present form of government of this nation as embodying the greatest amount of virtue and principles best calculated to maintain and preserve the rights of man...

I deem it of much importance that these principles should be well understood and thoroughly impressed upon the minds of the Latter-day Saints throughout the world, and especially those dwelling upon this American Continent and within the pale of this government, that they may implant in the hearts of our children a love of freedom and human rights, and a desire to preserve them, and to aid in maintaining and defending them in all lawful and proper ways; and to study the constitutional laws of the land, and make others acquainted with them; knowing the principles contained therein, and of learning how to apply them to ourselves, to our children, and to our fellowmen who are willing to be governed thereby; study them that we may also learn how to use them in suppressing tyranny, misrule and other evils that affect mankind ... and at no time will the Latter-day Saints, as a people, ever stand approval before God in violating those principles or slackening their efforts to maintain and defend them. They are closely allied to the teachings of the Savior and His disciples. ...

We have come to the understanding that every soul of man, both male and female, high and low, is the offspring of God, that their spirits are immortal, eternal, intelligent beings, and that their entity depends upon their agency and independent action, which is neither trammeled by God himself nor allowed to be restrained by any of His creatures with His sanction and approval; that the whole theory of God's rule and government in heaven and on earth is founded upon this principle of agency—self, independent action. And it is upon the free and independent exercise of this agency that the decree of God is founded, that all men shall be judged according to the deeds done in the body, none having it in his power to say that he was not at liberty to exercise this agency untrammeled. ...

I testify unto all Israel, and unto all the world, that God has called us, and required us to observe and practice these things; and that it is not the work of man, and that the institutions of this Church are not the institutions of man. And when we speak of the institutions of our common country, we say in the main, though God has used man in instituting this form of government, and in establishing its institutions and maintaining freedom upon this land, they are nevertheless the institutions of heaven; and God has revealed unto us that He did establish them by the hands of wise men, whom He raised up for that special purpose, and redeemed the land by the shedding of blood. It is

> therefore part of His great work, as much so as the part of revealing the keys of the Priesthood to Joseph, and the ordinances thereof, for the salvation of His people.[58]

Elder Snow reinforces that government based on the U.S. Constitution is the best form of government known to man and that it was revealed by God. Therefore, it is important that God's people, the Latter-day Saints, understand, uphold, and disseminate constitutional principles, for "[t]hey are closely allied to the teachings of the Savior and His disciples."

In the April, 1957 General Conference of the Church, Elder J. Reuben Clark of the First Presidency gave an address. Below are a few brief excerpts from that address:

> What a group of men of surpassing abilities, attainments, experience, and achievements! There has not been another such group of men in all the one hundred seventy years of our history, no group that ever challenged the supremacy of this group.
>
> When God puts his hand to the plow, his furrow is deep and straight, clear to the end. God gave us the heritage; ours is the duty to cherish and protect it. We have, as a people, a special relationship to these men and their work.
>
> No more clearly does it appear that Moses was so trained in the royal Egyptian courts that he could lead ancient Israel out of bondage, or that Brother Brigham was so trained, in directing the exodus of the Saints from Missouri to Nauvoo, that he could lead modern Israel from the mobbings and persecutions of the East to the freedom of the mountain fastnesses of the West; neither one was more clearly trained for his work than these Framers were trained for theirs—rich in intellectual endowment and ripened in experience. They were equally as the others in God's hands; he guided them in their epoch—making deliberations in Independence Hall.
>
> The Framers were deeply read in the facts of history; they were learned in the forms and practices and systems of the governments of the world, past and present; they were, in matters political, equally at home in Rome, in Athens, in Paris, and in London; they had a long, varied, and intense experience in the work of governing their various Colonies.[59]

---

[58] Ralph C. Hancock, *Just and Holy Principles*, 1998, pp. 44-48

[59] J. Reuben Clark, General Conference, April-1957

At a Freedom Festival celebration held in 1992 in Provo, Utah, Elder M. Russell Ballard of the Quorum of the Twelve Apostles gave an address. In that address, he made the below statements:

> The principles and philosophies upon which the U.S. constitutional law is based are not simply the result of the best efforts of a remarkable group of brilliant men. They were inspired by God, and the rights and privileges guaranteed in the Constitution are God-given, not man-derived. The freedom and independence afforded by the Constitution and Bill of Rights are divine rights—sacred, essential, and inalienable.[60]
>
> ...[I]t would not be politically expedient to say that the values that the Founding Fathers drew upon are eternal, unchanging values. But that is a fact. The values that made America great are, in reality, the commandments of God. They provide the foundation upon which the American republic was built.[61]

At a similar Independence Day celebration the following year, Elder Neal A. Maxwell of the Quorum of the Twelve Apostles delivered an address in which he stated the following:

> Being worthy of America's past and deserving God's blessings in the future are vital not only for America but also for the world. More hinges on what happens in America than we realize.[62]
>
> Our inspired Constitution is wisely designed to protect us from our excess of power, but it can do little to protect us from excesses of appetite or from our indifference to great principles or institutions.
>
> Any significant unraveling of the moral fiber of the American people, therefore, finally imperils the Constitution. The moral fabric of this society can become dangerously and relentlessly frayed as too few strands strain to hold us together. Hence shared patriotic, spiritual, and moral commitments within this nation's borders are as vital as defending those borders!
>
> Therefore, while great leaders are needed, so also are informed and wise followers. John Stuart Mill counseled as follows:
>
> "A people may prefer a free government, but if, from indolence, or carelessness, or cowardice, or want of public spirit, they are unequal to the exertions necessary for preserving it; if they will not fight for it when it is directly attacked; if they can be deluded by the artifices used to cheat them out of it; if by momentary discouragement, or

[60] Ralph C. Hancock, *Just and Holy Principles*, 1998, p. 160
[61] Ibid., p. 165
[62] Ibid., p. 176

> temporary panic, or a fit of enthusiasm for an individual, they can be induced to lay their liberties at the feet even of a great man, or trust him with powers which enable him to subvert their institutions, in all these cases they are more or less unfit for liberty: and though it may be for their good to have had it even for a short time, they are unlikely long to enjoy it."[63]

Elder Maxwell refers here to the collective morality of American society. It is easy to think of that morality as only meaning sexual morality, but that can be a mistake. Morality is a general distinction between right and wrong and doesn't have to pertain to sexual intimacy and relations. It is this author's opinion that the pervasive belief in America today that society, or the community, or the government, somehow has claim to a private citizen's property merely because that citizen earns more than others, has more than others, or can afford it by society's determination, is contrary to proper moral standards. If the individual cannot lay a just claim to his neighbor's property, then neither can he send the government in his place to do it. Ezra Taft Benson treats this concept more thoroughly below.

In a devotional address delivered at Brigham Young University in 1986, President Ezra Taft Benson taught the following:

> Rights are either God-given as part of the divine plan, or they are granted by government as part of the political plan. If we accept the premise that human rights are granted by government, then we must be willing to accept the corollary that they can be denied by government. I for one, shall never accept that premise. ...
>
> The fifth and final principle that is basic to our understanding of the Constitution is that governments should have only limited powers. The important thing to keep in mind is that the people who have created their government can give to that government only such powers as they, themselves, have in the first place. Obviously, they cannot give that which they do not possess.
>
> By deriving its just powers from the governed, government becomes primarily a mechanism for defense against bodily harm, theft, and involuntary servitude. It cannot claim the power to redistribute money or property nor to force reluctant citizens to perform acts of charity against their will. Government is created by the people. No individual possesses the power to take another's wealth or to force

[63] Ibid., p. 177

> others to do good, so no government has the right to do such things either.[64]

In a speech delivered on multiple different occasions, Ezra Taft Benson thoroughly and eloquently articulated many concepts regarding government and man's rights. Included in this speech is further elaboration on the concepts above regarding redistributing property. The speech is entitled *The Proper Role of Government* and one version of it can be found on the Latter-day Conservative website.[65] An abbreviated version of this speech was delivered as a General Conference Address in the October, 1968 General Conference.[66] Below are several excerpts from the speech:

> Since God created man with certain unalienable rights, and man, in turn, created government to help secure and safeguard those rights, it follows that man is superior to the creature which he created. Man is superior to government and should remain master over it, not the other way around. Even the non-believer can appreciate the logic of this relationship.
>
> Leaving aside, for a moment, the question of the divine origin of rights, it is obvious that a government is nothing more or less than a relatively small group of citizens who have been hired, in a sense, by the rest of us to perform certain functions and discharge certain responsibilities which have been authorized. It stands to reason that the government itself has no innate power or privilege to do anything. Its only source of authority and power is from the people who have created it. This is made clear in the Preamble to the Constitution of the United States, which reads: "WE THE PEOPLE... do ordain and establish this Constitution for the United States of America."
>
> The important thing to keep in mind is that the people who have created their government can give to that government only such powers as they, themselves, have in the first place. Obviously, they cannot give that which they do not possess. So, the question boils down to this. What powers properly belong to each and every person in the absence of and prior to the establishment of any organized governmental form? A hypothetical question? Yes, indeed! But, it is a question which is vital to an understanding of the principles which underlie the proper function of government. ...
>
> In a primitive state, there is no doubt that each man would be justified in using force, if necessary, to defend himself against physical

---

[64] Ezra Taft Benson, *The Constitution – A Heavenly Banner*, BYU, September-1986

[65] www.latterdayconservative.com

[66] Ezra Taft Benson, *The Proper Role of Government*, General Conference, October-1968

harm, against theft of the fruits of his labor, and against enslavement of another. This principle was clearly explained by Bastiat:

"Each of us has a natural right—from God—to defend his person, his liberty, and his property. These are the three basic requirements of life, and the preservation of any one of them is completely dependent upon the preservation of the other two. For what are our faculties but the extension of our individuality? And what is property but an extension of our faculties?" (The Law, p.6) ...

So far so good. But now we come to the moment of truth. Suppose pioneer "A" wants another horse for his wagon, He doesn't have the money to buy one, but since pioneer "B" has an extra horse, he decides that he is entitled to share in his neighbor's good fortune, Is he entitled to take his neighbor's horse? Obviously not! If his neighbor wishes to give it or lend it, that is another question. But so long as pioneer "B" wishes to keep his property, pioneer "A" has no just claim to it.

If "A" has no proper power to take "B's" property, can he delegate any such power to the sheriff? No. Even if everyone in the community desires that "B" give his extra horse to "A", they have no right individually or collectively to force him to do it. They cannot delegate a power they themselves do not have. This important principle was clearly understood and explained by John Locke nearly 300 years ago:

"For nobody can transfer to another more power than he has in himself, and nobody has an absolute arbitrary power over himself, or over any other, to destroy his own life, or take away the life or property of another." (Two Treatises of Civil Government, II, 135; P.P.N.S. p. 93)

This means, then, that the proper function of government is limited only to those spheres of activity within which the individual citizen has the right to act. By deriving its just powers from the governed, government becomes primarily a mechanism for defense against bodily harm, theft and involuntary servitude. It cannot claim the power to redistribute the wealth or force reluctant citizens to perform acts of charity against their will. Government is created by man. No man possesses such power to delegate. The creature cannot exceed the creator. ...

An important test I use in passing judgment upon an act of government is this: If it were up to me as an individual to punish my neighbor for violating a given law, would it offend my conscience to do so? Since my conscience will never permit me to physically punish my fellow man unless he has done something evil, or unless he has failed to do something which I have a moral right to require of him to do, I will never knowingly authorize my agent, the government to do this on

> my behalf. I realize that when I give my consent to the adoption of a law, I specifically instruct the police—the government—to take either the life, liberty, or property of anyone who disobeys that law. ...
>
> I believe we Americans should use extreme care before lending our support to any proposed government program. We should fully recognize that government is no plaything. ... It is an instrument of force and unless our conscience is clear that we would not hesitate to put a man to death, put him in jail or forcibly deprive him of his property for failing to obey a given law, we should oppose it. ...
>
> A category of government activity which, today, not only requires the closest scrutiny, but which also poses a grave danger to our continued freedom, is the activity NOT within the proper sphere of government. No one has the authority to grant such powers, as welfare programs, schemes for re-distributing the wealth, and activities which coerce people into acting in accordance with a prescribed code of social planning. There is one simple test. Do I as an individual have a right to use force upon my neighbor to accomplish this goal? If I do have such a right, then I may delegate that power to my government to exercise on my behalf. If I do not have that right as an individual, then I cannot delegate it to government, and I cannot ask my government to perform the act for me.[67]

Two more quotes on the responsibilities that these teachings bring will serve to close this section. First, J. Reuben Clark said:

> In broad outline, the Lord has declared through our Constitution his form of human government. Our own prophets have declared in our day the responsibility of the Elders of Zion in the preservation of the Constitution. We cannot, guiltless, escape our responsibility. We cannot be laggards, nor can we be deserters.[68]

Elder Clark reiterates the sentiments and counsel of many Church leaders of his day, that the Lord established the Constitution and that therefore members of the Church, particularly the Priesthood, have a responsibility to understand and maintain it. Priesthood holders will not be held guiltless in failing to discharge this duty.

Lastly, Elder Dallin H. Oaks wrote in the *Ensign* magazine in 1992:

---

[67] Ezra Taft Benson, *The Proper Role of Government*, www.latterdayconservative.com

[68] Ralph C. Hancock, *Just and Holy Principles*, 1998, p. 112

> U.S. citizens have an inspired Constitution, and therefore, what? Does the belief that the U.S. Constitution is divinely inspired affect citizens' behavior toward law and government? It should and it does.
>
> U.S. citizens should follow the First Presidency's counsel to study the Constitution. They should be familiar with its great fundamentals: the separation of powers, the individual guarantees in the Bill of Rights, the structure of federalism, the sovereignty of the people, and the principles of the rule of law. They should oppose any infringement of these inspired fundamentals.[69]

The counsel of the First Presidency to which Elder Oaks refers is a letter signed by the First Presidency on January 15, 1987, urging Church members and U.S. citizens to study and understand the U.S. Constitution, and to defend and uphold it in the face of increasing efforts to undermine and assail its principles.

Summary and Conclusions

This chapter has presented numerous scriptures and teachings from leaders of the Church regarding the subjects of agency, liberty, the U.S. Constitution, and the Founders. Many of the statements made were made by ordained and sustained general leaders of the Church during General Conference sessions. It is hard to deny that the Lord has taken a stance on these matters and it's equally difficult to not see which side He is on.

It is clear from the small sampling of evidence presented here that (1) agency is essential to the Plan of Salvation and Satan is therefore fighting against it; (2) Satan cannot directly take our agency but works to restrict us in its use by limiting our freedom; (3) he does this through governments and legislation among other methods; (4) our liberties are continually at risk and we have been repeatedly warned to be wary of efforts to destroy or undermine them; (5) God provided the U.S. Constitution as a safeguard for these liberties and we have a duty to sustain and uphold it for the benefit of all mankind. This argument, which is the core argument presented throughout this book, is completely congruent with revelation, scripture, and the teachings of many Church leaders over many years of Church history from Joseph Smith to the present day.

[69] Dallin H. Oaks, *The Divinely Inspired Constitution*, *Ensign*, 1992

Chapter 7 - Criticisms

The intent of this chapter is to anticipate in advance some of the criticisms that will be made against the arguments put forward in this book. These criticisms have been heard often in public discourse or as the subject matter of this book is brought up in conversation by the author with others, including Latter-day Saints. They are addressed here because it is anticipated that they will occur to many readers as they read and think on the arguments made herein.

The criticisms made against the Constitution and these arguments are many. Obviously, not all of them can be anticipated and the ones that can, cannot all be addressed here. This chapter will focus only on the more common ones that are heard, and the more fundamental ones on which other criticisms tend to be built.

This chapter will first give a brief overview of an anti-Constitution philosophy known as Progressivism. It is the Progressive movement that first introduced widespread argumentation against constitutional principles and gave rise to many of the detracting arguments still heard today. A few of those arguments are then addressed. The later arguments toward the end of the chapter are arguments made specifically by Christians and particularly Latter-day Saints.

Progressivism

Late in the nineteenth century there arose a new American political philosophy known as Progressivism. Progressivism is an ideology calculated to move, or progress, American society past the government system based on the U.S. Constitution and toward one of much greater scope and influence in the lives of American citizens. Ronald J. Pestritto and William J. Atto describe the Progressive Era as follows:

> The Progressive Era was the first major period in American political development to feature, as a primary characteristic, the open and direct criticism of the Constitution. While criticism of the Constitution could be found during any period of American history, the Progressive Era was unique in that such criticism formed the backbone of the entire movement. Progressive-Era criticism of the Constitution came not from a few fringe figures, but from the most prominent thinkers and politicians of that time. Readers are reminded, in almost any progressive text they pick up, that the Constitution is old, and that it

> was written to deal with circumstances that had long ago been replaced by a whole new set of pressing social and economic ills. The progressives understood the intention and structure of the Constitution very well; they knew that it established a framework for limited government, and that these limits were to be upheld by a variety of institutional restraints and checks. They also knew that the limits placed on the national government by the Constitution represented major obstacles to implementing the progressive policy agenda. Progressives had in mind a variety of legislative programs aimed at regulating significant portions of the American economy and society and at redistributing private property in the name of social justice. The Constitution, if interpreted and applied faithfully, stood in the way of this agenda.[1]

Woodrow Wilson, the twenty-eighth president of the United States, was a very prominent and outspoken leader in the Progressive movement. He advocated for this break from America's Founding and the Constitution when he stated that "we are not bound to adhere to the doctrines held by the signers of the Declaration of Independence."[2]

The Progressive movement was largely characterized by a disdain for the Founding principles and institutions of the United States. The Constitution and the free government that it formed were viewed by Progressives as barriers to the more energetic government that they desired. During the early twentieth century, before the second world war, much admiration could be found among American Progressives for many of the ideals found in the philosophies of Fascism, Socialism, and even Communism. Furthermore, the leaders of those movements, Benito Mussolini, Adolf Hitler, and Joseph Stalin respectively, were widely and publicly held in high estimation by American Progressive leadership. World War II and the subsequent Cold War then cast a very negative light on all of these philosophies and the significant historical figures that had championed them. Many American leaders and government officials continued to subscribe to these principles nonetheless, but this recasting made them more difficult to discuss and advocate for. Language then had to be changed, programs and groups had to be renamed, and some history had to be taken out of the spotlight. As a result, many people today have never been taught, forget (sometimes willingly), or deliberately ignore how influential socialist, communist, and fascist ideas were among many in American leadership during the Progressive Era, an era of substantial institutional change in American

---

[1] Ronald J. Pestritto, William J. Atto, *American Progressivism*, 2008, p. 3

[2] Ibid. p. 4

government and law. The principles underlying much of this substantive shift in American government have since been obfuscated, concealed, or disassociated from these ideologies. Many Americans today unknowingly advocate for philosophies and ideas that have their roots in Progressivism and thereby in the more nefarious collectivist philosophies. Many of the totalitarian principles of old are today decoupled from their original totalitarian philosophies and taught as independent and new ideas of progress, taking in many who have good intentions but who fail to recognize the true nature and origins of the ideas they are promoting.

Progressivism sought to incorporate many of the utopian ideals from the aforementioned collectivist philosophies into American society. Progressives sought to do this, however, not through violent revolution as it was accomplished in other places of the world, but through a gradual, step-by-step approach that would go largely unnoticed by the American public. Change was to be effected by continual "progress" toward the end of a benevolent totalitarianism. The mechanism of choice to accomplish this change was the continual reinterpretation of the Constitution and repeated experimentation in laws, regulation, and administration.

Progressives advocated the concept of Social Darwinism, that society and government are not mechanical in nature, but more akin to a living and evolving organism. Therefore, government and regulation should progress in response to the ever evolving society that they govern and administrate. The Constitution stood in the way of this Progressive evolution, and the most efficient way around it was not to rewrite or re-debate its principles and foundation, but to merely reinterpret it as circumstances were deemed to necessitate.

Woodrow Wilson, then a presidential candidate on the campaign trail in 1912, summed this up with the following explanation, "living political constitutions must be Darwinian in structure and in practice. Society is a living organism and must obey the laws of Life ... it must develop. ... [A]ll that progressives ask or desire is permission—in an era when 'development,' 'evolution,' is the scientific word—to interpret the Constitution according to the Darwinian principle."[3] Jonah Goldberg then follows this quotation with the following conclusion, "this interpretation leads to a system where the Constitution means whatever the reigning interpreters of 'evolution' say it means."[4] Of course, to arbitrarily and continually reinterpret the Constitution renders it near useless as an instrument of government restraint, as it was originally constructed to be. But then, that is exactly the objective of those that advocate for such reinterpretation.

---

[3] Jonah Goldberg, *Liberal Fascism*, 2007, p. 88

[4] Ibid.

In his work, *Congressional Government*, Wilson wrote that "[g]overnment is not a machine, but a living thing ... [i]t falls not under the [Newtonian] theory of the universe, but under the [Darwinian] theory of organic life."[5] The result of classifying government under Darwinian theory is that government can now do "whatever experience permits or the times demand,"[6] as Wilson wrote in another work he titled *The State*. It also allowed Progressive leaders to energetically pursue two of Progressivism's fundamental objectives, a powerful and influential federal government and the sacrifice of the individual for the benefit of the collective society.

Jane Addams was a Progressive activist of the era, she declared that "we must demand that the individual shall be willing to lose the sense of personal achievement, and shall be content to realize his activity only in connection to the activity of the many."[7] Walter Rauschenbusch was a prominent intellectual contributor to Progressive ideals. He said that "[n]ew forms of association must be created. Our disorganized competitive life must pass into an organic cooperative life."[8] Or, in other words, "[i]ndividualism means tyranny."[9]

Also at odds with American constitutional government is Progressivism's view of property. Theodore Roosevelt was another influential Progressive leader and the twenty-sixth president of the United States. He campaigned on his platform of "New Nationalism." Roosevelt described the property aspect of his platform as follows, "[t]he New Nationalism rightly maintains that every man holds his property subject to the general right of the community to regulate its use to whatever degree the public welfare may require of it."[10] This is in obvious contradiction to the Lockean view espoused by those who framed the Constitution and places the security of the individual and his property at the mercy of the state and whatever might be considered beneficial to the public welfare.

The basic philosophy of Progressivism is summed up nicely by Woodrow Wilson when he said, "[y]ou know that it was Jefferson who said that the best government is that which does as little governing as possible ... But that time is passed. America is not now and cannot in the future be a place for unrestricted individual enterprise."[11]

---

[5] Ibid., p. 86

[6] Ronald J Pestritto, *Woodrow Wilson and the Roots of Modern Liberalism*, 2005, p. 255

[7] Jonah Goldberg, *Liberal Fascism*, 2007, p. 87

[8] Ibid.

[9] Ibid.

[10] Ibid., p. 92

[11] Ronald J Pestritto, *Woodrow Wilson and the Roots of Modern Liberalism*, 2005, p. 255

Progressivism, at its core, is an ideology of big, controlling government, of one select group of people ruling over the rest of society. Perhaps this is illustrated best by Senator Albert J. Beveridge, a Progressive senator and legislative ally to Theodore Roosevelt and his New Nationalism, Progressive agenda. Senator Beveridge boldly declared, "[t]he opposition tells us we ought not to rule a people without their consent. I answer, the rule of liberty, that all just governments derive their authority from the consent of the governed, applies only to those who are capable of self-government."[12] This declaration by Beveridge of course begs the question, who decides whether people are capable of self-government? Presumably, this decision is left to their would-be rulers.

Note the direct opposition to constitutional principles of liberty, property, and Natural Rights being inherent in each individual. In their place are found the philosophies of some men being more fit to rule and make decisions for the rest of society, of individual rights necessarily being forfeited for the benefit of the social collective, of government evolving to do anything and everything it "needs" to as determined by different times and ever changing circumstances. While the terminology may vary and the language is now couched in more moderate rhetoric, there is no great strain to see these same Progressive ideas alive and widely disseminated throughout American society today.

It is essential for the reader to recognize that Progressivism, as defined by its founders and most prominent thought leaders, is an anti-Constitution movement. This is not an accusation leveled by critics, but a badge of intellectual honor worn by adherents and boasted by the intellectual and philosophical leaders of the movement. Progressives sought to reframe the historical context of America's Founding so that it could be interpreted in a manner more friendly to their legislative objectives. The principal goal of this reinterpretation was to create a gap between the nation and its Founding in order to lessen the influence of the Constitution and the Declaration of Independence and thereby weaken the restraints they placed on the federal government, enabling leaders to enact reforms that would otherwise be prohibited. Unfortunately, they saw a good deal of success and were able to reshape a number of aspects of American government and society. It is during the Progressive Era that noticeable shifts in power can be observed. It is during this era that the federal government began to grow in power and influence at the expense of the states and the people. These shifts were achieved through substantial legislation, through judicial decisions and opinions, and even through amendments to the Constitution itself.

---

[12] Jonah Goldberg, *Liberal Fascism*, 2007, p. 91

For example, it was in the midst of this Progressive political climate when the Supreme Court reversed the original intent of the Constitution by reinterpreting the "general welfare" clause in *Helvering v. Davis* as previously discussed in chapter 5. Additionally, during Woodrow Wilson's first year as president, the seventeenth amendment[13] to the Constitution was passed and ratified, weakening the constitutional congressional structure and advancing it a large step towards the parliamentary system he advocated. The federal government, since the Progressive Era, has undergone a more or less continuous trend of growth with few very brief periods of slight retreat. Meanwhile, the influence of the individual states and the people has continued to recede.

Many of the criticisms today directed at the American Founding and Founders were originated or made popular during the Progressive Era. While this was occurring, some general leaders of the Church spoke out against the philosophies of Progressivism and the criticisms it leveled at America's Founding.

In 1896 while serving as the First Counselor in the First Presidency, Elder George Q. Cannon wrote in the *Juvenile Instructor* magazine:

> In various ways, and by almost imperceptible degrees, the Constitution is being assailed. Sometimes its plain provisions are distorted if not openly violated, as can be remembered by many who are still young. Sometimes it is evaded and undermined, and by gradual processes is made to cover proceedings at which the fathers of the country would have stared. Laws which are not in accord with its spirit are sometimes enacted, and very frequently proposed. Men are becoming strangers to patriotism, and are striving after position and pelf.[14]

One of the objectives of Progressivism was to undermine constitutional institutions by the imperceptible degrees referred to by Elder Cannon. Additionally, through propaganda campaigns, they worked to dislodge the patriotism of Americans and thereby make them less likely to defend their sacred institutions of freedom.

In the October, 1912 General Conference of the Church, Elder James E. Talmage of the Quorum of the Twelve Apostles said:

> We stand for the Constitution and do not believe in any false notions of advancement and enlightenment and progressivism such as seeks to undermine that foundation of our liberties, for as a document we know that it was inspired and we believe that the men who framed it

[13] The direct election of senators briefly treated in chapter 5

[14] Jerreld L. Newquist, *Prophets, Principles and National Survival*, 1964, p. 106

> were raised up, as truly as was ever a prophet raised up in Israel in ancient or modern times, to frame that instrument and thereby provide for the fulfillment of prophetic utterances regarding the freedom and the liberty that should prevail in this choice land.[15]

Elder Talmage saw through the flattering rhetoric of the movement and recognized the proposed advancements and progress for what they were, carefully concealed efforts to undermine America's liberty and free institutions.

Levi Edgar Young, while serving in the Presidency of the Seventy and during the April, 1937 General Conference of the Church stated:

> A succession of small changes, a perpetual tampering with minute parts, steal away the breath, though they leave the body; for it is true that a Government may lose all its real character; its genius and its temper; without losing its appearance. So if we are not careful—very careful—we may find our government changed to a despotism, and yet called a Republic. It may have all the essential modes of freedom, and yet nothing of the essence, the vitality of freedom in it. The form may be left, but the spirit and the life will be gone.[16]

Elder Young counseled that continual innovating upon the text and principles of the Constitution was depriving the American government of the essence of its freedom. He also warns that freedom can be lost in such a manner while the outward appearance of the institution remains intact. This is extremely important to recognize in order to avoid complacency merely because the outward form of the American Republic yet remains. The reader is invited to think on what Elder Young might say regarding this subject at a Conference today were he still alive.

Progressivism is a large and complex subject, one that the reader is encouraged to pursue. Many people today assign themselves the thoughtful sounding label of "Progressive" without fully understanding its true meaning, its history, or its antagonism toward the U.S. Constitution and free government principles. Many also repeat the criticisms of the Constitution that were originated or made popular by the Progressive movement, not understanding the origins of or destructive designs behind such criticisms.

Constitution Outdated

It is increasingly popular and increasingly perceived as intelligent and insightful to label the U.S. Constitution as outdated or outmoded. This argument is usually

---

[15] James E. Talmage, General Conference, October-1912

[16] Levi Edgar Young, General Conference, April-1937

supported on specious pretexts regarding the Founders' shortsightedness or inability to foresee the advancements in population, transportation, technology, medicine, or whatever field of study or administration that best suits the discussion at hand. Another accusation made is at the Founders' supposed preference for social inequality and that the documents they produced served to form a government system based on that inequality to the end of protecting their own wealth, status, or influence.

The first important thing to understand about this argument is its origination. The argument originated with the initial advance of Progressivism, the American political philosophy described in the previous section. As mentioned above, Progressivism was founded on the premise that the Constitution was outdated, or outmoded, and unfit for governing the more modern and complex society. Progressives achieved a large amount of success in promulgating this idea as evidenced by the fact that the argument is still repeated today.

This criticism of the U.S. Constitution is especially interesting, however, when offered by Latter-day Saints, who claim as their most sacred and defining volume of scripture The Book of Mormon, which hasn't been added to in almost 1600 years. And yet the Church encourages its members to apply its principles and precepts to their modern lives on a daily basis.

The biggest problem with this criticism, however, is that it requires a fundamental misunderstanding of what the Constitution is in order to be believed. The Constitution is not an exhaustive list of all of the laws and regulations that were intended to govern all of society. It does not contain references to technology or modes of transportation. The Constitution is a set of principles on which those laws and regulations are to be made. It defines the governing bodies and institutions and their processes to be used to produce such laws and regulations. It defines the process by which officials are elected by citizens to their offices. It explicitly grants certain powers and authority to the federal government and forbids all others not so granted. And finally, through the first ten amendments, the Bill of Rights, the Constitution describes a set of Natural Rights, possessed by each individual citizen, that are not to be violated by the federal government.

In short, the Constitution is a set of principles on which civil laws and government should be based. It is not a comprehensive set of the laws and regulations themselves. Laws and regulations may have to change from time to time with changing circumstances. The principles on which sound and just government, laws, and regulations are based remain unchanged and everlasting. They do not vary with changes in technology, transportation, or other circumstances. The Constitution defines the way in which government should operate so as not to violate the Natural Rights of man, supreme among those rights including his liberty to exercise his God-given moral agency.

In addition, Latter-day Saints have even more compelling reasons to spurn this criticism and instead stand up for constitutional principles. These reasons have been treated in great detail throughout this entire book and are therefore only listed below and not reconsidered in any real detail here:

1. God established the U.S. Constitution
2. God justifies Constitutional government but not any form that is "more or less" than it
3. God justifies man in upholding Constitutional government and no other
4. God directed His prophet Joseph Smith to pray that Constitutional principles be "established forever"

It has been shown extensively throughout this book that God's power and principles are behind the U.S. Constitution. He established it, He justifies it and those who uphold it. He directed that it should be maintained and He revealed to Joseph Smith the prayer that it be established forever. He has not, since these revelations were given, revealed any new instructions or principles to the contrary. He has never rescinded His justification, His directive that it be maintained, or His sentiment that it be established forever. Latter-day Saints have been given clear and unequivocal direction on the matter of the Constitution, and that is that they should support, maintain, and uphold it.

Finally, If God established and justifies the Constitution and its precepts, then it follows that efforts to undermine and weaken that Constitution must originate with the Adversary since those efforts are working in opposition to God's designs. The argument that the Constitution is outdated and unfit for modern society is just such an effort. It was originated by those who openly disdained the limited government that the Constitution had constructed and advocated for a much more energetic, influential, and controlling national government.

In the October, 1940 General Conference of the Church, President David O. McKay said:

> Finally, if we would make the world better, let us foster a keener appreciation of the freedom and liberty guaranteed by the government of the United States as framed by the founders of this nation. Here again self-proclaimed progressives cry that such old-time adherence is out of date. But there are some fundamental principles of this Republic which, like eternal truths, never get out of date, and which are applicable at all times to liberty-loving peoples. Such are

> the underlying principles of the Constitution, a document framed by patriotic, freedom-loving men, who Latter-day Saints declare were inspired by the Lord.[17]

President McKay correctly identifies the authors of the outdated Constitution doctrine as Progressives and then reinforces the inspiration behind the Constitution's principles. These principles, "like eternal truths," said President McKay, "never get out of date."

Similarly, Elder J. Reuben Clark said:

> The Constitution is no more outmoded than the Ten Commandments, contrary to the claims of a new despotism. Without benefit of any prior blueprint, but prepared under God's guidance through study and experience, the remarkable body of men who framed the Constitution established certain fundamental principles ... This Constitution is part of my religion; it is our duty to uphold it.[18]

Elder Clark does not name the movement or philosophy directly, but the "new despotism" he refers to is the despotism of Progressivism, which, at the time that he spoke this, was vociferously making the case that the Constitution was outmoded or outdated. But the Constitution is not outdated. It is based on the just and holy principles of agency, liberty, and natural, God-given rights. These principles will not expire. It is the duty of Latter-day Saints to uphold the Constitution no matter the prevailing theories of the rest of the world.

Constitution Not Perfect

Another common criticism made of the Constitution is that it is not a perfect document, that the Founders knew it wasn't perfect and therefore created it with an accompanying mechanism to alter it with changing circumstances. Often the amendment process is used as evidence of the Founders' own lack of confidence in the document or their foresight that it would be severely lacking for future needs. Latter-day Saints will often take this argument a step further by saying that the Constitution is not scripture or a part of the LDS religion.

This argument is fascinating in that it is most often advanced by those that are advocating skirting, ignoring, or reinterpreting the Constitution as opposed to actually making use of the amendment process to make the alterations they seek. They point to the amendment process as evidence that the Constitution was meant to be kept up to date, and then advocate ignoring that process in

[17] David O. McKay, General Conference, October-1940

[18] Ralph C. Hancock, *Just and Holy Principles*, 1998, p. 104

favor of merely vaulting right over any constitutionally imposed barriers to whatever policy objective they hope to achieve.

It is conceded that the Constitution is not a perfect document, it is not scripture. In fact, Latter-day Saints have been cautioned against overzealousness in defending it. In 1992, Elder Dallin H. Oaks of the Quorum of the Twelve Apostles wrote an article in the *Ensign* magazine in which he counseled, "Reverence for the United States Constitution is so great that sometimes individuals speak as if its every word and phrase had the same standing as scripture. Personally, I have never considered it necessary to defend every line of the Constitution as scriptural."[19] Elder Oaks then follows this statement by referring to specific lines of text that don't seem to be particularly inspired in his mind. Note, however, that Elder Oaks is saying that the document is not equivalent to scripture, which is quite different than saying that it wasn't inspired or even that no part of it approaches a scriptural stature at all. The *Ensign* article that the quote was taken from is titled *The Divinely Inspired Constitution* and in it Elder Oaks praises the entire instrument, and the underlying fundamental principles on which it is built, as being divinely inspired. Later in the article, he writes the following paragraph regarding the Bill of Rights:

> I have always felt that the United States Constitution's closest approach to scriptural stature is in the phrasing of our Bill of Rights. ... I also see scriptural stature in the concept and wording of the freedoms of speech and press, the right to be secure against unreasonable searches and seizures, the requirements that there must be probable cause for an arrest and that accused persons must have a speedy and public trial by an impartial jury, and the guarantee that a person will not be deprived of life, liberty, or property without due process of law. President Ezra Taft Benson has said, "Reason, necessity, tradition, and religious conviction all lead me to accept the divine origin of these rights."[20]

Elder Oaks' caution against being overzealous in defending the Constitution is just that and nothing more. It should not be construed to detract from the inspired nature of the Constitution or the Heavenly principles on which it is built. As Elder Oaks demonstrates in this *Ensign* article, it is possible, and even advisable for Latter-day Saints, to understand, uphold, and defend the Constitution without being overzealous and without elevating the entire document to an expectation of being perfect, scripturally based doctrine.

---

[19] Dallin H. Oaks, *The Divinely Inspired Constitution*, *Ensign* Ferbruary-1992

[20] Ibid.

The U.S. Constitution was established by God, but through imperfect men. The Constitution is, however, the only form of government on the earth established by and justified by God, and so it is the best that man has until something new is revealed by Him.

Contrary to popular modern opinion, the Founders were far from displeased with the finished product of the Constitution. George Washington wrote to the Marquis de Lafayette in 1788, "It appears to me, then, little short of a miracle, that the delegates from so many different states (which states you know are also different from each other in their manners, circumstances, and prejudices) should unite in forming a system of national Government, so little liable to well-founded objections."[21]

Benjamin Franklin said to the Constitutional Convention, "when you assemble a number of men to have the advantage of their joint wisdom, you inevitably assemble with those men, all their prejudices, their passions, their errors of opinion, their local interests, and their selfish views. From such an Assembly can a perfect production be expected? It therefore astonishes me, Sir, to find this system approaching so near to perfection as it does."[22]

Thomas Jefferson said, "The Constitution ... is unquestionably the wisest ever yet presented to men, and some of the accommodations of interest which it has adopted are greatly pleasing to me, who have before had occasions of seeing how difficult those interests were to accommodate."[23]

Referring to the Constitutional Convention, James Madison wrote in *The Federalist* No. 37:

> The real wonder is that so many difficulties should have been surmounted, and surmounted with a unanimity almost as unprecedented as it must have been unexpected. It is impossible for any man of candor to reflect on this circumstance without partaking of the astonishment. It is impossible for the man of pious reflection not to perceive in it a finger of that Almighty hand which has been so frequently and signally extended to our relief in the critical stages of the revolution.[24]

The Constitution is not a perfect document and the Founders were aware of that fact. They were, nevertheless, quite pleased with the finished product of the Constitutional Convention. They made many statements of wonder and

---

[21] George Washington, Letter to Marquis de Lafayette, February 7, 1788

[22] Philip Kurland, Ralph Lerner, *The Founders' Constitution*, 1987, vol. 4, p. 658

[23] Andrew Allison, *The Real Thomas Jefferson*, 2008, pp. 379-380

[24] James Madison, *The Federalist*, 1787-1788, No. 37

astonishment at how well it turned out in the end and many acknowledgements of the divine intervention that had to be present for such an outcome.

The amendment process was included not because of their doubts in the document but with the hope that future generations would still be able to improve upon it or clarify its principles, not because of changing circumstances but as a result of increased wisdom and understanding. They knew they were fallible. In some cases, amendments have been made to the Constitution that have indeed clarified or improved on the principles originally intended by it. Unfortunately, on other occasions, amendments have been made that weaken the overall structure and work contrary to the Constitution's original spirit and intent. It is imperative that ordinary American citizens gain a deep enough understanding of the Constitution and its principles to be able to distinguish between these two and to not have to rely on self-proclaimed experts for the correct interpretations.

The reader is reminded again that the Constitution of the United States, as it was originally authored by the Founders and with the spirit in which they intended it, is justified by God and the only form of government that has received that particular accolade to date. That the document itself is not perfect is not sufficient reason to discard, disdain, or ignore it, especially for Latter-day Saints.

Elder Orson Pratt, as an Apostle of the Lord stated, "Many great and glorious principles are contained within the Constitution of our country, not to say that it is perfect, but it is perfect so far as it pertains to the rights and privileges of the children of men."[25]

The Founders Were Slave Owners

Many people today easily discard the Founders or what they accomplished largely based on the criticism that they were slave owners. Others, who wish to espouse the Constitution and Declaration of Independence and the corresponding philosophies imbued into them by the Founders, struggle to reconcile this seemingly glaring flaw of slave ownership with the principles of human freedom that they championed. It is easy to look back to the Founding Era through today's lens of post-civil rights America and make accusations of hypocrisy, or even racism, against individuals or groups that owned slaves while declaring the equality of all men. What is needed is to refocus our view through the appropriate historical lens to see the true complexity of the issue and the thoughts and actions of the Founders in relation to it.

---

[25] Ralph C. Hancock, *Just and Holy Principles*, 1998, p. 22

The first thing to recognize is that throughout the history of mankind, slavery has been a reality. It was not invented in America, nor was it invented by the Founders. In America, slavery had been forced onto the Colonies by the British Monarchy despite repeated attempts by many Colonists to abolish it. Henry Laurens, who served as both Vice President of South Carolina and as President of the Continental Congress lamented this fact in a letter he wrote in 1776:

> I abhor slavery. I was born in a country where slavery had been established by British Kings and Parliaments as well as by the laws of the country ages before my existence ... In former days there was no combating the prejudices of men supported by [economic] interest...[26]

Thomas Jefferson, in his original draft of the Declaration of Independence, included this British policy of forced slavery among the enumeration of injuries committed by Britain against the American Colonies, he wrote:

> [H]e [King George III] has waged cruel war against human nature itself, violating its most sacred rights of life & liberty in the persons of a distant people who never offended him, captivating and carrying them into slavery in another hemisphere or to incur miserable death in their transportation thither. ... Determined to keep open a market where men should be bought and sold, he has prostituted his negative for *suppressing every legislative attempt to prohibit or to restrain this execrable commerce* [that is, he has opposed efforts to prohibit the slave trade].[27]

Benjamin Franklin also wrote of this plight among the Colonies in 1773:

> A disposition to abolish slavery prevails in North America, that many of Pennsylvanians have set their slaves at liberty, and that even the Virginia Assembly have petitioned the King for permission to make a law for preventing the importation of more into that colony. This request, however, will probably not be granted as *their former laws of that kind have always been repealed*.[28]

Both Jefferson and Franklin here allude to the fact that repeated attempts had been made to weaken, diminish, or abolish the institution of slavery. Jefferson laments that King George had suppressed "every legislative attempt to prohibit or to restrain" the practice. Franklin points out that "former laws of that kind [preventing slave importation] have always been repealed." Both statements

---

[26] David Barton, *The Founding Fathers and Slavery*, 2011, www.wallbuilders.com
[27] Ibid. (emphasis added)
[28] Stephen McDowell, *The Bible, Slavery, and America's Founders*, 2003, www.wallbuilders.com (emphasis added)

attest to repeated and numerous attempts by many Colonists to work against the practice of slavery while being thwarted by the British monarch or by opposing factions in the Colonies.

It was into this world that the Founders were born, where slavery had been a reality their entire lives, forced onto them by law and tradition. Instead of being a blemish on their character, it is to their credit that they were able to see the evil in the practices and thinking of their fathers, their ancestors, and their fellow countrymen, and in the traditions and laws of their own country. Prior to Revolutionary America, little talk was heard anywhere in the world regarding the abolition of slavery, it was a longstanding and accepted practice throughout the history of mankind to that point in the world's history. John Jay pointed this out in 1788 in a letter to the English Anti-Slavery Society:

> Prior to the great Revolution, the great majority ... of our people had been so long accustomed to the practice and convenience of having slaves that very few among them even doubted the propriety and rectitude of it.[29]

It was the Founding of America, supported by the ideals of the Declaration of Independence, that popularized the philosophies of Natural Law, that all men are equally entitled to the same set of Natural Rights. The promulgation of these ideals throughout the world was a large factor in the near eradication of slavery that followed.

A large majority of the Founders were abolitionists and created or served in a number of organizations pursuing that end. In 1774, Benjamin Franklin and Benjamin Rush founded the first anti-slavery society in America. John Jay was the president of a similar society in New York. Other Founders who served in such societies included James Madison, James Monroe, Zephaniah Swift, John Marshall, Richard Stockton, Richard Bassett, Bushrod Washington, Charles Carroll, William Few and more.

The hostility held by Founders toward the practice of slavery was near universal, especially by those who contributed the most intellectually to the principles and documents we benefit from today. John Adams said:

> Every measure of prudence, therefore, ought to be assumed for the eventual total extirpation of slavery from the United States ... I have, through my whole life, held the practice of slavery in ... abhorrence.[30]

John Jay wrote:

---

[29] David Barton, *The Founding Fathers and Slavery*, 2011, www.wallbuilders.com

[30] Stephen McDowell, *The Bible, Slavery, and America's Founders*, 2003, www.wallbuilders.com

> I can safely promise them that neither my tongue, nor my pen, nor purse shall be wanting to promote the abolition of what to me appears so inconsistent with humanity and Christianity ... May the great and the equal Father of the human race, who has expressly declared His abhorrence of oppression, and that He is no respecter of persons, succeed a design so laudably calculated to undo the heavy burdens, to let the oppressed go free, and to break every yoke.[31]

James Otis of Massachusetts said in 1764 that "[t]he colonists are by law of nature freeborn, as indeed all men are, white or black."[32]

George Washington wrote in a letter to Robert Morris, "I can only say that there is not a man living who wishes more sincerely than I do to see a plan adopted for the abolition of [slavery]."[33]

Charles Carroll, who signed the Declaration of Independence wrote, "Why keep alive the question of slavery? It is admitted by all to be a great evil."[34]

The Founders of America were by and large abolitionists. The few who weren't were among the representation from the Southern states of North Carolina, South Carolina, and Georgia, where slavery was much more deeply entrenched and where it would take longer to abolish, as Thomas Jefferson explained:

> Where the disease [slavery] is most deeply seated, there it will be slowest in eradication. In the northern States, it was merely superficial and easily corrected. In the southern, it is incorporated with the whole system and requires time, patience, and perseverance in the curative process.[35]

Nevertheless, there were indeed slave owners among the American Founders, and many view this as being contradictory or even hypocritical. The two most prominent and notable examples are those of George Washington and Thomas Jefferson. Washington and Jefferson often suffer accusations of bigotry, racism, hypocrisy, and contradiction for their simultaneous parts in both the enlightened Revolution of America and slave ownership. Both men, however, were born into a country where slavery already existed and both inherited their slaves from relatives, Washington inheriting his first slaves at the young age of eleven.

But if they had slaves and abhorred the practice so much, why not just free them? This is the question no doubt occurring to every reader at this point. The answer is that those that supported slavery had used the government to

---

[31] Ibid.
[32] Ibid.
[33] Ibid.
[34] Ibid.
[35] David Barton, *George Washington, Thomas Jefferson & Slavery in Virginia*, 2000, www.wallbuilders.com

institutionalize the practice and make it financially prohibitive or otherwise objectionable to free one's slaves. For example, In 1692, Virginia passed a law mandating that slaves could not be set free "unless the emancipator pays for his transportation out of the country within six months,"[36] adding a substantial economic burden to the prospect of freeing one's slaves. Subsequent laws added provisions requiring the slave owner to provide for education, livelihood, and other financial support under the auspices of ensuring that the freed slave would not end up a burden to the rest of society. This increased the financial hardship for anyone wanting to free slaves. Additionally, these laws usually imposed severe penalties for anyone caught freeing slaves without abiding by these measures. In 1723, an even stricter law was passed making any emancipation of slaves illegal except for cases of "meritorious service"[37] as could only be determined by the Governor and his Council. This law was in effect for the majority of the lives of both Washington and Jefferson, making it illegal to emancipate slaves in the state of Virginia.

Despite owning slaves, which they had inherited, both of these men spent the better part of their lives in efforts to reverse the trend and ultimately abolish the practice of slavery. Thomas Jefferson was elected to the Virginia legislature in 1769 and made an attempt at emancipation, he recounts:

> In 1769, I became a member of the legislature by the choice of the county in which I live, and so continued until it was closed by the Revolution. I made one effort in that body for the permission of the emancipation of slaves, which was rejected: and indeed, during the regal government, nothing could expect success.[38]

Jefferson here alludes to the British crown as being an influence behind the stifling of emancipation legislation. Similar to Jefferson's effort above, Washington, in July of 1774 chaired a committee in Fairfax County that passed the following resolution:

> Resolved, that it is the opinion of this meeting that during our present difficulties and distress, no slaves ought to be imported into any of the British colonies on this continent; and we take this opportunity of declaring our most earnest wishes to see an entire stop for ever put to such a wicked, cruel, and unnatural trade.[39]

---

[36] Ibid.
[37] Ibid.
[38] Ibid.
[39] Ibid.

Shortly before his death, in 1797, Washington wrote to his nephew, Lawrence Lewis, "I wish from my soul that the legislature of this State could see the policy of a gradual abolition of slavery."[40] Unfortunately, neither Washington nor Jefferson saw much success in their native state of Virginia.

After the Declaration of Independence in 1776, which proclaimed equal rights for all men, and a successful Revolution that unshackled America from British rule, slavery began to be outlawed in much of the nation. Pennsylvania and Massachusetts abolished slavery in 1780, Connecticut and Rhode Island in 1784, New Hampshire in 1792, Vermont in 1793, New York in 1799, and New Jersey in 1804.[41]

The Northwest Ordinance was authored by Rufus King who signed the Constitution. it governed the admission of new states into the union from the Northwest Territories. The Northwest Ordinance prohibited slavery as a condition to enter the union. It was signed into law by President George Washington.

In 1784, Jefferson participated in a committee with two others that introduced a law in the Continental Congress to ban slavery from the "western territory."[42] But, the measure failed by a single vote.

In 1782, Virginia relaxed their anti-emancipation laws slightly and allowed for the emancipation of slaves in a slave owner's last will or deed. It was this law that George Washington took advantage of in order to free his slaves in his last will and testament upon his death in 1799. In 1806, however, the Virginia legislature amended this policy by again adding substantial financial burdens to the emancipator, requiring his estate to provide for and financially support many of the slaves freed in this manner. This restrictive environment for emancipation persisted to the time of Jefferson's death and beyond.

Washington and Jefferson were neither racist nor bigoted. They were slave owners, yes, but they had that position forced on them by circumstance and tradition that were difficult to overcome, though they fought toward that end their entire lives. By all accounts of contemporaries and witnesses, they treated their slaves very well and not like slaves at all. This is even attested to by the slaves themselves who didn't view these men as slave masters, but as family. John Quincy Adams was a staunch abolitionist, renowned for his efforts against slavery. He gave a speech commemorating the signing of the Declaration of Independence on July 4, 1837. In this speech, he said the following:

---

[40] Ibid.
[41] Stephen McDowell, *The Bible, Slavery, and America's Founders*, 2003, www.wallbuilders.com
[42] David Barton, *George Washington, Thomas Jefferson & Slavery in Virginia*, 2000, www.wallbuilders.com

> The inconsistency of the institution of domestic slavery with the principles of the Declaration of Independence was seen and lamented by all the southern patriots of the Revolution; by no one with deeper and more unalterable conviction than by the author of the Declaration himself [Jefferson]. No charge of insincerity or hypocrisy can be fairly laid to their charge. Never from their lips was heard one syllable of attempt to justify the institution of slavery. They universally considered it as a reproach fastened upon them by the unnatural step-mother country [Great Britain] and they saw that before the principles of the Declaration of Independence, slavery, in common with every other mode of oppression, was destined sooner or later to be banished from the earth. Such was the undoubting conviction of Jefferson to his dying day. In the Memoir of His Life, written at the age of seventy-seven, he gave to his countrymen the solemn and emphatic warning that the day was not distant when they must hear and adopt the general emancipation of their slaves.[43]

It is lamentable that Washington, Jefferson, and others didn't achieve more success against slavery in the state of Virginia, and that slavery persisted as long as it did in the United States. But it was not for want of trying. And it should not be overlooked that it was the American Revolution, and particularly the words phrased by Thomas Jefferson himself in the Declaration of Independence, that fueled emancipation of slaves and legislative banning of the practice of slavery across the globe. Because of this, it could be argued that Jefferson, and his colleagues, did more for the eventual emancipation of the slave than any other figure in history, though the seeds he planted didn't produce until after his lifetime.

Politics and Religion Don't Mix

Many Latter-day Saints today believe that politics and religion don't mix. This sentiment is often summed up with catchy colloquialisms like "Jesus isn't Republican or Democrat" or "my salvation isn't based on how I vote."

It is true that the Church as an organization does its best to remain apolitical. The author concedes that Church is not an appropriate setting to discuss candidates, campaigns, and most current events, and that a member's voting record is not likely to be a large deciding factor in his or her salvation.

At the same time, however, it is contained in the LDS canon of scripture "that [God] holds men accountable for their acts in relation to [governments]."[44] It appears from this scripture that at least some accounting will have to be made

---

[43] David Barton, *The Founding Fathers and Slavery*, 2011, www.wallbuilders.com

[44] D&C 134:1

for our acts in relation to government. The extent of that accounting is not known, but it will still evidently need to be made.

Furthermore, matters of government always have a moral component to consider. Everything that government does is done by force and so should always be done with the question of whether the force is justified. The use of force necessarily reduces freedom. The practice and application of government is a continual consideration of how much it is just and appropriate to restrict the freedom of others. In other words, it is a constant consideration of force versus freedom. As seen throughout this book, this is a very moral issue. The question of force versus freedom was the central issue over which the War in Heaven commenced and continues to play a key role in the ongoing struggle between good and evil, Christ and Satan, today.

In a 2009 speech given at BYU Idaho, Elder Dallin H. Oaks said, "I speak about religious freedom under the United States Constitution. There is a battle over the meaning of that freedom. The contest is of eternal importance."[45] Elder Oaks declares that this contest over religious freedom under the Constitution is of eternal importance. Elder Oaks speaks specifically of religious freedom, but the statement could very well be made without the "religious" qualifier. Many of the freedoms protected under the U.S. Constitution are rooted in religious freedom and the loss of any of those other freedoms would place society on a path toward the eventual loss of religious freedom as well. It is wise to heed the counsel given by James Madison, discussed in chapter 5, "to take alarm at the first experiment on our liberties."[46] Once any freedom under the Constitution is lost or weakened, the entire instrument of the Constitution is weakened and all freedoms under it are then found to be in jeopardy.

Another factor that makes government a moral matter is that the American form of government is executed through elected representation and delegated authority. That means that if the government is acting wickedly, the people, who retain ultimate power and authority and who delegate that power and authority to their elected representatives, bear some measure of accountability for that wickedness.

Furthermore, the principles of civil government are principles that have been revealed by God. As has been shown, agency and liberty are taught throughout the scriptures. God Himself saw fit to divulge through revelation His own involvement in raising the Founders and establishing the U.S. Constitution, and revealed the reason for doing so was to protect man's freedom and allow him to exercise his agency. He has revealed the principles on which the Constitution is

---

[45] Dallin H. Oaks, *Religious Freedom*, October 13, 2009, BYU Idaho

[46] Philip Kurland, Ralph Lerner, *The Founders' Constitution*, 1987, vol. 5, p. 82

based because they are among the "just and holy principles" of eternity. His prophets and Apostles have taught and warned about these constitutional principles and the morality of liberty since the Church of Jesus Christ was restored on the earth.

If anyone has made civil government and law into a religious and moral matter, it is God Himself who has done so. He has seen fit to give revelation on the matter, He saw fit to intervene in man's history to protect freedom and erect a standard of civil government for the benefit of all mankind, and He has inspired His prophets and apostles to speak on the matter over the course of centuries.

The Latter-day Saint religion teaches much about the just and holy principles on which civil law should be based. These principles, when understood, should drive the thoughts and actions of Latter-day Saints with respect to civil government and law. While neither the LDS religion or Church organization, with very few exceptions, expressly teach or counsel for whom or what their members and adherents should vote, they do teach the divinely revealed principles that should be applied to those votes. So, while candidates and most political issues and events should not be discussed in Church settings, the correct principles that undergird just government and that are taught in the scriptures and by revelation do indeed find appropriate settings in Church service to be discussed and taught.

Jesus Christ Taught to Care for the Poor

A very core fundamental of the Gospel of Jesus Christ is to impart of one's substance for the benefit of those less fortunate or in need of assistance. This is something on which most, if not all, Christian denominations and sects agree as being part of Christ's Gospel, including Latter-day Saints. The desire to care for the poor and needy, albeit commendable, often leads to misguided uses of force in order to be implemented on grand scales and for political expediency.

First, let it be acknowledged that there is no question regarding Jesus' teachings about caring for the poor, and about not being so attached to material possessions that they can't be used or given for the benefit of others. This is not in question.

But there is a very distinct characteristic to the teachings of Jesus Christ on this matter that is very often overlooked. In every case that Jesus taught to care for the poor and needy, He taught and encouraged individuals to impart of *their own* substance for such care. A classic example is the parable of the Good Samaritan. In this familiar story, a Samaritan happens upon a Jewish man on the road who had been robbed, beaten, and left for dead. The Samaritan tends to his wounds, gets him to an inn, and then pays the innkeeper for the Jewish man's food and room, and leaves with a commitment to return and pay for any additional charges the Jewish man incurs. Then Jesus commanded His disciples to go and do likewise.

Note that in this parable, like the rest of Jesus' teachings regarding using our substance to care for others, there is a conspicuous lack of any third party orchestrating the relief and care of the stricken Jew. The Samaritan used his own resources, his own private property to do what he could for another man in need.

In The Book of Mormon, the prophet Alma calls and ordains priests to preach and teach to a small group of people who are secretly starting a small gospel-centered society while trying to avoid the notice of the wicked King Noah. Contrary to the priests of King Noah, with whom Alma had much experience, Alma teaches that these priests were not to be supported through taxation on the people. Instead, the people "should impart of their substance *of their own free will* and good desires towards God, and to those priests that stood in need, yea, and to every needy, naked soul."[47] Alma, like Jesus Christ, teaches that care for the needy is to be done in accordance with the free will of the caregiver. We are commanded to impart of our own substance for those in need and not to forcefully take the substance of another for that care.

Government instituted social programs stand in stark contrast to Christ's teachings in that they are implemented and executed through the use of force. It is essential to recognize that government does not produce and has no possessions or substance of its own accord. Government can only come to possess substance by forcefully taking it from somewhere or someone. This is usually accomplished through taxation. Whenever government speaks of providing for the poor, caring for a certain group of people, funding or paying for this or that initiative or project, or offering "free" services, it is important to note that they are *always* speaking of achieving these ends through the use of money and resources that had to be either forcefully or surreptitiously taken from others. Government cannot spend or fund with its own resources, it can only redistribute the resources of others. Government cannot inject its own capital to stimulate an economy, but of necessity must make use of capital that it removes from elsewhere in the economy. Government can only divert resources from one place to another, or redistribute property from one group to another, and this is always accomplished through force. If one sector of the economy is stimulated, then it is always at the expense of another. This principle is often expertly concealed by examining very narrowly the effects of policies and

[47] Mosiah 18:28 (emphasis added)

legislation. The effects are often observed in too narrow a period of time or too narrowly focused on a specific group of people. The true and total impact of legislation is seldom fully analyzed. This principle is excellently illustrated by Henry Hazlitt in his work, *Economics in One Lesson* and further expanded in Thomas Sowell's *Applied Economics: Thinking Beyond Stage One*.

The reader is invited to consider a scenario. Two people, A and B, are walking down the street and happen upon X who is in need of money for whatever reason. If A produces some money and hands it to X, then a charitable service has been performed. If B then produces some money and hands it to X, then another charitable service has been performed. This is the spirit in which Jesus Christ has commanded us to care for the poor and needy, with our own substance and by our own choice.

Now consider if A first takes money from B, either forcefully or without B's knowledge, and then hands it to X. Has a charity been performed? X benefits the same as before, but A has committed a crime and violated B's right to private property. And, although it is B's money that ultimately benefits X, is this counted to B as charity? Likely not.

Finally, consider if A and B see X's need and decide to pool their money together to help. But they also notice well-to-do C walking the other way down the street and decide that C can also afford to help. So, A and B force money from C and give all of it to X. Again, X benefits the same. A and B have used their own money, which is laudable, but also forced additional money from C, which is a crime. And the money forced from C is not counted to C as charity.

The reader is now invited to consider which of these scenarios most closely resembles government social programs, and the impact that each scenario has on agency, freedom, and Natural Rights. Elder Howard W. Hunter of the Quorum of the Twelve Apostles delivered a BYU Devotional address in 1966 that largely dealt with this subject. In it, he states:

> The government will take from the "haves" and give to the "have nots." Both have lost their freedom. Those who "have," lost their freedom to give voluntarily of their own free will and in the way they desire. Those who "have not," lost their freedom because they did not earn what they received. They got "something for nothing" and they will neither appreciate the gift nor the giver of the gift.[48]

Very similar to the principle that Elder Hunter teaches above, J. Reuben Clark, taught the following:

---

[48] Howard W. Hunter, *The Law of the Harvest*, March 8, 1966

> There is an infinity of difference between the sack of flour that comes over the back fence from your next door neighbor and a sack that is sent to you from Washington. The one hallows the giver, and raises and enspirits, with the human love and sympathy behind it, him who thankfully eats it. The other debauches the hand which doles out that which is not his, and embitters and enslaves him who with maledictions devours it.[49]

Late in the nineteenth century, a Yale Philosopher by the name of William Graham Sumner wrote an essay titled *The Forgotten Man* that describes a scenario very similar to the ones above. The object of his essay was the nature of government social programs. In it he wrote: "As soon as A observes something which seems to him to be wrong, from which X is suffering, A talks it over with B, and A and B then propose to get a law passed to remedy the evil and help X. Their law always proposes to determine ... what A, B, and C shall do for X." Amity Shlaes follows this up with, "But what about C? There was nothing wrong with A and B helping X. What was wrong was the law, and the indenturing of C to the cause. C was the forgotten man, the man who paid."[50] The flaws in these types of policies are easily overlooked as corresponding commentary and analysis tend to focus most of the attention on the benefit received by X and some little mention of A and B who sponsor the legislation. C is almost always left out of the conversation, he is forgotten. Amity Shlaes wrote a fantastic historical work documenting the effects of such laws and programs on C, and titled it *The Forgotten Man*.[51]

To give of one's own substance for those in need is divine and holy and in line with the spirit of the teachings of the Savior, Jesus Christ. To forcefully take the possessions of another, whatever the intended cause to do so, is evil and of the devil. It has been shown previously that the right and control of private property is one of the key aspects of true liberty. Property rightfully belongs to the individual who earns or produces it, it does not belong to the entire collective of society.

To deprive individuals of their private property merely because it is deemed by society that they can afford it or that they already have enough is out of step with the teachings of Jesus Christ and is certainly "more or less"[52] than the civil government established by the U.S. Constitution.

---

[49] Jerreld L. Newquist, *Prophets, Principles and National Survival*, 1964, pp. 387-388

[50] Amity Shlaes, *The Forgotten Man*, 2007, p. 12

[51] Amity Shlaes, *The Forgotten Man*, 2007

[52] D&C 98:7

Chapter 5 treated in great detail the concept of Natural Rights, including the right to property. Recall that it is a usurped government power to unduly deprive a citizen of his private property. It is often easy to advocate for the government to remedy the ills of others while remaining removed from the situation ourselves and not realizing, or not caring, that to do so, the government must take the resources of those that have them. It is important to realize that in doing so, while we are not ourselves depriving another of his property, we are advocating for the government to do it in our stead and we cannot then remain wholly unsullied by this action of taking the property of another without their consent.

This is the way the Founders understood redistributive government policies and so advocated for private property as a Natural Right granted by God. James Madison, addressing the Virginia House of Representatives, said that "charity is no part of the legislative duty of the government."[53] Madison understood that government is incapable of charity because it must first take from one before it can give to another.

Thomas Jefferson gave one definition of tyranny as follows, "To compel a man to furnish contributions of money for the propagation of ideas he disbelieves and abhors, is sinful and tyrannical."[54] Jefferson further reinforces that property should remain under the control of its owner so that each individual has the freedom to decide how their resources will be used to accomplish the ends that they themselves believe in.

Alexander Hamilton warned of another serious threat to freedom when the government is allowed to provide for its citizens. In *The Federalist*, he wrote, "In the general course of human nature, a power over a man's subsistence amounts to a power over his will."[55] The more power a government accumulates over the subsistence of a man, the more control that government can exercise over the man's will and behavior.

Jesus Christ taught that individuals should freely decide to part with their own resources and substance for the benefit of others. This is charity. To compel an individual, through force or theft, to furnish funds, money, or resources for the benefit of another is more akin to Satan's plan than to the one proposed by our Father and His Christ.

As mentioned above, James Madison, considered the father of the Constitution, stated that "charity is no part of the legislative duty of the

---

[53] Jonathan Elliot, *The Debates in the Several State Conventions*, 1888, p. 431

[54] Thomas Jefferson, Virginia Statute for Religious Freedom, 1779, Virginia State Legislature, Bill 82

[55] Alexander Hamilton, *The Federalist*, 1787-1788, No. 79

government"[56] because government is incapable of charity as it only has what it takes from others. Latter-day Saints, and all Christians, should be careful to factor this into their considerations of government programs and policies.

Brethren Not Saying These Things

Many Latter-day Saints are wondering why, if this topic is so critical and essential, aren't the general leaders and authorities of the Church speaking of it in General Conference and other official Church forums.

The short answer to this question is that it's difficult to know. The long answer necessitates a little up front clarification. First and foremost, nothing in this book should be taken to be critical or contradictory to what the leaders of the Church teach. Nothing herein is claimed to be new information or new revelation that hasn't yet been taught over the years by Prophets and the Apostles. The aim of this writing is to assemble together teachings from ancient scripture and modern revelation to make a specific argument that is not considered contrary to existing doctrine or teachings of the Church, but rather as presenting multiple facets of existing Church doctrine and teachings in a way that will hopefully bring a unique focus and perspective to a particular subject matter consisting of existing Gospel principles.

In the April, 2015 General Conference of the Church, Elder Dallin H. Oaks opened his address with the following statement:

> Subjects for general conference talks are assigned—not by mortal authority but by the impressions of the Spirit. Many subjects would address the mortal concerns we all share. But just as Jesus did not teach how to overcome the mortal challenges or political oppression of His day, He usually inspires His modern servants to speak about what we must do to reform our personal lives to prepare us to return to our heavenly home.[57]

It is the opinion and testimony of the author that the General Authorities of The Church of Jesus Christ of Latter-day Saints are called and inspired by God to do His work on the earth. He is inspiring them on the subjects that they teach and preach through General Conference and other Church forums. His ways are not man's ways and so it will not be presumed to know the mind of God regarding which topics He chooses for His Children to hear and when He chooses for them to hear them.

---

[56] Jonathan Elliot, *The Debates in the Several State Conventions*, 1888, p. 431

[57] Dallin H. Oaks, *The Parable of the Sower*, General Conference, April-2015

All that being said, that it is not a commonly recurring topic of discussion during Conferences and other speeches given by leaders now does not detract from the teachings and messages already given in the past on this subject. As has been seen extensively throughout the present work, Prophets, Apostles, and other leaders and authorities have spoken much on these matters and continue to do so today. It is not a subject that is treated as prominently nor as much as the more spiritual topics that are central to the Gospel of Jesus Christ, but that is to be expected from servants of the Lord who are called to preach His Atonement, His Resurrection, and the way back to Heaven through Him.

Moreover, God has not retracted nor withdrawn the things that He has spoken on these matters: that He justifies constitutional government and nothing "more or less" than it; that He established the Constitution; and that He raised up the Founders for the work that they did and that they were wise.

In 1992, Elder Dallin H. Oaks gave an address to the Brigham Young University Management Society. In that address, he stated that "[a]s a matter of prudence, our church has confined its own political participation within a far smaller range than is required by the law or the Constitution."[58] He does not elaborate on all that prudence entails, but it does appear evident from this statement that the Church leaders have made conscious decisions to limit what they say regarding matters of government and law.

Perhaps one reason for this is that it would put the Church's tax-exempt status under U.S. tax law in jeopardy. If the Church were to have their tax-exempt status revoked, it would impact the finances of the Church and all of its members.

The IRS website summarizes the restrictions on charitable organizations as follows:

> Under the Internal Revenue Code, all section 501(c)(3) organizations are absolutely prohibited from directly or indirectly participating in, or intervening in, any political campaign on behalf of (or in opposition to) any candidate for elective public office. Contributions to political campaign funds or public statements of position (verbal or written) made on behalf of the organization in favor of or in opposition to any candidate for public office clearly violate the prohibition against political campaign activity. Violating this prohibition may result in denial or revocation of tax-exempt status and the imposition of certain excise taxes.[59]

---

[58] Ralph C. Hancock, *Just and Holy Principles*, 1998, p. 154

[59] www.irs.gov

The language to add these restrictions to tax-exempt organizations was introduced into the U.S. tax code in 1954. It's hard to say definitively how much of an influence, if any, this and other similar regulations have on Church leaders' decisions regarding how much to speak out on matters of government. It does seem as though it at least must play some role in it. There seem to be a lot more statements before 1954 regarding this subject than there have been since. But, this is not data that has been quantified and this is admittedly mere speculation on the part of the author.

Church leaders, Elder Dallin H. Oaks being especially prominent among them, have spoken out on a number of occasions on the deterioration of religious freedoms provided for under the U.S. Constitution. In a 2011 speech he delivered to an audience at Chapman University, Elder Oaks said:

> Notwithstanding its special place in our Constitution, a number of trends are eroding both the protections the free exercise clause was intended to provide and the public esteem this fundamental value has had during most of our history. For some time we have been experiencing laws and official actions that impinge on religious freedom.[60]

Elder Oaks is certainly of the opinion that religious freedom is under attack. On another occasion, at Utah Valley University, he said, "I am one of the many religious persons who have decried the alarming trajectory of theories, court decisions and executive actions that are diminishing the free exercise of religion."[61]

The free exercise of religion and church organizations have fallen under increasingly restrictive regulations over the past century. When Elder Oaks refers to these increasing restrictions, he *may* be including the Church's ability to speak out on political matters or those pertaining to government without fear of a corresponding retribution. This is highly speculative, admittedly, but a plausible possibility nonetheless.

The more pertinent point, however, is that the simple fact that this subject is not one of the more common ones addressed by Church leaders today does not make these things untrue or the subject unimportant. The truth is that this subject has been treated throughout the Church's history by its leaders and continues to be addressed today. The treatment of this subject seems to have been more frequent in the past than it is now, but that does not detract from its importance. The key thing to note is that when the subject is treated, whether

---

60 Dallin H. Oaks, *Preserving Religious Freedom*, February 4, 2011

61 Dallin H. Oaks, *Hope for the Years Ahead*, April 16, 2014

past or present, the position of the Church and its leaders is consistent. The Latter-day Saint religion most assuredly teaches that man's liberty is of eternal significance, so much so that God has intervened in world events to protect it, He did so through the establishment of the U.S. Constitution, and He expects His people to understand and uphold it.

Chapter 8 – Summary Argument and Conclusions

This book is intended to be informative and educational, but it is also intended as a logical presentation of an argument. The information and evidence presented throughout this book is organized in a specific way in order to layout this logical argument. This chapter will summarize the argument that has been presented throughout the present work so it can be digested in a more concise manner.

Summary Argument

Below is the central argument made throughout this book.

1. God established agency as an essential eternal principle and gave it to man.
2. Liberty is the temporal extension of agency, it is the ability to exercise one's agency and is also granted unto man by God.
3. God foreordained and prepared the American Founders and instructed them in the principles of agency and liberty.
4. God, through the Founders, established the U.S. Constitution for the protection of man's liberty and his ability to exercise his agency.
5. God called the Founders wise and approved of and justified their work.
6. Latter-day Saints have all of this revealed to them by God and so have a unique responsibility to understand and uphold the U.S. Constitution.

Agency is a key and fundamental principle of eternity. God's teachings and behavior regarding agency in the pre-mortal existence firmly establish it as essential to His plan for His children. God gave agency to man and has decreed that it will never be taken from him. Agency is the principal issue over which the War in Heaven was fought. To be on the wrong side in that conflict, to rebel against the principle of agency, meant expulsion from God's presence forever with no means of ever returning. The Sons of Perdition are identified as such because they sought to exercise power and control over others at the expense of the agency of those they wished to control.

Liberty is a temporal extension of that supernal principle of agency. Liberty is the ability to exercise one's agency. While agency is innate in every man and cannot be taken from him, liberty can be taken by other men, but to do so is to restrict another in the full exercise of his agency and is an offense to God. Depriving another of his liberty is to exercise a power and control over that individual very similar to the power and control desired by Lucifer and his followers, which resulted in their expulsion from Heaven forever. Liberty is a Natural Right that each and every individual enters this life already possessing. Every man and woman has equal claim to this right to liberty.

The Founding Fathers of the United States of America were called and foreordained in the pre-mortal existence to perform an important work here on the earth. Their preparation consisted of instruction at the hand of the Almighty in the just and holy principles of eternity, including those of agency and liberty. They understood that God had created man with certain rights, including life, liberty, and property, and they constructed the American institutions of government on the foundation of these principles and rights. They were wise, intelligent, well educated, spiritual, religious, honest, and moral men. They comprehended eternal gospel principles before the gospel had been restored, and they saw many of the fallacies in the religious sects of their era. God referred to them as wise and gave His personal stamp of approval on the works that they produced.

God, through the Founders, established the United States Constitution. He did so for the explicitly stated purpose of protecting man's freedom to exercise his moral agency. He established it on just and holy principles, including agency and liberty. He did so by instructing the Founders in these principles and then prompting and guiding them through the process of founding the nation and its Constitution. God directed that the U.S. Constitution should be maintained. He declared that civil law based on the U.S. Constitution, as produced by the Founders, is justifiable before Him. He justifies man in befriending and upholding that same constitutional law. With respect to civil law, or law instituted by men among men, God has stated that anything more or less than the U.S. Constitution comes from evil. He has not rescinded, recanted, or further qualified any of these statements or declarations that He made. In fact, He revealed to Joseph Smith a prayer that included a supplication to God for the establishment of U.S. constitutional principles forever. The U.S. Constitution is the only form of government on the earth today that carries with it a personal justification by God Almighty.

Each of these points are substantially supported by revelation and scripture as demonstrated throughout this entire work. Latter-day Saints, therefore, are both uniquely qualified and uniquely duty bound to understand and support the U.S. Constitution and the just and holy principles on which it is based. Latter-day Saints have a similarly unique responsibility to understand who the Founders were and what they taught, especially regarding civil government and the principles on which they based America's government. In matters of the Gospel and spirituality, God has ever instructed his prophets and apostles so that they could, in turn, teach mankind. In matters of civil government and the principles on which it is justly based, God called and instructed the American Founders so that they could, in turn, teach those principles to mankind and establish a government based on them. The Founders of the United States of America are God's apostles of civil government and constitutional law.

Moroni's Warning

In the eighth chapter of the book of Ether there is a story about a man named Jared who enslaves his father, Omer. This Jared is not to be confused with the earlier Jared who crossed the ocean from the old world to the new and for whom the Jaredites as a people are named. This Jared is a wicked man who desired power and used force and secret combinations to gain it, as will be shown here below.

While Omer was king, Jared attacked and enslaved him to take the kingship for himself. Jared kept his father, Omer, in captivity for many years until Jared's brothers were finally upset with him enough to take action. They gathered together their military might, overthrew Jared, and liberated their father, Omer.

Seeing her father's distress over losing the kingship, Jared's beautiful daughter proposes a plan to dance in front of a man named Akish to entice him to desire her as a wife. The plan is executed and works. When Akish asks for Jared's daughter to wife, Jared says, "I will give her unto you, if ye will bring unto me the head of my father, the king."[1]

Akish agrees and gathers a group of people together to swear their fealty to him and his plan. The swearing of allegiance to a clandestine group for the execution of covert plans for the benefit of that group, or its members, at the expense of others and their rights is what The Book of Mormon refers to as secret combinations. These are the secret combinations that ultimately destroyed the Jaredites. Moroni says of them, "And it came to pass that they formed a secret combination, even as they of old; which combination is most abominable and wicked above all, in the sight of God."[2] A little further down in the chapter, Moroni also states that "whatsoever nation shall uphold such secret combinations, to get power and gain, until they shall spread over the nation, behold, they shall be destroyed."[3]

---

[1] Ether 8:12
[2] Ether 8:18
[3] Ether 8:22

"Secret combination" is a term used many times throughout The Book of Mormon in varying forms. They are characterized by groups who work in the dark, or in secret, to obtain power, influence, wealth, and gain. Moroni writes the following description of them while telling this story of Jared and Akish and their secret combination:

> And they were kept up by the power of the devil to administer these oaths unto the people, to keep them in darkness, to help such as sought power to gain power, and to murder, and to plunder, and to lie, and to commit all manner of wickedness and whoredoms.[4]

One characteristic of secret combinations that is commonly noted is that of committing murder. Though it is a mistake to think that a secret combination is not had without the murder component. Note the entire list in the above scripture that includes seeking power, plunder, lying, whoredoms, and "all manner of wickedness." The evil in secret combinations is that they are people working in secret to do evil and get gain, murder is only one form of the evil they commit. If an organization, society, or group of people is found to be participating in all of the above listed evils except for murder, then they are a secret combination as defined by Moroni. Furthermore, that group can be reasonably expected to eventually add murder to their list of perpetuated evils in order to maintain their power, influence, wealth, status, or whatever they have gained through the commission of the other evils in the list.

One other notable characteristic of secret combinations is that every time they are mentioned in the scriptures, they refer to a group of people that are either already operating within a government or are working to take control of a government through subversion or force. But they are always in and around governments and the power and influence they seek always has some relation to government. They are not mentioned for seeking wealth in conjunction with industry or enterprise, but by inserting their members into government positions and setting themselves up as rulers over others. This is not to say that evil cannot be committed in the name of industry or enterprise, but the pattern described throughout The Book of Mormon suggests that the principal goal of secret combinations is to seek power as the rule makers and to gain and preserve their wealth and status through manipulating and bending law and regulation to their own advantage, or through placing themselves and their operatives in positions of power in order to exercise control over the law, to whom the law applies, and for whom the law looks the other way.

---

[4] Ether 8:16 (see also: 2 Nephi 10:15, 26:22, 28:9; Helaman 2:8; 3 Nephi 3:9; Mormon 8:27; Ether 11:22; Moses 6:15)

What makes this story so extremely interesting is that after Moroni describes the formation of this secret combination and describes the wickedness of the same, he then breaks in his narrative and interrupts it to speak directly to the Gentiles who would one day become the recipients of the record being kept. He says:

> Wherefore, ***O ye Gentiles***, it is wisdom in God that these things should be shown unto you, that thereby ye may repent of your sins, and suffer not that these murderous combinations shall get above you, which are built up to get power and gain—and the work, yea, even the work of destruction come upon you, yea, even the sword of the justice of the Eternal God shall fall upon you, to your overthrow and destruction if ye shall suffer these things to be.
>
> Wherefore, the Lord commandeth you, when ye shall see these things come among you that ye shall awake to a sense of your awful situation, because of this secret combination which shall be among you; or wo be unto it, because of the blood of them who have been slain; for they cry from the dust for vengeance upon it, and also upon those who built it up.
>
> For it cometh to pass that whoso buildeth it up seeketh to overthrow the freedom of all lands, nations, and countries; and it bringeth to pass the destruction of all people, for it is built up by the devil, who is the father of all lies; even that same liar who beguiled our first parents, yea, even that same liar who hath caused man to commit murder from the beginning; who hath hardened the hearts of men that they have murdered the prophets, and stoned them, and cast them out from the beginning.
>
> Wherefore, I, Moroni, am commanded to write these things that evil may be done away, and that the time may come that Satan may have no power upon the hearts of the children of men, but that they may be persuaded to do good continually, that they may come unto the fountain of all righteousness and be saved.[5]

This passage of scripture is extremely important. First, it is directed explicitly to "ye Gentiles." The Gentiles referred to here could possibly mean all Gentiles throughout the world. But, it seems more likely that Moroni is referring to a more specific group of Gentiles, those that would be the initial recipients of The Book of Mormon record and then carry it out to the rest of the world. Throughout The Book of Mormon, references are made to Gentiles in varying contexts. For example, in the thirteenth chapter of the First Book of Nephi,

[5] Ether 8:23-26 (emphasis added)

references are clearly made to two distinct groups of Gentiles, those that "went forth out of captivity"[6] to colonize America and their "mother Gentiles"[7] who gathered together to battle against them. Note that the unqualified reference is used for the American colonizers and a separate group is qualified in relation to those colonizers, suggesting that the American colonizers were the primary group in Nephi's mind.

Later in the same book (1 Nephi), numerous references are made to the Gentiles that will receive the fullness of the Gospel[8], be established as a mighty nation[9] and as a standard[10], scatter the descendants of Lehi[11], and then bring the Gospel to the descendants of Lehi.[12] These references are clearly not being made to all the Gentiles across the world but to those in America that would receive the Gospel and then preach it to the rest of the world, including to the descendants of Lehi. The authors of The Book of Mormon, and especially Mormon and Moroni, seem at times to reference or directly address a specific group of Gentiles, and that group always seems to be those who would initially receive The Book of Mormon and then take it to the rest of the world. This is the group of Gentiles who seem at times throughout The Book of Mormon record to be addressed personally, and that appears to be the case in the quoted verses above.

Further evidence of this is given earlier in the book of Ether where Moroni, just like he does in the passage above, addresses "ye Gentiles." He is describing the covenant that is upon this land of promise that any people keeping the commandments of God will be blessed and prospered, but those who do not, will ultimately be destroyed and removed from the land. Verses 10-11 read:

> For behold, this is a land which is choice above all other lands; wherefore he that doth possess it shall serve God or shall be swept off; for it is the everlasting decree of God. And it is not until the fulness of iniquity among the children of the land, that they are swept off.
>
> And this cometh unto you, ***O ye Gentiles***, that ye may know the decrees of God—that ye may repent, and not continue in your iniquities until the fulness come, that ye may not bring down the

6 1 Nephi 13:16
7 1 Nephi 13:17
8 1 Nephi 13:34-36
9 1 Nephi 13:15,30; 22:7
10 1 Nephi 21:22; 22:6
11 1 Nephi 13:14; 22:7
12 1 Nephi 13:38-39; 15:13; 22:8

> fulness of the wrath of God upon you as the inhabitants of the land have hitherto done.[13]

This reference to "ye Gentiles" is clearly and obviously intended to only apply to Gentiles that are living within the covenant land of promise. As was demonstrated in chapter 6, this area must at a minimum include the present day geographic United States of America and wherever the events of The Book of Mormon took place.

Not only is Moroni addressing a specific audience, but he is addressing an audience that he has seen in vision and whose works he knows. In another part of the record, Moroni speaks of the time "when these things shall come forth among you"[14] and says, "Behold, I speak unto you as if ye were present, and yet ye are not. But behold, Jesus Christ hath shown you unto me, and I know your doing."[15]

Moroni, who has seen the present time and knows the doings of the recipients of The Book of Mormon, interrupts his narrative to directly address the specific group of Gentiles that will receive The Book of Mormon and then says that "it is wisdom in God that these things should be shown unto you, that thereby ye may repent of your sins, and suffer not that these murderous combinations shall get above you , which are built up to get power and gain."

This is a clear warning from Moroni to a specific group of Gentiles to be on guard against these same secret combinations that he was describing as being had among the Jaredites. Moroni does not warn merely of the risk, but appears instead to be calling his target audience to repentance for the things he has already observed among them, as he goes on to declare that "the Lord commandeth you, when ye shall see these things come among you that ye shall awake to a sense of your awful situation."

Finally, Moroni also warns "that whoso buildeth it up seeketh to overthrow the freedom of all lands, nations, and countries." This last statement is notable for two reasons. First, note that the secret combinations, which are "most abominable and wicked above all, in the sight of God" have as their primary objective the overthrow of freedom. This reinforces the argument made throughout this entire book, that God sanctions freedom as important and righteous and that those that seek to overthrow it are "most abominable and wicked" in His sight. Next, note that the threat of the loss of freedom is to "all lands, nations, and countries." This could mean one of two things, either there is

---

[13] Ether 2:10-11 (emphasis added)
[14] Mormon 8:34
[15] Mormon 8:35

one particular secret combination or society that is very large and threatening the entire world or there are many different secret groups, not necessarily working together but ultimately all authored by the devil and all seeking the same end of power at the expense of others' freedom. Regardless of whether the threat is from a single large group or many disparate groups, the clear important message from Moroni here is that the threat is everywhere and so a constant guard is necessary to protect against it.

One interpretation of Moroni's warning in these verses is that it is referring to the spread of Soviet Communism that occurred through much of the twentieth century. Elder Ezra Taft Benson specifically identified it this way in a devotional address given at Brigham Young University in May of 1968.[16] Many of the teachings and quotes given throughout this book by leaders of the Church were originally spoken or written around the middle third of the twentieth century while Communism was rapidly spreading throughout the world. Interestingly, Church leaders were resolutely warning against the philosophies of Communism during a time when it was still largely viewed in a positive light in the United States during the 1920s and 30s. Communism later became much more widely criticized around the close of World War II and the subsequent onset of the Cold War. The Church and many of its leaders were outspoken and direct on matters relating to Communism during this time. For example, The First Presidency of the Church, in 1936, published *A Warning to Church Members* in the *Improvement Era* magazine. In the published warning, the below points are made (quoted directly from the text). The full text of the Warning to Church Members is included as an appendix at the end of this book.

1. Communism ... is a system of government that is the opposite of our Constitutional government
2. to support Communism is treasonable to our free institutions
3. no patriotic American citizen may become either a Communist or supporter of Communism
4. Communism is not the United Order, and bears only the most superficial resemblance thereto
5. Communism is based upon intolerance and force, the United Order upon love and freedom of conscience
6. no loyal American citizen and no faithful Church member can be a Communist
7. We call upon all Church members completely to eschew Communism

[16] Ezra Taft Benson, *The Book of Mormon Warns America*, BYU, May-1968

8. The safety of our divinely inspired Constitutional government and the welfare of our Church imperatively demand that Communism shall have no place in America[17]

Similarly, in the April, 1966 General Conference of the Church an official statement was read by President David O. McKay during the Priesthood session of that Conference. Below are listed several key points from that statement. The entire text of the statement can be found in an appendix at the end of this book.

1. The position of this Church on the subject of Communism has never changed
2. We consider it the greatest satanical threat to peace, prosperity, and the spread of God's work among men that exists on the face of the earth
3. We therefore commend and encourage every person and every group who is sincerely seeking to study Constitutional principles and awaken a sleeping and apathetic people to the alarming conditions that are rapidly advancing about us
4. We wish all of our citizens throughout the land were participating in some type of organized self-education in order that they could better appreciate what is happening and know what they can do about it
5. The entire concept and philosophy of Communism is diametrically opposed to everything for which the Church stands
6. Communism debases the individual and makes him the enslaved tool of the state
7. Communism destroys man's God-given free agency
8. No member of this Church can be true to his faith ... while lending aid, encouragement, or sympathy to any of these false philosophies; for if he does, they will prove snares to his feet[18]

The official Church position on Communism is quite clear from these and other statements and declarations made by its leaders. It is a mistake, however, to suppose that these teachings are only applicable to Soviet Communism and that the threat of Communism and similar ideologies died with the dissolution of the Soviet Union. The ideology of Communism is still very much alive in the world today and many still exist that desire to see it become the principal governing

[17] The First Presidency of The Church of Jesus Christ of Latter-day Saints, *A Warning to Church members*, 1936 (numbered list added)

[18] David O. McKay, *Statement Concerning the Position of the Church on Communism*, General Conference, April-1966 (numbered list added)

philosophy of America or even the entire globe. Unfortunately, some of these people are Americans. It is naïve to assume that America, its people, and its government institutions, are completely insulated from this school of thought by mere virtue of being American. Furthermore, many similar, more benign sounding ideologies exist that borrow concepts, ideas, and principle from Communism and Socialism. Recall how Progressivism in America, as described in chapter 7, grew out of the philosophies of Communism and Socialism. Progressivism remains an influential ideology in American government today.

Item number 7 in *A Warning to Church Members* above calls on all members to *completely* eschew Communism. In order to completely eschew communism, it is not enough to be comfortable in the demise of the Soviet Union. An understanding of the principles underlying the Communist form of government is required and a total rejection of those principles then necessary. The particular principles on which Communism is based that drew such forceful criticism from the Lord's servants are listed below.

1. A government system opposite to Constitutional government
2. A government system based on force as opposed to freedom
3. A government system that opposes what the Church and Gospel stand for
4. A government system that debases the individual and enslaves him to the state
5. A government system that restricts man in his exercise of agency

In addition to these principles above, an investigation into the implementation of Communist governments would be instructive in just how the use of force was applied to debase the individual and exalt the state. Such an investigation is outside the scope of the present work, but one fundamental difference between government under the U.S. Constitution and that of Communist regimes needs to be noted and that difference is in respect to the treatment of property.

It has been shown extensively throughout this book that property under the U.S. Constitution is to be considered a sacred and Natural Right from God and is not to be violated. The Socialist and Communist concept of property is one of communal ownership or appropriation. Under collectivist governments (Socialist and Communist), certain properties (particularly those considered means of production and subsistence) are considered to be state property or, in more mild forms, under the jurisdiction of the state and subject to re-appropriation if a greater need can be met with it as determined by the government.

The level to which governments respect or violate property rights is not necessarily measured in absolute degrees. In other words, there are not only two forms of government, one form that completely respects private property rights and another that does not. Instead, it is a continuum along which an infinite number of levels of respect can be observed. The reader is invited to reflect on how much present day America respects the individual's right to private property, and to also compare that to what the Founders thought and taught regarding that property. There is much discussion in present day America regarding the proper distribution and use of wealth, giving rise to programs calculated at redistributing that wealth. The arguments advocating for these measures justify redistribution by the state because some individuals have enough, or can afford it, and the government can make use of it for the benefit of the public. Is this manner of thinking regarding property closer to the principles taught and advocated by the Founders or the ideals of Socialism and Communism? Perhaps more importantly, towards which end of the spectrum is the trend advancing? These questions are left to the reader to consider, but it is hoped that the reader is now much better equipped to address these and similar questions.

Another way to view Moroni's warning is less as a single organization or group that seeks to overthrow freedom across the entire world and more as a common philosophy or ideology held by disparate groups. This is more likely as it more closely reflects the world today. The Soviet Union collapsed in the 1980s and so the world lost the most powerful purveyor of Communism it had ever seen. The only trouble is that during its time in power, the U.S.S.R. sowed numerous seeds of their ideology and those seeds continue to germinate and bear fruit today.

Many of the ideas and philosophies of collectivist ideologies like Communism continue to thrive in the world today. They are known by varying labels and are promulgated by different groups in different societies and cultures. Many have been successfully disassociated from Communism and are now gaining in popularity under new and more attractive sounding names. American Progressivism is an example of such. It is a mistake to assume that an idea is in no way associated with Socialism or Communism merely because it lacks one of those labels. It is imperative to correctly and thoroughly understand the principles on which Socialism and Communism are based, how they differ from U.S. constitutional principles, and judge policies, laws, and programs on those principles and not on mere labels alone.

The overall trend in the present world, alarmingly, is largely in one direction: toward more government control, more government influence, more of government absorbing the consequences of the decisions of its citizens and spreading the risk and consequences of those decisions across all of society. The principles adhered to and advocated by the Founding Fathers of America are on the retreat.

It is Given unto you to Judge

In the Second Book of Nephi in The Book of Mormon, Lehi teaches that "it must needs be, that there is an opposition in all things."[19] Satan is the opposition to Jesus Christ. Where Jesus loves and leads to salvation, Satan hates and works to lead astray of that salvation.

It was demonstrated in great detail in chapters 1 through 3 that it is God and Jesus Christ that are the source of agency, liberty, the nation of America, and the U.S. Constitution. It is God and Jesus Christ that called and prepared the Founding Fathers for the work they were to perform. It follows then that what the Founders understood and advocated regarding liberty is what they learned at the hand of the Almighty, and that their teachings on liberty are in line with the teachings of God and Jesus Christ on that subject. It was a revelation from Jesus Christ that declared the Founders as "wise men."[20] And it was with God's allowance that those men were permitted to cross back from the next life to request their temple work be performed.

It follows logically then that Satan will oppose all of these things. It has already been seen that Satan opposed agency in the premortal existence. There is no reason to believe that he doesn't persist in that effort today. As Elder D. Todd Christofferson has taught, "Satan has not ceased his effort 'to destroy the agency of man.'"[21] One effective way to oppose agency is to oppose liberty as well and work to limit or eliminate liberty wherever he can. If Jesus Christ is the source of the Constitution, then it stands to reason that Satan opposes it. And finally, if God and Jesus are behind raising the Founders for their work, then it is expected that Satan will be found opposing the Founders and working against them wherever he can.

In the seventh chapter of the Book of Moroni, Moroni teaches: "For behold, my brethren, it is given unto you to judge, that ye may know good from evil; and the way to judge is as plain, that ye may know with a perfect knowledge, as the daylight is from the dark night."[22]

Moroni declared that it is as easy to distinguish good from evil as it is to know the day from the night. After making the declaration, he gives us the formula to do so:

---

[19] 2 Nephi 2:11
[20] D&C 101:80
[21] D. Todd Christofferson, *Moral Agency*, BYU, January-2006
[22] Moroni 7:15

> For behold, the Spirit of Christ is given to every man, that he may know good from evil; wherefore, I show unto you the way to judge; for every thing which inviteth to do good, and to persuade to believe in Christ, is sent forth by the power and gift of Christ; wherefore ye may know with a perfect knowledge it is of God.
>
> But whatsoever thing persuadeth men to do evil, and believe not in Christ, and deny him, and serve not God, then ye may know with a perfect knowledge it is of the devil; for after this manner doth the devil work, for he persuadeth no man to do good, no, not one; neither do his angels; neither do they who subject themselves unto him.[23]

If Jesus Christ is the author of man's agency, then efforts to limit the exercise of that agency, or to revoke or restrict liberty must arise from Satan. If Jesus Christ is the one that established the U.S. Constitution as part of His work, and to protect man's freedom to exercise his agency, then it follows that efforts to subvert or undermine that Constitution or the American form of government that it defines are efforts led by Satan. And if Jesus Christ is the one who raised up those wise men to author the Constitution, then it is Satan who seeks to demean their character, despoil their reputations, undermine their philosophies, and diminish their influence.

In a speech delivered at Brigham Young University in 1957, Elder Marion G. Romney of the Quorum of the Twelve Apostles, said:

> One of the fundamental doctrines of the revealed truth is that, in the Garden of Eden, God endowed men with free agency. The preservation of this free agency is more important than the preservation of life itself ... everything which militates against man's enjoyment of this endowment persuades not to believe in Christ, for Christ is the author of free agency.
>
> Now the world today in which we live is in the throes of a great social and political revolution. In almost every department of our society laws and practices are being daily proposed and adopted which greatly alter the course of our lives. Indeed, some of them are literally shaking the foundations of our political and social institutions. If you would know truth from error in this bitterly contested arena, apply Mormon's test to these innovations. Do they facilitate or restrict the exercise of man's divine endowment of free agency? Tested by this standard, most of them will fall quickly into their proper category as between good and evil.[24]

---

[23] Moroni 7:16-17

[24] Marion G. Romney, *Your Quest for Truth*, BYU, May-1957

It has been pointed out in several places of the present work that the exercise of government always carries with it a consideration of force versus freedom and that just government can only act with delegated authority from its citizens. For these reasons, the application of government force always carries with it a moral consideration and must be executed with extreme caution and care. Latter-day Saints, more than any other people, have been given the tools to know right from wrong with respect to civil law and governments. Latter-day Saints know better than any other people the source of man's freedom and the divine hand behind the Founding of America and the U.S. Constitution. Latter-day Saints, of all people, know exactly who the Founders of this great nation are. We know these things because we possess direct revelation from God declaring them. The question that now needs to be asked is what are we doing with that knowledge?

In the October, 1987 General Conference of the Church, President Ezra Taft Benson stated that "we must learn the principles of the Constitution in the tradition of the Founding Fathers."[25] He then followed that statement with:

> Have we read *The Federalist* papers? Are we reading the Constitution and pondering it? Are we aware of its principles? Are we abiding by these principles and teaching them to others? Could we defend the Constitution? Can we recognize when a law is constitutionally unsound? Do we know what the prophets have said about the Constitution and the threats to it?
>
> As Jefferson said, "If a nation expects to be ignorant and free ... it expects what never was and never will be" (Letter to Colonel Charles Yancey, 6 Jan. 1816).[26]

After Mormon dies, his son, Moroni, takes upon himself the task of completing The Book of Mormon record. Moroni begins his portion of the book by describing detailed elements of the record itself. In one part early in his writings, Moroni suggests that one benefit that the Gentiles in the last days could gain from The Book of Mormon is "that ye may learn to be more wise than we have been."[27]

Have we been and are we being more wise than the Nephites were? No doubt Moroni was referring in large part to the Nephites failing or refusing to live the spiritual law of the gospel that had been revealed to them. But, ample evidence in The Book of Mormon record suggests that part of their wickedness and lack of wisdom was also in their allowance of secret combinations and corrupt

---

[25] Ezra Taft Benson, *Our Divine Constitution*, General Conference, October-1987

[26] Ibid.

[27] Mormon 9:31

government, in not living up to the civil law that also had been given to them by God, and in not appropriately maintaining and defending their rights, their privileges, and their liberty.

Latter-day Saints cannot fall into the same traps today as the Nephites did of old. We need to be more wise than they were. We need to understand what God has revealed to us regarding liberty and civil government and work to maintain and uphold true principles of freedom and the government institutions that were originally based on those principles. True liberty and freedom can only be secured with a free and just government firmly rooted in the Constitution of the United States. No other form of government will do for Latter-day Saints until another is revealed by God.

Appendix I. LDS Canon

The volumes of scripture that together comprise the Latter-day Saint canon, or "standard works" as named by Latter-day Saints, are listed below so the reader might know where to find scripture references used throughout this book.

King James Bible

Old Testament

Genesis
Exodus
Leviticus
Numbers
Deuteronomy
Joshua
Judges
Ruth
1 Samuel
2 Samuel
1 Kings
2 Kings
1 Chronicles
2 Chronicles
Ezra
Nehemiah
Esther
Job
Psalms
Proverbs
Ecclesiastes
The Song of Solomon
Isaiah
Jeremiah
Lamentations
Ezekiel
Daniel
Hosea
Joel
Amos
Obadiah
Jonah
Micah
Nahum
Habakkuk
Zephaniah
Haggai
Zechariah
Malachi

New Testament

Matthew
Mark
Luke
John
Acts
Romans
1 Corinthians
2 Corinthians
Galatians
Ephesians
Philippians
Colossians
1 Thessalonians
2 Thessalonians
1 Timothy
2 Timothy
Titus
Philemon
Hebrews
James
1 Peter
2 Peter
1 John
2 John
3 John
Jude
Revelation

Book of Mormon

1 Nephi
2 Nephi
Jacob
Enos
Jarom
Omni
Words of Mormon
Mosiah
Alma
Helaman
3 Nephi
4 Nephi
Mormon
Ether
Moroni

Doctrine & Covenants

Sections 1-138
Official Declaration 1
Official Declaration 2

Pearl of Great Price

Moses
Abraham
Joseph Smith – Matthew
Joseph Smith – History
Articles of Faith

Appendix II. Warning to Church Members

WARNING TO CHURCH MEMBERS[1]

The First Presidency

With great regret we learn from credible sources, governmental and others, that a few Church members are joining directly or indirectly, the communists and are taking part in their activities.

The Church does not interfere, and has no intention of trying to interfere with the fullest and freest exercise of the political franchise of its members, under and within our Constitution which the Lord declared: "I established ... by the hands of wise men whom I raised up unto this very purpose," and which, as to the principles thereof, the Prophet, dedicating the Kirtland Temple, prayed should be "established forever."

But Communism is not a political party nor a political plan under the Constitution; it is a system of government that is the opposite of our constitutional government, and it would be necessary to destroy our government before Communism could be set up in the United States.

Since Communism, established, would destroy our American constitutional government, to support Communism is treasonable to our free institutions, and no patriotic American citizen may become either a Communist or supporter of Communism.

To our Church members we say: Communism is not the United Order, and bears only the most superficial resemblance thereto; Communism is based upon intolerance and force, the United Order upon love and freedom of conscience and action; Communism involves forceful despoliation of confiscation, the United Order voluntary consecration and sacrifice.

Communists cannot establish the United Order, nor will Communism bring it about. The United Order will be established by the Lord in His own due time and in accordance with the regular prescribed order of the Church.

Furthermore, it is charged by universal report, which is not successfully contradicted or disproved, that Communism undertakes to control, if not indeed to prescribe the religious life of the people living within its jurisdiction, and that it even reaches into the sanctity of the family circle itself, disrupting the normal relationship of parent and child, all in a manner unknown and unsanctioned

[1] Published as an editorial in *The Improvement Era*, August, 1936

under the constitutional guarantees under which we in America live. Such interference would be contrary to the fundamental precepts of the Gospel and to the teachings and order of the Church.

Communism being thus hostile to loyal American citizenship and incompatible with true Church membership, of necessity no loyal American citizen and no faithful Church member can be a Communist.

We call upon all Church members completely to eschew Communism. The safety of our divinely inspired constitutional government and the welfare of our Church imperatively demand that Communism shall have no place in America.

Appendix III. Church Statement on Communism

Church Statement on Communism[1]
President David O. McKay

In order that there may be no misunderstanding by bishops, stake presidents, and others regarding members of the Church participating in non-church meetings to study and become informed on the Constitution of the United States, Communism, etc., I wish to make the following statements that I have been sending out from my office for some time and that have come under question by some stake authorities, bishoprics, and others.

Church members are at perfect liberty to act according to their own consciences in the matter of safeguarding our way of life. They are, of course, encouraged to honor the highest standards of the gospel and to work to preserve their own freedoms. They are free to participate in nonchurch meetings that are held to warn people of the threat of Communism or any other theory or principle that will deprive us of our free agency or individual liberties vouchsafed by the Constitution of the United States.

The Church, out of respect for the rights of all its members to have their political views and loyalties, must maintain the strictest possible neutrality. We have no intention of trying to interfere with the fullest and freest exercise of the political franchise of our members under and within our Constitution, which the Lord declared he established "by the hands of wise men whom [he] raised up unto this very purpose" (D&C 101:80) and which, as to the principles thereof, the Prophet Joseph Smith, dedicating the Kirtland Temple, prayed should be "established forever." (D&C 109:54) The Church does not yield any of its devotion to or convictions about safeguarding the American principles and the establishments of government under federal and state constitutions and the civil rights of men safeguarded by these.

The position of this Church on the subject of Communism has never changed. We consider it the greatest satanical threat to peace, prosperity, and the spread of God's work among men that exists on the face of the earth.

In this connection, we are continually being asked to give our opinion concerning various patriotic groups or individuals who are fighting Communism and speaking up for freedom. Our immediate concern, however, is not with

[1] Read at general priesthood session of General Conference, April 9, 1966

parties, groups, or persons, but with principles. We therefore commend and encourage every person and every group who is sincerely seeking to study constitutional principles and awaken a sleeping and apathetic people to the alarming conditions that are rapidly advancing about us. We wish all of our citizens throughout the land were participating in some type of organized self-education in order that they could better appreciate what is happening and know what they can do about it.

Supporting the FBI, the police, the congressional committee investigating Communism, and various organizations that are attempting to awaken the people through educational means is a policy we warmly endorse for all our people.

The entire concept and philosophy of Communism is diametrically opposed to everything for which the Church stands—belief in Deity, belief in the dignity and eternal nature of man, and the application of the gospel to efforts for peace in the world. Communism is militantly atheistic and is committed to the destruction of faith wherever it may be found.

The Russian Commissioner of Education wrote: "We must hate Christians and Christianity. Even the best of them must be considered our worst enemies. Christian love is an obstacle to the development of the revolution. Down with love for one's neighbor. What we want is hate. Only then shall we conquer the universe."

On the other hand, the gospel teaches the existence of God as our Eternal and Heavenly Father and declares: "... him only shalt thou serve." (Matt. 4:10)

Communism debases the individual and makes him the enslaved tool of the state, to which he must look for sustenance and religion. Communism destroys man's God-given free agency.

No member of this Church can be true to his faith, nor can any American be loyal to his trust, while lending aid, encouragement, or sympathy to any of these false philosophies; for if he does, they will prove snares to his feet.

Appendix IV. The Communist Manifesto

Excerpts taken from *The Communist Manifesto*[1]

In this sense, the theory of the Communists may be summed up in the single sentence: Abolition of private property.[2] ...

Abolition of the family! Even the most radical flare up at this infamous proposal of the Communists.[3] ...

... we replace home education by social.[4] ...

We have seen above, that the first step in the revolution by the working class, is to raise the proletariat to the position of ruling as to win the battle of democracy.

The proletariat will use its political supremacy to wrest, by degrees, all capital from the bourgeoisie, to centralise all instruments of production in the hands of the State, ...

Of course, in the beginning, this cannot be effected except by means of despotic inroads on the rights of property, and on the conditions of bourgeois production; by means of measures, therefore, which appear economically insufficient and untenable, but which, in the course of the movement, outstrip themselves, necessitate further inroads upon the old social order, and are unavoidable as a means of entirely revolutionizing the mode of production.

These measures will of course be different in different countries.

Nevertheless in the most advanced countries, the following will be pretty generally applicable.

1. Abolition of property in land and application of all rents of land to public purposes.
2. A heavy progressive or graduated income tax.
3. Abolition of all right of inheritance.
4. Confiscation of the property of all emigrants and rebels.
5. Centralisation of credit in the hands of the State, by means of a national bank with State capital and an exclusive monopoly.
6. Centralisation of the means of communication and transport in the hands of the State.

---

[1] Karl Marx, Frederick Engels, *The Communist Manifesto*, 2005

[2] Ibid., p. 24

[3] Ibid., p. 29

[4] Ibid., p. 30

7. Extension of factories and instruments of production owned by the State; the bringing into cultivation of wastelands, and the improvement of the soil generally in accordance with a common plan.
8. Equal liability of all to labour. Establishment of industrial armies, especially for agriculture.
9. Combination of agriculture with manufacturing industries; gradual abolition of the distinction between town and country, by a more equable distribution of the population over the country.
10. Free education for all children in public schools. Abolition of children's factory labour in its present form. Combination of education with industrial production, &c., &c.[5]

[5] Ibid., pp. 34-36

Appendix V. The Constitution of the U.S.S.R.

Chapter X – Fundamental Rights and Duties of Citizens[1]

ARTICLE 118. Citizens of the U.S.S.R. have the right to work, that is, are guaranteed the right to employment and payment for their work in accordance With its quantity and quality.

The right to work is ensured by the socialist organization of the national economy, the steady growth of the productive forces of Soviet society, the elimination of the possibility of economic crises, and the abolition of unemployment.

ARTICLE 119. Citizens of the U.S.S.R. have the right to rest and leisure. The right to rest and leisure is ensured by the reduction of the working day to seven hours for the overwhelming majority of the workers, the institution of annual vacations with full pay for workers and employees and the provision of a wide network of sanatoria, rest homes and clubs for the accommodation of the working people.

ARTICLE 120. Citizens of the U.S.S.R. have the right to maintenance in old age and also in case of sickness or loss of capacity to work. This right is ensured by the extensive development of social insurance of workers and employees at state expense, free medical service for the working people and the provision of a wide network of health resorts for the use of the working people.

ARTICLE 121. Citizens of the U.S.S.R. have the right to education. This right is ensured by universal, compulsory elementary education; by education, including higher education, being free of charge; by the system of state stipends for the overwhelming majority of students in the universities and colleges; by instruction in schools being conducted in the native language, and by the organization in the factories, state farms, machine and tractor stations and collective farms of free vocational, technical and agronomic training for the working people.

ARTICLE 122. Women in the U.S.S.R. are accorded equal rights with men in all spheres of economic, state, cultural, social and political life. The possibility of exercising these rights is ensured to women by granting them an equal right with men to work, payment for work, rest and leisure, social insurance and education, and by state protection of the interests of mother and child, prematernity and maternity leave with full pay, and the provision of a wide network of maternity homes, nurseries and kindergartens.

[1] Taken from the Constitution of the U.S.S.R. adopted December, 1936

ARTICLE 123. Equality of rights of citizens of the U.S.S.R., irrespective of their nationality or race, in all spheres of economic, state, cultural, social and political life, is an indefeasible law. Any direct or indirect restriction of the rights of, or, conversely, any establishment of direct or indirect privileges for, citizens on account of their race or nationality, as well as any advocacy of racial or national exclusiveness or hatred and contempt, is punishable by law.

ARTICLE 124. In order to ensure to citizens freedom of conscience, the church in the U.S.S.R. is separated from the state, and the school from the church. Freedom of religious worship and freedom of antireligious propaganda is recognized for all citizens.

ARTICLE 125. In conformity with the interests of the working people, and in order to strengthen the socialist system, the citizens of the U.S.S.R. are guaranteed by law:

a. freedom of speech;
b. freedom of the press;
c. freedom of assembly, including the holding of mass meetings;
d. freedom of street processions and demonstrations.

These civil rights are ensured by placing at the disposal of the working people and their organizations printing presses, stocks of paper, public buildings, the streets, communications facilities and other material requisites for the exercise of these rights.

ARTICLE 126. In conformity with the interests of the working people, and in order to develop the organizational initiative and political activity of the masses of the people, citizens of the U.S.S.R. are ensured the right to unite in public organizations—trade unions, cooperative associations, youth organizations,' sport and defense organizations, cultural, technical and scientific societies; and the most active and politically most conscious citizens in the ranks of the working class and other sections of the working people unite in the Communist Party of the Soviet Union (Bolsheviks), which is the vanguard of the working people in their struggle to strengthen and develop the socialist system and is the leading core of all organizations of the working people, both public and state.

ARTICLE 127. Citizens of the U.S.S.R. are guaranteed inviolability of the person. No person may be placed under arrest except by decision of a court or with the sanction of a procurator.

ARTICLE 128. The inviolability of the homes of citizens and privacy of correspondence are protected by law.

ARTICLE 129. The U.S.S.R. affords the right of asylum to foreign citizens persecuted for defending the interests of the working people, or for their scientific activities, or for their struggle for national liberation.

ARTICLE 130. It is the duty of every citizen of the U.S.S.R. to abide by the Constitution of the Union of Soviet Socialist Republics, to observe the laws, to maintain labor discipline, honestly to perform public duties, and to respect the rules of socialist intercourse.

ARTICLE 131. It is the duty of every citizen of the U.S.S.R. to safeguard and strengthen public, socialist property as the sacred and inviolable foundation of the Soviet system, as the source of the wealth and might of the country, as the source of the prosperous and cultured life of all the working people.

Persons committing offenses against public, socialist property are enemies of the people.

ARTICLE 132. Universal military service is law. Military service in the Workers' and Peasants' Red Army is an honorable duty of the citizens of the U.S.S.R.

ARTICLE 133. To defend the fatherland is the sacred duty of every citizen of the U.S.S.R. Treason to the country—violation of the oath of allegiance, desertion to the enemy, impairing the military power of the state, espionage is punishable with all the severity of the law as the most heinous of crimes.

Appendix VI. The Platform of the Nazi Party

Platform of the National Socialist German Workers' Party

1933

1. We demand the union of all Germans in a Great Germany on the basis of the principle of self-determination of all peoples.

2. We demand that the German people have rights equal to those of other nations; and that the Peace Treaties of Versailles and St. Germain shall be abrogated.

3. We demand land and territory (colonies) for the maintenance of our people and the settlement of our surplus population.

4. Only those who are our fellow countrymen can become citizens. Only those who have German blood, regardless of creed, can be our countrymen. Hence no Jew can be a countryman.

5. Those who are not citizens must live in Germany as foreigners and must be subject to the law of aliens.

6. The right to choose the government and determine the laws of the State shall belong only to citizens. We therefore demand that no public office, of whatever nature, whether in the central government, the province, or the municipality, shall be held by anyone who is not a citizen.

We wage war against the corrupt parliamentary administration whereby men are appointed to posts by favor of the party without regard to character and fitness.

7. We demand that the State shall above all undertake to ensure that every citizen shall have the possibility of living decently and earning a livelihood. If it should not be possible to feed the whole population, then aliens (non-citizens) must be expelled from the Reich.

8. Any further immigration of non-Germans must be prevented. We demand that all non-Germans who have entered Germany since August 2, 1914, shall be compelled to leave the Reich immediately.

9. All citizens must possess equal rights and duties.

10. The first duty of every citizen must be to work mentally or physically. No individual shall do any work that offends against the interest of the community to the benefit of all.

Therefore we demand:

11. That all unearned income, and all income that does not arise from work, be abolished.

12. Since every war imposes on the people fearful sacrifices in blood and treasure, all personal profit arising from the war must be regarded as treason to the people. We therefore demand the total confiscation of all war profits.

13. We demand the nationalization of all trusts.

14. We demand profit-sharing in large industries.

15. We demand a generous increase in old-age pensions.

16. We demand the creation and maintenance of a sound middle-class, the immediate communalization of large stores which will be rented cheaply to small tradespeople, and the strongest consideration must be given to ensure that small traders shall deliver the supplies needed by the State, the provinces and municipalities.

17. We demand an agrarian reform in accordance with our national requirements, and the enactment of a law to expropriate the owners without compensation of any land needed for the common purpose. The abolition of ground rents, and the prohibition of all speculation in land.

18. We demand that ruthless war be waged against those who work to the injury of the common welfare. Traitors, usurers, profiteers, etc., are to be punished with death, regardless of creed or race.

19. We demand that Roman law, which serves a materialist ordering of the world, be replaced by German common law.

20. In order to make it possible for every capable and industrious German to obtain higher education, and thus the opportunity to reach into positions of leadership, the State must assume the responsibility of organizing thoroughly the entire cultural system of the people. The curricula of all educational establishments shall be adapted to practical life. The conception of the State Idea (science of citizenship) must be taught in the schools from the very beginning. We demand that specially talented children of poor parents, whatever their station or occupation, be educated at the expense of the State.

21. The State has the duty to help raise the standard of national health by providing maternity welfare centers, by prohibiting juvenile labor, by increasing physical fitness through the introduction of compulsory games and gymnastics, and by the greatest possible encouragement of associations concerned with the physical education of the young.

22. We demand the abolition of the regular army and the creation of a national (folk) army.

23. We demand that there be a legal campaign against those who propagate deliberate political lies and disseminate them through the press. In order to make possible the creation of a German press, we demand:

(a) All editors and their assistants on newspapers published in the German language shall be German citizens.

(b) Non-German newspapers shall only be published with the express permission of the State. They must not be published in the German language.

(c) All financial interests in or in any way affecting German newspapers shall be forbidden to non-Germans by law, and we demand that the punishment for transgressing this law be the immediate suppression of the newspaper and the expulsion of the non-Germans from the Reich.

Newspapers transgressing against the common welfare shall be suppressed. We demand legal action against those tendencies in art and literature that have a disruptive influence upon the life of our folk, and that any organizations that offend against the foregoing demands shall be dissolved.

24. We demand freedom for all religious faiths in the state, insofar as they do not endanger its existence or offend the moral and ethical sense of the Germanic race.

The party as such represents the point of view of a positive Christianity without binding itself to any one particular confession. It fights against the Jewish materialist spirit within and without, and is convinced that a lasting recovery of our folk can only come about from within on the principle:

COMMON GOOD BEFORE INDIVIDUAL GOOD

25. In order to carry out this program we demand: the creation of a strong central authority in the State, the unconditional authority by the political central parliament of the whole State and all its organizations.

The formation of professional committees and of committees representing the several estates of the realm, to ensure that the laws promulgated by the central authority shall be carried out by the federal states.

The leaders of the party undertake to promote the execution of the foregoing points at all costs, if necessary at the sacrifice of their own lives.

Appendix VII. The Declaration of Independence

IN CONGRESS, July 4, 1776.

The unanimous Declaration of the thirteen united States of America,

When in the Course of human events, it becomes necessary for one people to dissolve the political bands which have connected them with another, and to assume among the powers of the earth, the separate and equal station to which the Laws of Nature and of Nature's God entitle them, a decent respect to the opinions of mankind requires that they should declare the causes which impel them to the separation.

We hold these truths to be self-evident, that all men are created equal, that they are endowed by their Creator with certain unalienable Rights, that among these are Life, Liberty and the pursuit of Happiness.—That to secure these rights, Governments are instituted among Men, deriving their just powers from the consent of the governed,—That whenever any Form of Government becomes destructive of these ends, it is the Right of the People to alter or to abolish it, and to institute new Government, laying its foundation on such principles and organizing its powers in such form, as to them shall seem most likely to effect their Safety and Happiness. Prudence, indeed, will dictate that Governments long established should not be changed for light and transient causes; and accordingly all experience hath shewn, that mankind are more disposed to suffer, while evils are sufferable, than to right themselves by abolishing the forms to which they are accustomed. But when a long train of abuses and usurpations, pursuing invariably the same Object evinces a design to reduce them under absolute Despotism, it is their right, it is their duty, to throw off such Government, and to provide new Guards for their future security.—Such has been the patient sufferance of these Colonies; and such is now the necessity which constrains them to alter their former Systems of Government. The history of the present King of Great Britain is a history of repeated injuries and usurpations, all having in direct object the establishment of an absolute Tyranny over these States. To prove this, let Facts be submitted to a candid world.

He has refused his Assent to Laws, the most wholesome and necessary for the public good.

He has forbidden his Governors to pass Laws of immediate and pressing importance, unless suspended in their operation till his Assent should be obtained; and when so suspended, he has utterly neglected to attend to them.

He has refused to pass other Laws for the accommodation of large districts of people, unless those people would relinquish the right of Representation in the Legislature, a right inestimable to them and formidable to tyrants only.

He has called together legislative bodies at places unusual, uncomfortable, and distant from the depository of their public Records, for the sole purpose of fatiguing them into compliance with his measures.

He has dissolved Representative Houses repeatedly, for opposing with manly firmness his invasions on the rights of the people.

He has refused for a long time, after such dissolutions, to cause others to be elected; whereby the Legislative powers, incapable of Annihilation, have returned to the People at large for their exercise; the State remaining in the mean time exposed to all the dangers of invasion from without, and convulsions within.

He has endeavoured to prevent the population of these States; for that purpose obstructing the Laws for Naturalization of Foreigners; refusing to pass others to encourage their migrations hither, and raising the conditions of new Appropriations of Lands.

He has obstructed the Administration of Justice, by refusing his Assent to Laws for establishing Judiciary powers.

He has made Judges dependent on his Will alone, for the tenure of their offices, and the amount and payment of their salaries.

He has erected a multitude of New Offices, and sent hither swarms of Officers to harrass our people, and eat out their substance.

He has kept among us, in times of peace, Standing Armies without the Consent of our legislatures.

He has affected to render the Military independent of and superior to the Civil power.

He has combined with others to subject us to a jurisdiction foreign to our constitution, and unacknowledged by our laws; giving his Assent to their Acts of pretended Legislation:

For Quartering large bodies of armed troops among us:

For protecting them, by a mock Trial, from punishment for any Murders which they should commit on the Inhabitants of these States:

For cutting off our Trade with all parts of the world:

For imposing Taxes on us without our Consent:

For depriving us in many cases, of the benefits of Trial by Jury:

For transporting us beyond Seas to be tried for pretended offences

For abolishing the free System of English Laws in a neighbouring Province, establishing therein an Arbitrary government, and enlarging its Boundaries so as to render it at once an example and fit instrument for introducing the same absolute rule into these Colonies:

For taking away our Charters, abolishing our most valuable Laws, and altering fundamentally the Forms of our Governments:

For suspending our own Legislatures, and declaring themselves invested with power to legislate for us in all cases whatsoever.

He has abdicated Government here, by declaring us out of his Protection and waging War against us.

He has plundered our seas, ravaged our Coasts, burnt our towns, and destroyed the lives of our people.

He is at this time transporting large Armies of foreign Mercenaries to compleat the works of death, desolation and tyranny, already begun with circumstances of Cruelty & perfidy scarcely paralleled in the most barbarous ages, and totally unworthy the Head of a civilized nation.

He has constrained our fellow Citizens taken Captive on the high Seas to bear Arms against their Country, to become the executioners of their friends and Brethren, or to fall themselves by their Hands.

He has excited domestic insurrections amongst us, and has endeavoured to bring on the inhabitants of our frontiers, the merciless Indian Savages, whose known rule of warfare, is an undistinguished destruction of all ages, sexes and conditions.

In every stage of these Oppressions We have Petitioned for Redress in the most humble terms: Our repeated Petitions have been answered only by repeated injury. A Prince whose character is thus marked by every act which may define a Tyrant, is unfit to be the ruler of a free people.

Nor have We been wanting in attentions to our British brethren. We have warned them from time to time of attempts by their legislature to extend an unwarrantable jurisdiction over us. We have reminded them of the circumstances of our emigration and settlement here. We have appealed to their native justice and magnanimity, and we have conjured them by the ties of our common kindred to disavow these usurpations, which, would inevitably interrupt our connections and correspondence. They too have been deaf to the voice of justice and of consanguinity. We must, therefore, acquiesce in the necessity, which denounces our Separation, and hold them, as we hold the rest of mankind, Enemies in War, in Peace Friends.

We, therefore, the Representatives of the united States of America, in General Congress, Assembled, appealing to the Supreme Judge of the world for the rectitude of our intentions, do, in the Name, and by Authority of the good People of these Colonies, solemnly publish and declare, That these United Colonies are, and of Right ought to be Free and Independent States; that they are Absolved from all Allegiance to the British Crown, and that all political connection between them and the State of Great Britain, is and ought to be totally dissolved; and that as Free and Independent States, they have full Power to levy War, conclude Peace, contract Alliances, establish Commerce, and to do all other Acts and Things which Independent States may of right do. And for the support of this Declaration, with a firm reliance on the protection of divine Providence, we mutually pledge to each other our Lives, our Fortunes and our sacred Honor.

Appendix VIII. The Constitution of the United States

The U.S. Constitution and Bill of Rights as originally ratified in 1790 and 1791 respectively.

We the People of the United States, in Order to form a more perfect Union, establish Justice, insure domestic Tranquility, provide for the common defence, promote the general Welfare, and secure the Blessings of Liberty to ourselves and our Posterity, do ordain and establish this Constitution for the United States of America.

Article. I.

Section. 1.

All legislative Powers herein granted shall be vested in a Congress of the United States, which shall consist of a Senate and House of Representatives.

Section. 2.

The House of Representatives shall be composed of Members chosen every second Year by the People of the several States, and the Electors in each State shall have the Qualifications requisite for Electors of the most numerous Branch of the State Legislature.

No Person shall be a Representative who shall not have attained to the Age of twenty five Years, and been seven Years a Citizen of the United States, and who shall not, when elected, be an Inhabitant of that State in which he shall be chosen.

Representatives and direct Taxes shall be apportioned among the several States which may be included within this Union, according to their respective Numbers, which shall be determined by adding to the whole Number of free Persons, including those bound to Service for a Term of Years, and excluding Indians not taxed, three fifths of all other Persons. The actual Enumeration shall be made within three Years after the first Meeting of the Congress of the United States, and within every subsequent Term of ten Years, in such Manner as they shall by Law direct. The Number of Representatives shall not exceed one for every thirty Thousand, but each State shall have at Least one Representative; and until such enumeration shall be made, the State of New Hampshire shall be entitled to chuse three, Massachusetts eight, Rhode-Island and Providence Plantations one, Connecticut five, New-York six, New Jersey four, Pennsylvania eight, Delaware one, Maryland six, Virginia ten, North Carolina five, South Carolina five, and Georgia three.

When vacancies happen in the Representation from any State, the Executive Authority thereof shall issue Writs of Election to fill such Vacancies.

The House of Representatives shall chuse their Speaker and other Officers; and shall have the sole Power of Impeachment.

Section. 3.

The Senate of the United States shall be composed of two Senators from each State, chosen by the Legislature thereof, for six Years; and each Senator shall have one Vote.

Immediately after they shall be assembled in Consequence of the first Election, they shall be divided as equally as may be into three Classes. The Seats of the Senators of the first Class shall be vacated at the Expiration of the second Year, of the second Class at the Expiration of the fourth Year, and of the third Class at the Expiration of the sixth Year, so that one third may be chosen every second Year; and if Vacancies happen by Resignation, or otherwise, during the Recess of the Legislature of any State, the Executive thereof may make temporary Appointments until the next Meeting of the Legislature, which shall then fill such Vacancies.

No Person shall be a Senator who shall not have attained to the Age of thirty Years, and been nine Years a Citizen of the United States, and who shall not, when elected, be an Inhabitant of that State for which he shall be chosen.

The Vice President of the United States shall be President of the Senate, but shall have no Vote, unless they be equally divided.

The Senate shall chuse their other Officers, and also a President pro tempore, in the Absence of the Vice President, or when he shall exercise the Office of President of the United States.

The Senate shall have the sole Power to try all Impeachments. When sitting for that Purpose, they shall be on Oath or Affirmation. When the President of the United States is tried, the Chief Justice shall preside: And no Person shall be convicted without the Concurrence of two thirds of the Members present.

Judgment in Cases of Impeachment shall not extend further than to removal from Office, and disqualification to hold and enjoy any Office of honor, Trust or Profit under the United States: but the Party convicted shall nevertheless be liable and subject to Indictment, Trial, Judgment and Punishment, according to Law.

Section. 4.

The Times, Places and Manner of holding Elections for Senators and Representatives, shall be prescribed in each State by the Legislature thereof; but the Congress may at any time by Law make or alter such Regulations, except as to the Places of chusing Senators.

The Congress shall assemble at least once in every Year, and such Meeting shall be on the first Monday in December, unless they shall by Law appoint a different Day.

Section. 5.

Each House shall be the Judge of the Elections, Returns and Qualifications of its own Members, and a Majority of each shall constitute a Quorum to do Business; but a smaller Number may adjourn from day to day, and may be authorized to compel the Attendance of absent Members, in such Manner, and under such Penalties as each House may provide.

Each House may determine the Rules of its Proceedings, punish its Members for disorderly Behaviour, and, with the Concurrence of two thirds, expel a Member.

Each House shall keep a Journal of its Proceedings, and from time to time publish the same, excepting such Parts as may in their Judgment require Secrecy; and the Yeas and Nays of the Members of either House on any question shall, at the Desire of one fifth of those Present, be entered on the Journal.

Neither House, during the Session of Congress, shall, without the Consent of the other, adjourn for more than three days, nor to any other Place than that in which the two Houses shall be sitting.

Section. 6.

The Senators and Representatives shall receive a Compensation for their Services, to be ascertained by Law, and paid out of the Treasury of the United States. They shall in all Cases, except Treason, Felony and Breach of the Peace, be privileged from Arrest during their Attendance at the Session of their respective Houses, and in going to and returning from the same; and for any Speech or Debate in either House, they shall not be questioned in any other Place.

No Senator or Representative shall, during the Time for which he was elected, be appointed to any civil Office under the Authority of the United States, which shall have been created, or the Emoluments whereof shall have been encreased during such time; and no Person holding any Office under the United States, shall be a Member of either House during his Continuance in Office.

Section. 7.

All Bills for raising Revenue shall originate in the House of Representatives; but the Senate may propose or concur with Amendments as on other Bills.

Every Bill which shall have passed the House of Representatives and the Senate, shall, before it become a Law, be presented to the President of the United States; If he approve he shall sign it, but if not he shall return it, with his Objections to that House in which it shall have originated, who shall enter the Objections at large on their Journal, and proceed to reconsider it. If after such Reconsideration two thirds of that House shall agree to pass the Bill, it shall be sent, together with the Objections, to the other House, by which it shall likewise be reconsidered, and if approved by two thirds of that House, it shall become a Law. But in all such Cases the Votes of both Houses shall be determined by yeas and Nays, and the Names of the Persons voting for and against the Bill shall be entered on the Journal of each House respectively. If any Bill shall not be returned by the President within ten Days (Sundays excepted) after it shall have been presented to him, the Same shall be a Law, in like Manner as if he had signed it, unless the Congress by their Adjournment prevent its Return, in which Case it shall not be a Law.

Every Order, Resolution, or Vote to which the Concurrence of the Senate and House of Representatives may be necessary (except on a question of Adjournment) shall be presented to the President of the United States; and before the Same shall take Effect, shall be approved by him, or being disapproved by him, shall be repassed by two thirds of the Senate and House of Representatives, according to the Rules and Limitations prescribed in the Case of a Bill.

Section. 8.

The Congress shall have Power To lay and collect Taxes, Duties, Imposts and Excises, to pay the Debts and provide for the common Defence and general Welfare of the United States; but all Duties, Imposts and Excises shall be uniform throughout the United States;

To borrow Money on the credit of the United States;

To regulate Commerce with foreign Nations, and among the several States, and with the Indian Tribes;

To establish an uniform Rule of Naturalization, and uniform Laws on the subject of Bankruptcies throughout the United States;

To coin Money, regulate the Value thereof, and of foreign Coin, and fix the Standard of Weights and Measures;

To provide for the Punishment of counterfeiting the Securities and current Coin of the United States;

To establish Post Offices and post Roads;

To promote the Progress of Science and useful Arts, by securing for limited Times to Authors and Inventors the exclusive Right to their respective Writings and Discoveries;

To constitute Tribunals inferior to the supreme Court;

To define and punish Piracies and Felonies committed on the high Seas, and Offences against the Law of Nations;

To declare War, grant Letters of Marque and Reprisal, and make Rules concerning Captures on Land and Water;

To raise and support Armies, but no Appropriation of Money to that Use shall be for a longer Term than two Years;

To provide and maintain a Navy;

To make Rules for the Government and Regulation of the land and naval Forces;

To provide for calling forth the Militia to execute the Laws of the Union, suppress Insurrections and repel Invasions;

To provide for organizing, arming, and disciplining, the Militia, and for governing such Part of them as may be employed in the Service of the United States, reserving to the States respectively, the Appointment of the Officers, and the Authority of training the Militia according to the discipline prescribed by Congress;

To exercise exclusive Legislation in all Cases whatsoever, over such District (not exceeding ten Miles square) as may, by Cession of particular States, and the Acceptance of Congress, become the Seat of the Government of the United States, and to exercise like Authority over all Places purchased by the Consent of the Legislature of the State in which the Same shall be, for the Erection of Forts, Magazines, Arsenals, dock-Yards, and other needful Buildings;—And

To make all Laws which shall be necessary and proper for carrying into Execution the foregoing Powers, and all other Powers vested by this Constitution in the Government of the United States, or in any Department or Officer thereof.

Section. 9.

The Migration or Importation of such Persons as any of the States now existing shall think proper to admit, shall not be prohibited by the Congress prior to the Year one thousand eight hundred and eight, but a Tax or duty may be imposed on such Importation, not exceeding ten dollars for each Person.

The Privilege of the Writ of Habeas Corpus shall not be suspended, unless when in Cases of Rebellion or Invasion the public Safety may require it.

No Bill of Attainder or ex post facto Law shall be passed.

No Capitation, or other direct, Tax shall be laid, unless in Proportion to the Census or enumeration herein before directed to be taken.

No Tax or Duty shall be laid on Articles exported from any State.

No Preference shall be given by any Regulation of Commerce or Revenue to the Ports of one State over those of another: nor shall Vessels bound to, or from, one State, be obliged to enter, clear, or pay Duties in another.

No Money shall be drawn from the Treasury, but in Consequence of Appropriations made by Law; and a regular Statement and Account of the

Receipts and Expenditures of all public Money shall be published from time to time.

No Title of Nobility shall be granted by the United States: And no Person holding any Office of Profit or Trust under them, shall, without the Consent of the Congress, accept of any present, Emolument, Office, or Title, of any kind whatever, from any King, Prince, or foreign State.

Section. 10.

No State shall enter into any Treaty, Alliance, or Confederation; grant Letters of Marque and Reprisal; coin Money; emit Bills of Credit; make any Thing but gold and silver Coin a Tender in Payment of Debts; pass any Bill of Attainder, ex post facto Law, or Law impairing the Obligation of Contracts, or grant any Title of Nobility.

No State shall, without the Consent of the Congress, lay any Imposts or Duties on Imports or Exports, except what may be absolutely necessary for executing it's inspection Laws: and the net Produce of all Duties and Imposts, laid by any State on Imports or Exports, shall be for the Use of the Treasury of the United States; and all such Laws shall be subject to the Revision and Controul of the Congress.

No State shall, without the Consent of Congress, lay any Duty of Tonnage, keep Troops, or Ships of War in time of Peace, enter into any Agreement or Compact with another State, or with a foreign Power, or engage in War, unless actually invaded, or in such imminent Danger as will not admit of delay.

Article. II.

Section. 1.

The executive Power shall be vested in a President of the United States of America. He shall hold his Office during the Term of four Years, and, together with the Vice President, chosen for the same Term, be elected, as follows

Each State shall appoint, in such Manner as the Legislature thereof may direct, a Number of Electors, equal to the whole Number of Senators and Representatives to which the State may be entitled in the Congress: but no Senator or Representative, or Person holding an Office of Trust or Profit under the United States, shall be appointed an Elector.

The Electors shall meet in their respective States, and vote by Ballot for two Persons, of whom one at least shall not be an Inhabitant of the same State with themselves. And they shall make a List of all the Persons voted for, and of the Number of Votes for each; which List they shall sign and certify, and transmit sealed to the Seat of the Government of the United States, directed to the President of the Senate. The President of the Senate shall, in the Presence of the Senate and House of Representatives, open all the Certificates, and the Votes shall then be counted. The Person having the greatest Number of Votes shall be the President, if such Number be a Majority of the whole Number of Electors appointed; and if there be more than one who have such Majority, and have an equal Number of Votes, then the House of Representatives shall immediately chuse by Ballot one of them for President; and if no Person have a Majority, then from the five highest on the List the said House shall in like Manner chuse the President. But in chusing the President, the Votes shall be taken by States, the Representation from each State having one Vote; A quorum for this Purpose shall consist of a Member or Members from two thirds of the States, and a Majority of all the States shall be necessary to a Choice. In every Case, after the Choice of the President, the Person having the greatest Number of Votes of the Electors shall be the Vice President. But if there should remain two or more who have equal Votes, the Senate shall chuse from them by Ballot the Vice President.

The Congress may determine the Time of chusing the Electors, and the Day on which they shall give their Votes; which Day shall be the same throughout the United States.

No Person except a natural born Citizen, or a Citizen of the United States, at the time of the Adoption of this Constitution, shall be eligible to the Office of President; neither shall any Person be eligible to that Office who shall not have attained to the Age of thirty five Years, and been fourteen Years a Resident within the United States.

In Case of the Removal of the President from Office, or of his Death, Resignation, or Inability to discharge the Powers and Duties of the said Office, the Same shall devolve on the Vice President, and the Congress may by Law provide for the Case of Removal, Death, Resignation or Inability, both of the President and Vice President, declaring what Officer shall then act as President, and such Officer shall act accordingly, until the Disability be removed, or a President shall be elected.

The President shall, at stated Times, receive for his Services, a Compensation, which shall neither be encreased nor diminished during the Period for which he shall have been elected, and he shall not receive within that Period any other Emolument from the United States, or any of them.

Before he enter on the Execution of his Office, he shall take the following Oath or Affirmation:—"I do solemnly swear (or affirm) that I will faithfully execute the Office of President of the United States, and will to the best of my Ability, preserve, protect and defend the Constitution of the United States."

Section. 2.

The President shall be Commander in Chief of the Army and Navy of the United States, and of the Militia of the several States, when called into the actual Service of the United States; he may require the Opinion, in writing, of the principal Officer in each of the executive Departments, upon any Subject relating to the Duties of their respective Offices, and he shall have Power to grant Reprieves and Pardons for Offences against the United States, except in Cases of Impeachment.

He shall have Power, by and with the Advice and Consent of the Senate, to make Treaties, provided two thirds of the Senators present concur; and he shall nominate, and by and with the Advice and Consent of the Senate, shall appoint Ambassadors, other public Ministers and Consuls, Judges of the supreme Court, and all other Officers of the United States, whose Appointments are not herein otherwise provided for, and which shall be established by Law: but the Congress may by Law vest the Appointment of such inferior Officers, as they think proper, in the President alone, in the Courts of Law, or in the Heads of Departments.

The President shall have Power to fill up all Vacancies that may happen during the Recess of the Senate, by granting Commissions which shall expire at the End of their next Session.

Section. 3.

He shall from time to time give to the Congress Information of the State of the Union, and recommend to their Consideration such Measures as he shall judge necessary and expedient; he may, on extraordinary Occasions, convene both Houses, or either of them, and in Case of Disagreement between them, with Respect to the Time of Adjournment, he may adjourn them to such Time as he shall think proper; he shall receive Ambassadors and other public Ministers; he shall take Care that the Laws be faithfully executed, and shall Commission all the Officers of the United States.

Section. 4.

The President, Vice President and all civil Officers of the United States, shall be removed from Office on Impeachment for, and Conviction of, Treason, Bribery, or other high Crimes and Misdemeanors.

Article III.

Section. 1.

The judicial Power of the United States, shall be vested in one supreme Court, and in such inferior Courts as the Congress may from time to time ordain and establish. The Judges, both of the supreme and inferior Courts, shall hold their Offices during good Behaviour, and shall, at stated Times, receive for their Services, a Compensation, which shall not be diminished during their Continuance in Office.

Section. 2.

The judicial Power shall extend to all Cases, in Law and Equity, arising under this Constitution, the Laws of the United States, and Treaties made, or which shall be made, under their Authority;—to all Cases affecting Ambassadors, other public Ministers and Consuls;—to all Cases of admiralty and maritime Jurisdiction;—to Controversies to which the United States shall be a Party;—to Controversies between two or more States;— between a State and Citizens of another State,—between Citizens of different States,—between Citizens of the same State claiming Lands under Grants of different States, and between a State, or the Citizens thereof, and foreign States, Citizens or Subjects.

In all Cases affecting Ambassadors, other public Ministers and Consuls, and those in which a State shall be Party, the supreme Court shall have original Jurisdiction. In all the other Cases before mentioned, the supreme Court shall have appellate Jurisdiction, both as to Law and Fact, with such Exceptions, and under such Regulations as the Congress shall make.

The Trial of all Crimes, except in Cases of Impeachment, shall be by Jury; and such Trial shall be held in the State where the said Crimes shall have been committed; but when not committed within any State, the Trial shall be at such Place or Places as the Congress may by Law have directed.

Section. 3.

Treason against the United States, shall consist only in levying War against them, or in adhering to their Enemies, giving them Aid and Comfort. No Person shall be convicted of Treason unless on the Testimony of two Witnesses to the same overt Act, or on Confession in open Court.

The Congress shall have Power to declare the Punishment of Treason, but no Attainder of Treason shall work Corruption of Blood, or Forfeiture except during the Life of the Person attainted.

Article. IV.

Section. 1.

Full Faith and Credit shall be given in each State to the public Acts, Records, and judicial Proceedings of every other State. And the Congress may by general Laws prescribe the Manner in which such Acts, Records and Proceedings shall be proved, and the Effect thereof.

Section. 2.

The Citizens of each State shall be entitled to all Privileges and Immunities of Citizens in the several States.

A Person charged in any State with Treason, Felony, or other Crime, who shall flee from Justice, and be found in another State, shall on Demand of the executive Authority of the State from which he fled, be delivered up, to be removed to the State having Jurisdiction of the Crime.

No Person held to Service or Labour in one State, under the Laws thereof, escaping into another, shall, in Consequence of any Law or Regulation therein, be discharged from such Service or Labour, but shall be delivered up on Claim of the Party to whom such Service or Labour may be due.

Section. 3.

New States may be admitted by the Congress into this Union; but no new State shall be formed or erected within the Jurisdiction of any other State; nor any State be formed by the Junction of two or more States, or Parts of States, without the Consent of the Legislatures of the States concerned as well as of the Congress.

The Congress shall have Power to dispose of and make all needful Rules and Regulations respecting the Territory or other Property belonging to the United States; and nothing in this Constitution shall be so construed as to Prejudice any Claims of the United States, or of any particular State.

Section. 4.

The United States shall guarantee to every State in this Union a Republican Form of Government, and shall protect each of them against Invasion; and on Application of the Legislature, or of the Executive (when the Legislature cannot be convened), against domestic Violence.

Article. V.

The Congress, whenever two thirds of both Houses shall deem it necessary, shall propose Amendments to this Constitution, or, on the Application of the Legislatures of two thirds of the several States, shall call a Convention for proposing Amendments, which, in either Case, shall be valid to all Intents and Purposes, as Part of this Constitution, when ratified by the Legislatures of three fourths of the several States, or by Conventions in three fourths thereof, as the one or the other Mode of Ratification may be proposed by the Congress; Provided that no Amendment which may be made prior to the Year One thousand eight hundred and eight shall in any Manner affect the first and fourth Clauses in the Ninth Section of the first Article; and that no State, without its Consent, shall be deprived of its equal Suffrage in the Senate.

Article. VI.

All Debts contracted and Engagements entered into, before the Adoption of this Constitution, shall be as valid against the United States under this Constitution, as under the Confederation.

This Constitution, and the Laws of the United States which shall be made in Pursuance thereof; and all Treaties made, or which shall be made, under the Authority of the United States, shall be the supreme Law of the Land; and the Judges in every State shall be bound thereby, any Thing in the Constitution or Laws of any State to the Contrary notwithstanding.

The Senators and Representatives before mentioned, and the Members of the several State Legislatures, and all executive and judicial Officers, both of the United States and of the several States, shall be bound by Oath or Affirmation, to support this Constitution; but no religious Test shall ever be required as a Qualification to any Office or public Trust under the United States.

Article. VII.

The Ratification of the Conventions of nine States, shall be sufficient for the Establishment of this Constitution between the States so ratifying the Same.

done in Convention by the Unanimous Consent of the States present the Seventeenth Day of September in the Year of our Lord one thousand seven hundred and Eighty seven and of the Independence of the United States of America the Twelfth In witness whereof We have hereunto subscribed our Names,

Amendment I

Congress shall make no law respecting an establishment of religion, or prohibiting the free exercise thereof; or abridging the freedom of speech, or of the press; or the right of the people peaceably to assemble, and to petition the Government for a redress of grievances.

Amendment II

A well regulated Militia, being necessary to the security of a free State, the right of the people to keep and bear Arms, shall not be infringed.

Amendment III

No Soldier shall, in time of peace be quartered in any house, without the consent of the Owner, nor in time of war, but in a manner to be prescribed by law.

Amendment IV

The right of the people to be secure in their persons, houses, papers, and effects, against unreasonable searches and seizures, shall not be violated, and no Warrants shall issue, but upon probable cause, supported by Oath or affirmation, and particularly describing the place to be searched, and the persons or things to be seized.

Amendment V

No person shall be held to answer for a capital, or otherwise infamous crime, unless on a presentment or indictment of a Grand Jury, except in cases arising in the land or naval forces, or in the Militia, when in actual service in time of War or public danger; nor shall any person be subject for the same offence to be twice put in jeopardy of life or limb; nor shall be compelled in any criminal case to be a witness against himself, nor be deprived of life, liberty, or property, without due process of law; nor shall private property be taken for public use, without just compensation.

Amendment VI

In all criminal prosecutions, the accused shall enjoy the right to a speedy and public trial, by an impartial jury of the State and district wherein the crime shall have been committed, which district shall have been previously ascertained by law, and to be informed of the nature and cause of the accusation; to be confronted with the witnesses against him; to have compulsory process for obtaining witnesses in his favor, and to have the Assistance of Counsel for his defence.

Amendment VII

In Suits at common law, where the value in controversy shall exceed twenty dollars, the right of trial by jury shall be preserved, and no fact tried by a jury, shall be otherwise re-examined in any Court of the United States, than according to the rules of the common law.

Amendment VIII

Excessive bail shall not be required, nor excessive fines imposed, nor cruel and unusual punishments inflicted.

Amendment IX

The enumeration in the Constitution, of certain rights, shall not be construed to deny or disparage others retained by the people.

Amendment X

The powers not delegated to the United States by the Constitution, nor prohibited by it to the States, are reserved to the States respectively, or to the people.

Appendix IX. Recommended Resources

General Conference Addresses

James E. Talmage, October-1912
J. Reuben Clark, April-1935
Levi Edgar Young, April-1937
Steven L. Richards, April-1939
J. Reuben Clark, Message of the First Presidency, April-1942
J. Reuben Clark, October-1942
J. Reuben Clark, April-1944
Heber J. Grant, October-1944
David O. McKay, April-1950
Joseph Fielding Smith, April-1950
J. Reuben Clark, April-1957
J. Reuben Clark, October-1959
Ezra Taft Benson, October-1961
David O. McKay, October-1962
Ezra Taft Benson, October-1963
Two Great Forces, David O. McKay, October-1965
Protecting Freedom – An Urgent Duty, Ezra Taft Benson, October-1966
The Proper Role of Government, Ezra Taft Benson, October-1968
A Witness and a Warning, Ezra Taft Benson, October-1979
Our Divine Constitution, Ezra Taft Benson, October-1987

Other Speeches and Articles

The Proper Role of Government, Ezra Taft Benson, BYU, October 21, 1968
The Proper Role of Government, Ezra Taft Benson, latterdayconservative.com
Preserving Religious Freedom, Dallin H. Oaks, Chapman University, February 4, 2011
The Constitution – A Heavenly Banner, Ezra Taft Benson, BYU, September 16, 1986
Hope for the Years Ahead, Dallin H. Oaks, UVU, April 16, 2014
Fundamentals of Our Constitutions, Dallin H. Oaks, Salt Lake City, September 17, 2010
Religious Freedom, Dallin H. Oaks, BYU-Idaho, October 13, 2009

Moral Agency, D. Todd Christofferson, BYU, January 31, 2006
The Divinely Inspired Constitution, Dallin H. Oaks, *Ensign*, February, 1992
Moral Free Agency, Daniel H. Ludlow, BYU, July 2, 1974
Free Agency and Freedom, Dallin H. Oaks, BYU, October 11, 1987
Pay Thy Debt and Live, Ezra Taft Benson, BYU, February 28, 1962
Prophecies, Penalties, and Blessings, J. Reuben Clark, *Improvement Era*, July-1940
Human Liberties and the Gospel of Jesus Christ, Albert E. Bowen, *Improvement Era*, May-1938
Socialism and the United Order, Marion G. Romney, BYU, March 1, 1966
America at a Crossroads, Ezra Taft Benson, New Era, July-1978
Two Contending Forces, David O. McKay, BYU, May 18, 1960
The Law of the Harvest, Howard W. Hunter, BYU, March 8, 1966
The Book of Mormon Warns America, Ezra Taft Benson, BYU, May 21, 1968

Websites

http://www.lds.org
http://www.latterdayconservative.com
http://www.wallbuilders.com
http://archive.org
http://speeches.byu.edu

Books

Just and Holy Principles, Ralph C. Hancock
An Enemy Hath Done This, Jerreld L. Newquist
Prophets, Principles, and National Survival, Jerreld L. Newquist
The Real Thomas Jefferson, W. Cleon Skousen et al.
The Jefferson Lies, David Barton
The Real Benjamin Franklin, W. Cleon Skousen et al.
The Real George Washington, W. Cleon Skousen et al.
George Washington's Sacred Fire, Peter A. Lillback
Benjamin Rush: Signer of the Declaration of Independence, David Barton
Samuel Adams: A Life, Ira Stoll
John Adams, David McCullough
Original Intent, David Barton
By the People, Charles Murray
The Dirty Dozen, Robert A. Levy, William Mellor
Economics in One Lesson, Henry Hazlitt
Applied Economics: Thinking Beyond Stage One, Thomas Sowell

The Federalist Papers, Alexander Hamilton, James Madison, John Jay
Liberal Fascism, Jonah Goldberg
American Progressivism, Ronald J. Pestritto, William Atto
Woodrow Wilson and the Roots of Modern Liberalism, Ronald J. Pestritto
The Forgotten Man, Amity Shlaes
Seven Miracles That Saved America, Chris Stewart

Bibliography

Adams, Charles Francis. 1856. *The Works of John Adams, Second President of the United States.* Boston: Little, Brown and Company.

Allison, Andrew, M. Richard Maxfield, K. DeLynn Cook, and W. Cleon Skousen. 2008. *The Real Thomas Jefferson: The True Story of America's Philospher of Freedom.* National Center for Constitutional Studies.

Allison, Andrew, W. Cleon Skousen, and M. Richard Maxfield. 2008. *The Real Benjamin Franklin: The True Story of America's Greatest Diplomat.* National Center for Constitutional Studies.

Barnett, Randy E. 2004. *Restoring the Lost Constitution: The Presumption of Liberty.* Princeton: Princeton University Press.

Barton, David. 2015. http://www.wallbuilders.com.

—. 1999. *Benjamin Rush: Signer of the Declaration of Independence.* Aledo: WallBuilder Press.

—. 2008. *Original Intent: The Courts, the Constitution, and Religion.* Aledo: WallBuilder Press.

—. 2007. *Separation of Chruch and State: What the Founders Meant.* Aledo: WallBuilder Press.

—. 2012. *The Jefferson Lies.* Nashville: Thomas Nelson Inc.

—. 2000. *The Second Amendment: Preserving the Inalienable Right of Individual Self-Protection.* Aledo: WallBuilder Press.

—. 2008. "A Few Declarations of Founding Fathers and Early Statements on Jesus, Christianity, and the Bible." *WallBuilders*, May.

—. 1787. "Franklin's Appeal for Prayer at the Constitutional Convention." *WallBuilders.*

—. 2000. "George Washington, Thomas Jefferson, & Slavery in Virginia." *WallBuilders*, January.

—. 2011. "The Founding Fathers and Slavery." *WallBuilders*, July.

Bastiat, Frederic. 1998. *The Law.* Irvington: Foundation for Economic Education.

Benson, Ezra Taft. 1961. *One Hundred Thirty-First Semi-Annual Conference of The Church of Jesus Christ of Latter-day Saints.* October.

—. 1963. *One Hundred Thirty-Third Semi-Annual Conference of The Church of Jesus Christ of Latter-day Saints.* October.

—. 1979. "A Witness and a Warning." *One Hundred Forty-Ninth Semi-Annual Conference of The Church of Jesus Christ of Latter-day Saints.* October.

—. 1968. "Americans Are Destroying America." *One Hundred Thirty-Eighth Annual Conference of The Church of Jesus Christ of Latter-day Saints.* April.

—. 1962. "Pay Thy Debt and Live." *BYU Speeches*, February 28.

—. 1968. "The Book of Mormon Warns America." *BYU Speeches*, May 21.

—. 1986. "The Constitution - A Heavenly Banner." *BYU Speeches*, September 16.

—. 1968. "The Proper Role of Government." *BYU Speeches*, October 21.

—. 1967. "Civil Rights - Tool of Communist Deception." *One Hundred Thirty-Seventh Semi-Annual Conference of The Church of Jesus Christ of Latter-day Saints.* October.

—. n.d. "The Proper Role of Government." *http://www.latterdayconservative.com.*

—. 1978. "America at a Crossroads." *New Era*, July.

—. 1965. "Not Commanded in All Things." *One Hundred Thirty-Fifth Annual Conference of The Church of Jesus Christ of Latter-day Saints.* April.

—. 1987. "Our Divine Constitution." *One Hundred Fifty-Seventh Semi-Annual Conference of The Church of Jesus Christ of Latter-day Saints.* October.

—. 1966. "Protecting Freedom - An Urgent Duty." *One Hundred Thirty-Sixth Semi-Annual Conference of The Church of Jesus Christ of Latter-day Saints.* October.

—. 1968. "The Proper Role of Government." *One Hundred Thirty-Eighth Semi-Annual Conference of The Church of Jesus Christ of Latter-day Saints.* October.

Blackstone, William. 1979. *Commentaries on the Laws of England: A Facsimile of the First Edition of 1765--1769.* Chicago: University of Chicago Press.

Bowen, Albert E. 1938. "Human Liberties and the Gospel of Jesus Christ." *Improvement Era*, May.

Brigham Young University. 2015. *BYU Speeches.* http://speeches.byu.edu.

Buck, Charles. 1823. *A Theological Dictionary, Containing Definitions of All Religious Terms.* Philadelphia: E.T. Scott.

Carey, George W. 2000. *The Political Writings of John Adams.* Washington, DC: Regnery Publishing.

Christofferson, D. Todd. 2006. "Moral Agency." *BYU Speeches*, January 31.

Clark, J. Reuben. 1935. *One Hundred Fifth Annual Conference of The Church of Jesus Christ of Latter-day Saints.* April.

—. 1942. *One Hundred Thirteenth Semi-Annual Conference of The Church of Jesus Christ of Latter-day Saints.* October.

—. 1944. *One Hundred Fourteenth Annual Conference of The Church of Jesus Christ of Latter-day Saints.* April.

—. 1957. *One Hundred Twenty-Seventh Annual Conference of The Church of Jesus Christ of Latter-day Saints.* April.

—. 1959. *One Hundred Twenty-Ninth Semi-Annual Conference of The Church of Jesus Christ of Latter-day Saints.* October.

—. 1940. "Prophecies, Penalties, and Blessings." *Improvement Era*, July.

—. 1942. "Message of the First Presidency." *One Hundred Twelfth Annual Conference of The Church of Jesus Christ of Latter-day Saints.* April.

Elliot, Jonathan. 1888. *The Debates in the Several State Conventions on the Adoption of the Federal Constitution as Recommended by the General Convention at Philadelphia, in 1787.* New York: Burt Franklin.

Ewbank, Henry. 1835. *The Influences of Democracy on Liberty, Property, and The Happiness of Society, Considered.* London: J.W. Parker.

Feiler, Bruce. 2009. *America's Prophet: Moses and the American Story.* New York: HarperCollins Publishers.

Galbraith, Richard C. 1993. *Scriptural Teachings of the Prophet Joseph Smith.* Salt Lake City: Deseret Book Company.

Goldberg, Jonah. 2007. *Liberal Fascism: The Secret History of the American Left from Mussolini to the Politics of Meaning.* New York: Doubleday.

Grant, Heber J. 1944. *One Hundred Fifteenth Semi-Annual Conference of The Church of Jesus Christ of Latter-day Saints.* October.

Grant, Michael. 1960. *Cicero: Selected Works.* London: The Penguin Group.

Hancock, Ralph C. 1998. *Just and Holy Principles: Latter-Day Saint Readings on America and the Constitution.* Boston: Pearson Custom Publishing.

Hart, Benjamin. 1997. *Faith and Freedom: The Christian Roots of American Liberty.* Christian Defense Fund.

Hazlitt, Henry. 1946. *Economics in One Lesson.* New York: Harper & Brothers.

Hunter, Howard W. 1966. "The Law of the Harvest." *BYU Speeches*, March 8.

Internal Revenue Service. 2015. http://www.irs.gov.

Johnson, William J. 1919. *George Washington, The Christian.* New York: The Abingdon Press.

2015. *Joseph Smith Academy.* http://www.josephsmithacademy.org/wiki/eminent-spirits-appear-to-wilford-woodruff.

Kurland, Philip B., and Ralph Lerner. 1987. *The Founders' Constitution.* 5 vols. Chicago: University of Chicago.

Laslett, Peter. 2010. *Locke: Two Treatises of Government.* Cambridge: Cambridge University Press.

Lee, Harold B. 1952. *One Hundred Twenty-Third Semi-Annual Conference of The Church of Jesus Christ of Latter-day Saints.* October.

Levy, Robert A., and William Mellor. 2009. *The Dirty Dozen: How Twelve Supreme Court Cases Radically Expanded Government and Eroded Freedom.* Washington, D.C.: Cato Institute.

Lillback, Peter A., and Jerry Newcombe. 2006. *George Washington's Sacred Fire.* Bryn Mawr: Providence Forum Press.

Locke, John. 2015. *The John Locke Collection.* Lexington: First Rate Publishers.

Ludlow, Daniel H. 1974. "Moral Free Agency." *BYU Speeches*, July 2.

Lund, Gerald N. 1971. *The Coming of the Lord.* Salt Lake City: Deseret Book.

M., Brian. n.d. *Latter-day Conservative.* Accessed 2015. http://www.latterdayconservative.com.

Madison, James. 1884. *Letters and Other Writings of James Madison.* 4 vols. New York: R. Worthington.

McCullough, David. 2001. *John Adams.* New York: Simon & Schuster.

McDowell, Stephen. 2003. "The Bible, Slavery, and America's Founders." *WallBuilders.*

McKay, David O. 1940. *One Hundred Eleventh Semi-Annual Conference of The Church of Jesus Christ of Latter-day Saints.* October.

—. 1951. *One Hundred Twenty-Second Semi-Annual Conference of The Church of Jesus Christ of Latter-day Saints.* October.

—. 1950. *One Hundred Twentieth Annual Conference of The Church of Jesus Christ of Latter-day Saints.* April.

—. 1962. *One Hundred Thirty-Second Semi-Annual Conference of The Church of Jesus Christ of Latter-day Saints.* October.

—. 1960. "Two Contending Forces." *BYU Speeches*, May 18.

—. 1965. "Two Great Forces." *One Hundred Thirty-Fifth Semi-Annual Conference of The Church of Jesus Christ of Latter-day Saints.* October.

Montesquieu, Charles de Secondat Baron de. 1900. *The Spirit of Laws.* New York: Colonial Press.

Mooy, Kees de. 2003. *The Wisdom of John Adams.* New York: Kensington Publishing Corp.

Moyle, Henry D. 1947. *One Hundred Eighteenth Semi-Annual Conference of The Church of Jesus Christ of Latter-day Saints.* October.

Newquist, Jerreld L. 1969. *An Enemy Hath Done This.* Salt Lake City: Parliament Publishers.

—. 1964. *Prophets, Principles and National Survival.* Salt Lake City: Publishers Press.

Nibley, Charles. 1925. *Ninety-Fifth Annual Conference of The Church of Jesus Christ of Latter-day Saints.* April.

Oaks, Dallin H. 1987. "Free Agency and Freedom." *BYU Speeches*, October 11.

—. 2009. "Religious Freedom." *BYU-Idaho*, October 13.

—. 2011. "Preserving Religious Freedom." *Chapman University School of Law*, February 4.

—. 1992. "The Divinely Inspired Constitution." *Ensign*, February.

—. 2010. "Fundamentals of Our Constitutions." September 17.

—. 2014. "Hope for the Years Ahead." *Utah Valley University*, April 16.

Parry, Jay A., Andrew M. Allison, and W. Cleon Skousen. 2008. *The Real George Washington: The True Story of America's Most Indespensible Man.* National Center for Constitutional Studies.

Pestritto, Ronald J. 2005. *Woodrow Wilson and the Roots of Modern Liberalism.* Lanham: Rowand & Littlefield Publishers.

Pestritto, Ronald J., and William J. Atto. 2008. *American Progressivism: A Reader.* Lanham: Lexington Books.

Platt, Suzy. 1989. *Respectfully Quoted: A Dictionary of Quotations Requested from the Congressional Research Service.* Washington D.C.: Library of Congress.

Richards, Steven L. 1939. *One Hundred Ninth Annual Conference of The Church of Jesus Christ of Latter-day Saints.* April.

Romney, Marion G. 1960. *One Hundred Thirtieth Semi-Annual Conference of The Church of Jesus Christ of Latter-day Saints.* October.

—. 1966. "Socialism and the United Order." *BYU Speeches*, March 1.

Rossiter, Clinton. 1961. *The Federalist Papers.* New York: The Penguin Group.

Schweikart, Larry. 2009. *48 Liberal Lies About American History (That You Probably Learned in School).* New York: The Penguin Group.

Schweikart, Larry, and Michael Allen. 2004. *A Patriot's History of the United States: From Columbus's Great Discovery to the War on Terror.* New York: The Penguin Group.

Shlaes, Amity. 2007. *The Forgotten Man: A New History of The Great Depression.* New York: HarperCollins Publishers.

Smith, George Albert. 1948. *One Hundred Eighteenth Annual Conference of The Church of Jesus Christ of Latter-day Saints.* April.

Smith, Joseph Fielding. 1950. *One Hundred Twentieth Annual Conference of The Church of Jesus Christ of Latter-day Saints.* April.

Sowell, Thomas. 2009. *Applied Economics: Thinking Beyond Stage One.* New York: Basic Books.

Stewart, Chris. 2009. *Seven Miracles That Saved America.* Salt Lake City: Shadow Mountain.

Stoll, Ira. 2008. *Samuel Adams: A Life.* New York: Free Press.

Talmage, James E. 1912. *Eighty-Third Semi-Annual Conference of The Church of Jesus Christ of Latter-day Saints.* October.

The Church of Jesus Christ of Latter-day Saints. 2015. http://www.lds.org.

—. 1880-2015. "General Conference of The Church of Jesus Christ of Latter-day Saints."

—. 1980. *History of the Church.* 7 vols. Salt Lake City: Deseret Book Company.

—. 2015. *The Book of Mormon: Another Testament of Jesus Christ.*

—. 2015. *The Doctrine and Covenants of The Church of Jesus Christ of Latter Day Saints.*

—. 2015. *The Holy Bible.* King James.

—. 2015. *The Pearl of Great Price.*

United States. Dept. of State. 1889. *Foreign Relations of the United States.* Washington, DC: U.S. Government Printing Office.

Wilson, Bird. 1804. *The Works of the Honourable James Wilson, L.L.D.* Philadelphia: Lorenzo Press.

Wright, John. 1894. *Early Bibles of America: Being a Descriptive Account of Bibles Published in the United States, Mexico and Canada.* New York: Thomas Whittaker, 2 and 3 Bible House.

Young, Levi Edgar. 1937. *One Hundred Seventh Annual Conference of The Church of Jesus Christ of Latter-day Saints.* April.

About the Author

Jason Hackett grew up in Fairfax County, Virginia. He joined The Church of Jesus Christ of Latter-day Saints at the age of fifteen. He served a mission in Concepcion, Chile. He has a bachelor's degree from Brigham Young University in Computer Science. He currently lives in Layton, Utah with his wife and four children.

Made in the USA
Las Vegas, NV
17 April 2023